MYTH
INFORMATION

MYTH
INFORMATION

J. Allen Varasdi

BALLANTINE BOOKS · NEW YORK

Copyright © 1989 by J. Allen Varasdi

All rights reserved under International and Pan-American Copyright Conventions. Published in the United States by Ballantine Books, a division of Random House, Inc., New York, and simultaneously in Canada by Random House of Canada Limited, Toronto.

http://www.randomhouse.com

Library of Congress Catalog Card Number: 96-96699

ISBN: 345-41049-1

Manufactured in the United States of America

First Ballantine Books Mass Market Edition: November 1989
First Ballantine Books Trade Edition: August 1996

10 9 8 7 6 5 4 3 2 1

"A man doesn't know what he knows
until he knows what he doesn't know."

Thomas Carlyle

Contents

Contents

Contents xiii

xvi   Contents

Contents   xvii

Introduction

Everyone knows that hemophiliacs bleed to death, piranhas are a dangerous, man-eating fish, the Boston Tea Party resulted from higher taxes on British tea, and teenagers have the highest rate of suicide. Yet everyone would be wrong to accept these beliefs, because they are not true. They also would be mistaken to think the Hippocratic oath is required of doctors, Paul Revere rode alone and completed his intended journey, the center of the earth is molten rock, and chameleons can change color to match their surroundings.

In fact, many of our common beliefs turn out to have no factual support. Indeed, the truth is often the exact opposite of what is usually thought to be true. Despite the fact that these ideas can be easily disproved, misconceptions, fallacies, and misbeliefs seem to be everywhere.

I will define a belief as the acceptance of a proposition as fact without the full intellectual knowledge required to guarantee its truth. In terms of certainty, a belief is above a surmise, conjecture, or opinion, but below the level of fact, knowledge, and truth. A misbelief is any idea or assumption held by a large number of people that violates correct and readily available information. In fact, one of the more interesting aspects of popular misinformation is just how easily it can be disproved and how surprised we are to discover our error.

In this book, I have collected more than 550 of these popular misconceptions which are as baffling to our sense of reality as they are easy to disprove. Although I have accumulated a considerable amount of unusual and interesting information, this is more than a collection of trivia and factual oddity. *Myth Infor-*

mation debunks many of these common fallacies, challenges our reason, and encourages us to question our other beliefs.

Misbelieving involves more than just not knowing that a fact is true. That phenomenon is usually called ignorance—something we have all experienced. There is a difference between not knowing something and knowing something that is untrue.

For example, how many people really know the size of the world's great pyramids? Yet, most of us believe that the largest ones are in Egypt. They are not. Similarly, few people, except medical experts, know the exact location of the human heart. Nevertheless, we all place our hand over the left side of our chest when pledging allegiance, so we believe the heart must be there. But to be correctly placed over the heart, the hand should actually be over the center of the chest.

Misbelieving is not just an individual act. In fact, it is usually the result of the collective, common mentality that we call society. Misconceptions are shared and reinforced by others, particularly through the highly influential and pervasive media—especially television and movies. But the media alone cannot be blamed, since misbeliefs have existed all through history. Even widespread literacy has failed to stem the tide of error in popular thought. Somehow these beliefs become accepted as truth, and no amount of available fact can dispel them from the minds of people.

The study of misconceptions and fallacies has only infrequently been addressed by academicians. Psychologists dwell on attitude, which includes thought, feeling, and behavior. Sociologists dabble in attitude, opinion, and group events in society, but seldom consider the acceptance of unfounded, individual beliefs. Philosophy grapples with profound issues of epistemology—the origin, nature, and validity of knowledge—but ignores the down-to-earth question of why people believe nonsense in the first place.

Why do we believe things that are not true? That is a complex question, the answer to which is beyond the scope of this discussion. But misbelieve we do, and with great persistence, despite the wealth of factual information available everywhere.

Many fallacies become established throughout history in art, particularly paintings, and then prove highly resistant to change. Others become fixed in folklore and legend and are not easily altered by the truth. Some are simply the products of our imaginations striving to create a reality that intuitively makes sense by fulfilling some basic, psychoemotional need for stability and closure in our lives. Because they are shared by others, their apparent truth becomes even more self-evident.

There also seems to be a human propensity to believe things that are read or told by an authoritative person, such as a parent or teacher. These misconceptions are then passed on from one generation to the next without anyone bothering to ask if they are true. A perception is created producing a barrier against the simple truth, which is nearly impossible to erase from the collective mind. These beliefs also become quite strong. History is filled with examples of how men are willing to die for their cherished beliefs rather than the support of the truth.

The consequences of readily accepting our beliefs without question is also the power behind the placebo effect, faith healers, horoscopes, occults, impostors, and charlatans. Misbeliefs also underlie the acceptance of fanatic religious groups, pseudo sciences, and are a factor in the success of heroes and great and not-so-great leaders.

But the fallacies presented in this book are of a much less serious nature. They deal with common, everyday misconceptions most of us share that are, in fact, unsupported by fact. Most will surprise and delight you. Many will inform and enlighten. Hopefully, by recognizing the fallacy in our popular ideas about the world, we may also begin to question the truth in our other beliefs, assumptions, and attitudes.

Finally, although much of the information contained in this book came from standard encyclopedias and reference sources, many times a question still remained unanswered. In these instances, correspondence to professional associations and societies proved invaluable. I would like to thank those individuals who took the time to share their considerable knowledge by responding to what must have seemed to them rather odd questions. There were so many people who contributed in this manner that, unfortunately, they cannot be mentioned individually. My appreciation is also extended to the many people—family and friends—who contributed so much to this effort by offering ideas or simply putting up with me as I regularly corrected them about their misconceptions.

A

" 'Tain't what a man don't know that hurts him,
it's what he knows that just ain't so."

Frank McKinney Hubbard

A–OK

The phrase A–OK was never used by Alan Shepard in the first
U.S. suborbital space flight on May 5, 1961. Although attributed
to him, quoted in newspapers, and even adopted as a catchword
for the early years of the space program, the transcript of the
pilot-voice communications reveals that no such expression was
ever used by Shepard.

A–OK existed only in the mind of Colonel "Shorty" Powers,
the NASA public relations officer. In a briefing to newsmen
following Shepard's mission, Powers related a routine "OK"
from Shepard and replaced it with "A–OK."

Powers liked the term and repeated it often. A–OK caught
on with reporters and the public, although the astronauts generally disliked it. However, the nonexistent term became
closely identified with the first launches of the Mercury space
program despite the fact that none of the astronauts ever used
it in flight.

Abacus

The bead and frame device used to perform arithmetic operations called the abacus is not Chinese as most people believe. Although its origins are not known for certain, it is fairly well established that the instrument did not originate in China. It appears likely that this type of counting device was first used by the Egyptians around 2000 B.C. The word itself is derived from the Greek *abax*, meaning a writing or ciphering tablet.

The abacus has actually been used for thousands of years in many different countries. The device was commonly used to perform arithmetic calculations when more ancient numbering systems, such as Roman numerals, made written computations difficult.

When our current system of Arabic numerals supplanted Roman numerals throughout the world, the abacus as an aid in calculating became obsolete. However, it remained useful and popular primarily in China due to the cumbersome written numerical system that the Chinese retained. Since it is now used mainly in China, the abacus has become popularly identified as a Chinese device.

Abdication

Although most sovereign rulers may generally abdicate at will, in Great Britain, where utmost propriety is the rule, the monarch simply cannot voluntarily decide to quit. The king or queen must request permission to abdicate.

Following such a request, Parliament draws up an article of abdication which stipulates the full requirements and conditions for the royal resignation. It is signed by the monarch and then must be approved by Parliament. There are also provisions that force a monarch to abdicate should the situation arise.

A.D.

Nearly everyone is correct in believing that when used with the date, B.C. stands for "Before Christ." However, it is not true, as most people think, that A.D. means "after death." It is actually an abbreviation for the Latin *anno Domini*, meaning "in the year of the Lord." A.D. refers to dates in the Christian era occurring after the birth of Christ, and should precede the date rather than follow it as does B.C. It should also be noted that there is no year zero in the Christian-era calendar.

Adam and Eve's children

Adam and Eve did not have just two children as is usually believed. According to the Bible (Genesis 4:1–2), there were three named sons—Cain, Abel, and Seth. Also, Adam is said to have sired an additional unspecified number of ''sons and daughters'' (Genesis 5:4), a fact not so surprising considering that Adam is said to have lived for 930 years (Genesis 5:5).

Aggravate

It is not possible to aggravate a person. To aggravate means to make a thing or condition worse or more serious. Thus, only a problem or situation can be aggravated. People are irritated or annoyed.

Air

Because we move and see through air with relative ease, most people do not realize that air has weight, and a great deal of it too. The total weight of the earth's atmosphere is about fifty-six hundred trillion tons. A one-square-inch vertical column of air at sea level extended up into space weighs about 14.5 pounds, and a square-foot vertical column weighs more than a ton. Barometers and altimeters work only because of the weight of air.

We are enveloped in a ''fluid'' that actually has buoyant properties similar to water, a principle that allows birds and airplanes to ''float,'' or fly. This buoyancy is the result of the weight of air pressing in all directions with an equal force just like water. Depending on their size and skin area, the atmosphere weighs down on each human at sea level with a force of between ten and twenty tons. We are not crushed by the air around us only because this pressure is applied in all directions, including from within our bodies.

Air fresheners

Contrary to popular belief, air fresheners do not usually work by removing the offending odor from the air. Although this method is used in some products, most air fresheners rely on a more insidious technique.

Air fresheners produce their results through three different methods. One way is to actually remove the odor with absorbing agents, such as activated charcoal or silica gel. This is the most expensive method and usually requires mechanical and filtering devices.

However, aerosol and liquid air fresheners never remove odor in this manner. Instead, they often work by simply covering the smell of an offending odor with an even stronger scent which overwhelms the olfactory senses, but leaves the original odor undetectable, yet present.

Another method used by air fresheners consists of dispersing numbing agents into the air so that the smelling ability of the nose is actually anesthetized. Most commercial air fresheners, especially aerosols, work by masking with strong fragrances or using nasal anesthetics, neither of which removes the offending odor from the air.

Air pocket

As used in aviation, an air pocket is an interesting, but inaccurate, metaphor to describe what happens when an aircraft suddenly rises and falls during flight. There is no such thing as an empty pocket in the atmosphere where nothing exists. An airplane cannot fly without air, and would simply fall to the ground in a real "air pocket."

The sudden upward or downward motion of an airplane while in flight results from encountering streams of air, some quite powerful, in the atmosphere. Known as uplifts and downdrafts, these strong flows, usually vertical, temporarily alter the lifting action of an aircraft's wings. These currents cause the airplane to rise and fall abruptly until it passes through the turbulence. It is actually the effects of these streams of air that are referred to as air pockets.

Airplane, first

Most people would agree that the world's first airplane was made by Orville and Wilbur Wright. But then, most people would be wrong.

While it is true that the historic and famous flight by the Wright brothers was the first manned, powered, controlled, and sustained flight in a heavier-than-air craft, it was not the first airplane to fly. Others had actually flown before in various kinds of machines, but Samuel Pierpont Langley is generally credited with making the first heavier-than-air machine that could fly.

Serious efforts to fly date to the mid 1800s. Successful gliders had been built that carried men and provided an understanding of airfoils and the principles of lift. First attempts at powered flight utilized steam engines, but because of their weight and insufficient power, they were doomed to failure.

One of the early successes with steam-powered flight was made by Clément Ader, a Frenchman, who piloted his *Eole* in a 164-foot flight in 1890. This short hop, not considered true sustained flight, at least demonstrated that heavier-than-air machines could leave the ground.

Langley was an astronomer and aeronautical pioneer who was the first to experiment with the concept of lift and drag on objects as they move through the air. After giving up astronomy and devoting his energies to powered flight, Langley designed and built an unmanned, heavier-than-air, steam-propelled airplane in 1896. This craft, which was launched from a catapult, successfully flew forty-two hundred feet over the Potomac River, was refueled, and flew again the same day.

Spurred on by fifty thousand dollars from the War Department to build a manned aerodrome, Langley, using a test pilot, attempted to launch a larger airplane on December 8, 1903. This model, weighing 850 pounds, was about one hundred pounds heavier than the Wright brothers' first airplane. However, the attempt failed due to problems with the catapult system, and the plane crashed into the Potomac just nine days before the Wrights' successful flight at Kitty Hawk.

It is now believed that Langley would have been the first to build a manned, heavier-than-air flying machine had his catapult worked. Discouraged because of the unfortunate outcome, and after hearing about the flight of the Wright brothers, Langley abandoned aviation forever. However, his unmanned aerodrome which flew in 1896 is regarded as the world's first successful airplane.

Airplane shadows

Contrary to what one might think, the shadow produced by a high-flying airplane is not bigger than the shadow created by the same plane when it is on the ground. In fact, both shadows would be the same size, and each would be as big as the airplane itself.

The path of photons of light coming from the sun travel virtually in parallel lines since the sun is so far from the earth. Shadows produced by parallel rays of light are the same size as the object that causes them regardless of where or how far away the shadows are projected. For this reason, the shadow of an airplane will be as big as the plane itself no matter how high or low the plane is flying.

Airplane tire wear

Despite the smoking, screeching tires usually seen when a large jet aircraft lands, it is not true that landings produce the greatest tire wear for an airplane. Nor is it true that the tires wear out faster during takeoffs. The truth is, experts uniformly agree that the most severe conditions for airplane tire wear are when the plane is slowly taxiing on the ground.

During the taxi of commercial jet aircraft, the lateral, or sideways, scrubbing action on tires as the aircraft is steering through turns produces the most tire wear. This is usually evident at airports where large black tire marks, similar to skid marks, can be seen on the tarmac and taxiways where planes turn while on the ground.

Following conditions on the ground, other factors affecting tire wear involve landings and takeoffs. However these effects are variable and are mostly influenced by tire heat. On cold tires, takeoffs are more destructive due to greater speeds, longer distances, and heavier fuel loads on the relatively stiff tire rubber. But on short flights, when tires remain hot considerably longer than one might expect, heated tires will wear faster on landings due to the effects of impact, tire spin, and braking.

Aisle

Brides do not walk down the aisle of a church during a wedding. The center section, or passage, of a church is correctly called the nave. The aisle refers to the outer, or side, sections of a church that are separated from the center area by pillars or some other structural support. This confusion stems from the early use of the Old English word *isle*, meaning "a surrounding area," when referring to the "middle isle" of a church.

Alcohol

Because of the behavior usually associated with the consumption of alcohol, it is commonly believed that alcohol is a stimulant. It is not. Alcohol is really a depressant and, as such, its effects can range from mental disorganization to death.

The specific effects of alcohol are as a selective depressant on the brain and central nervous system. Small quantities depress the inhibitory, or controlling, center within the brain producing a sensation of relaxation and loss of inhibitions usually mistaken for stimulation.

However, larger doses begin to sedate and impair muscular coordination, speech, and mental functioning in general. As the effects slowly spread from the frontal centers of the brain back toward the cerebellum, severe depression of the vital centers of the central nervous system may be fatal.

Also, contrary to popular opinion, alcohol does not warm the body in cold weather. The small capillaries under the skin dilate in response to alcohol creating the sensation of warmth, but the body temperature actually drops following the intake of alcohol, producing dangerous chilling in the cold.

It is also untrue that the reason people urinate much more when drinking alcoholic beverages is because more liquids are being taken into the body. Instead, the alcohol itself is actually removing water from the body causing partial dehydration.

This happens because the body contains a natural antidiuretic which regulates the amount of water in the blood. Alcohol inhibits this agent which, in effect, tells the kidneys to remove more water from the body. Increased urination and the resulting dehydration and thirst are some of the more familiar symptoms of excessive alcohol intake.

Alger, Horatio

As the most popular American writer in the last half of the nineteenth century, and the most influential of his generation, Horatio Alger and his 135 books have led to the legend known as the

Horatio Alger story. This American ideal of hard work rewarded with success and wealth, however, is largely unsupported by the content of Alger's novels or of his life itself.

No American writer has been so misrepresented by biographers as Horatio Alger. The rags-to-riches theme so often associated with Alger is not evident in any of his stories. Not one of his characters ever became wealthy. Although the young boys he wrote about persevered with virtue and industry, their rewards were only respectability and moderate financial success, usually resulting from the precipitous luck of meeting a wealthy businessman.

Alger saw himself as a moral reformer, and did not advocate wealth to achieve happiness. However, he was not exactly the personification of the American ideal of morality. Alger was a slave to his pederastic desires that by any standard would be condemned as morally unacceptable.

As related in *Horatio's Boys*, by Edwin P. Hoyt, the little boys that Alger wrote about in his fiction were simply the objects of his own homosexual persuasion which first became an issue while Alger served as a minister in 1864. At that time, Alger was forced to leave his parish after it was revealed that he was guilty of "gross immorality" and an "unnatural familiarity with boys" in the parish.

Although no other such accusations were ever made against Alger, his life followed a familiar pattern of very close associations with young boys. He later ran a home for wayward boys, he never married, and Alger lived out his life with his housekeeper and her young sons. Alger's novels represented a lifelong perversion focused on young boys, and he failed to heed the lesson of his own stories, as he died destitute.

Alumni

Alumni does not mean the former students, male and female, of a college or university. Neither do alumnus, alumna, or alumnae refer to the men and women who have previously attended a university. In fact, there appears to be no single word that precisely means both the men and women graduates of a school.

Alumnus refers to a male who has attended or is a graduate of a school, college, or university. Alumni is the plural of alumnus and means more than one male former student. Alumna is a female former student, while alumnae is the plural of alumna and refers to more than one female graduate.

American

Although it may come as a surprise to most residents of the United States, the term American technically applies to all people from the Canadian Arctic to Tierra del Fuego in South America. This is because "American" means any resident of the continent of America—North or South. Certainly, it describes those people in Central America, Mexico, the United States, and Canada since all are residents of North America.

In its more limited, but familiar, sense, American describes only those people living in the United States of America. Because there is no term like "United Statesians" to refer to residents of the U.S., the less specific "American," meaning the country and both continents, will have to suffice.

American Revolutionary War

When asked how the American colonists defeated the British during the Revolutionary War, most people imagine scenes of hapless, red-coated British soldiers marching in formation while hiding minutemen pick them off in ambush. However, this is not really how the Americans won the Revolution.

In the initial confrontations of the war, the methods used by the colonists were, in fact, quite unlike the formal, controlled, frontal line assaults with which the British were familiar. However, the British had seventy-five years of experience with this type of "guerrilla" warfare in North America, especially during the French and Indian War.

The Americans were, with this method of fighting, largely ineffective militarily, and early actions in the conflict were indecisive. The colonists' appearance of disarray only served to bolster British morale while lowering the confidence of the Americans.

The military gains made by the colonists were not realized until the Continental Army was trained in the traditional and more formal methods of European warfare. Baron Frederick von Steuben, with experience in the Prussian War, was engaged by Washington for this purpose. Through his influence and discipline in creating a regular army matching the British in tactics, the Americans were then able to defeat the British on the battle-field.

However, the American victory was really more the result of British failures than of colonial superiority. Fighting three thousand miles from home, on unknown terrain, with inferior commanders, lacking overall coordination of large armies, and the inability to utilize their naval power actually contributed more to the British defeat than did the actions of the Americans.

Also, contrary to popular belief, support among the Americans themselves for the war was not overwhelming. Historians tend to agree with John Adams's estimate that only about one-third of the colonists were Patriots, about one-third were British Tories, and the rest did not really care who won.

America's Cup

The America's Cup, the symbol of international yachting supremacy, does not refer to the United States of America. Originally known as the Hundred-Guinea Cup, it was offered, along with about five hundred dollars, by Great Britain's Royal Yacht Squadron as its trophy for yacht races conducted during the London Exposition in 1851.

After years of domination by the British, the privately owned yacht *America* won the Guinea Cup over twenty-four other challengers. The new owners of the trophy returned to the United States and renamed it the America's Cup in honor of their winning boat. The America's Cup remained in the possession of the New York Yacht Club for the next 132 years as its name came to be associated more with the country than for the yacht from which it was named.

Anarchy

As used in everyday speech, anarchy is a negative term that denotes absence of control and is characterized by lawlessness, disorder, rioting, and social breakdown. But as a political philosophy, anarchy holds only that government interference, or even the mere existence of authority, is inherently bad. Anarchy is actually one of the most idealistic and peaceful of all political theories.

Anarchy assumes that man is rational, cooperative, and basically good when given the choice to act freely, and will coexist in complete social harmony. It envisions a society, not without order, but one based on voluntary associations of self-governing groups functioning for the common good.

Anarchy is simply a nonauthoritarian society that views all laws and government as the sources of social evil. As a theory, it does not advocate revolution or even unrest. Because it condemns all forms of authority, the conditions of lawlessness sometimes occurring have been incorrectly labeled as anarchistic. However, the term properly applies only to the evils of authority, and not to the chaos usually described as anarchy.

Angels

Nowhere in the Bible does it mention that angels have wings. According to the Bible, angels are spiritual beings created by God to serve as heavenly messengers between the Creator and mankind. As such, they are pure spirits, entirely unrelated to physical matter, and cannot have wings or any other bodily features.

It has largely been through the influence of painters and sculptors that angels were depicted with wings. They are also usually presented as feminine figures, although biblical angels are always referred to in the masculine gender. These images of angels in the popular mind have proven highly resistant to change despite the fact that they have little in common with the angels described in the Bible.

Antarctica

Antarctica is quite unlike what most people imagine this region at the "bottom" of the world to be. It is not a frozen, flat ocean as is the Arctic.

The Antarctic is a large landmass comprising ten percent of the earth's land area, and is the fifth largest continent on earth. It has many mountainous regions, the highest of which is 16,864 feet, higher than the highest peak in the continental United States or any mountain in the Swiss Alps.

The average elevation of Antarctica's landmass is about eight thousand feet, twice that of any other continent. With its dome-shaped mantle of snow and ice permanently covering much of the surface, the combined average elevation is about fourteen thousand feet. The elevation at the South Pole is ninety-two hundred feet.

Antarctica is also seldom recognized as the coldest and most icy place in the world. Its mean temperature is 20°F colder than the Arctic, and Antarctica contains ninety percent of the world's ice.

Antelope

Although the popular western song *Home on the Range* contains the line, "where the deer and the antelope play," there are no antelope in North America. The nearest relative to the antelope on this continent is the Rocky Mountain goat. The animals in North America commonly called antelope are actually pronghorn sheep, which are found in Wyoming and several other western states. True antelope are found only in Africa and Asia.

Antiperspirants

Antiperspirants do not stop the flow of perspiration simply by plugging up the little sweat pores in the skin as is commonly believed. Perspiration does not simply flow, drip, or ooze out of the body by a pushing, or pumping, action from within.

Instead, the droplets of sweat, which are electrically negatively charged, are pulled out of the pores by the positively charged skin surface. The main ingredient in all antiperspirants is aluminum, which is negatively charged. The aluminum short-circuits the electrical charges of the perspiration system by neutralizing the attraction between the sweat in the pores and the skin surface. This stops the secretion of sweat.

Aphrodisiacs

Despite long-standing popular interest and historical folklore, there is virtually no scientific evidence to support any validity to the existence of aphrodisiacs, except to the power of suggestion.

Aphrodisiacs include both psychophysiological—such as visual, olfactory, and tactile—stimuli and internal substances. Both the popular interest in and the scientific study of aphrodisiacs is usually focused on the internal types involving foods, alcohol, drugs, or so-called love potions. Psychophysiological stimuli are generally recognized as contributing to an increase in sexual desire.

However, no substance has yet to be found that produces an

increase in sexual desire beyond psychological suggestion. Some, such as alcohol and other drugs, create a euphoria that tends to reduce inhibitions, but they also reduce sexual performance. Other substances that are commonly considered to be sexual inhibitors, such as saltpeter, similarly produce no verifiable physical effects on sexual desire or ability.

Many so-called aphrodisiacs, including Spanish fly, and anaphrodisiacs are actually nothing more than diuretics that elicit effects only with toxic doses. Even with these substances, the effects are indirect and not physiologically significant.

Apple in the Garden of Eden

Nowhere in the Bible is the apple mentioned, or even suggested, as the forbidden fruit eaten by Adam and Eve in the Garden of Eden. The only reference made by the Bible is to the "fruit of the tree" (Genesis 3:3), but no fruits are specifically named.

Horticulturists consider it highly unlikely that apple trees ever grew in regions where the Garden of Eden is presumed to have existed. Because the apple has been the principal fruit through much of early history, it became part of the popular version of this story from Genesis despite the lack of evidence from the Bible to support it.

It is also commonly believed that it was Eve who enticed Adam into taking the first bite from the fruit of the forbidden tree. This is not true. Eve actually bit first, and then Adam (Genesis 3:6), although the concept of original sin stems from Adam's transgression of eating the fruit.

Appleseed, Johnny

Johnny Appleseed was not a myth or a legend as many people think. He was a real person who did, in fact, roam frontier America distributing apple seeds to thousands of settlers and farmers.

Born John Chapman on September 26, 1774, in Leominster, Massachusetts, he wandered for forty years from the Alleghenies to Indiana distributing and scattering apple seeds to the westward-bound travelers and settlers. He obtained his seeds from the ever-present cider mills and spread them, along with preachings of Swedenborgianism, a complex Christian theology. He contributed greatly to the westward spread of the apple orchard in America.

Arabic numbers

Our modern system of numbering, called Arabic numerical notation, in which the value of a digit depends on its position, is not of Arabic origin. It began in India about A.D. 500, and by the ninth century, this Hindu numbering system had spread and was commonly in use in Arabic and Persian regions.

The numbering system gradually reached the capitals of European Christendom about 1100, and it retained the name of its presumed, but incorrect, Arabic origin. Arabic numbers replaced the existing Roman system, which was useless for calculations, throughout most of the world.

Aristotle

Although Aristotle is considered a brilliant thinker, history has chosen to remember only some of his thoughts while ignoring others—and for good reason.

Aristotle believed that men have more teeth than women, that the wind direction determines the sex of a child, that earthquakes are caused by winds inside the earth, and that motion is impossible in a vacuum.

He also thought that heavy objects fall faster than light ones, that the center of mental life is the heart, and that the purpose of the brain is to cool the blood.

Ark

Despite the popular notion that two of each kind of animal were taken onto Noah's Ark, there is actually no consistent inventory given in the Bible for either the number of animals or the kinds of each that were on the Ark. Although "two of every sort" of "unclean beasts" were gathered (Genesis 6:19), the Bible also says that "clean beasts" were gathered "by sevens" (Genesis 7:2).

"Clean" meant an animal's fitness for sacrifice and referred to those animals with a single hoof, such as a pig. "Unclean" animals were those with a cloven, or divided, hoof, such as oxen, sheep, and goats, which were considered more suitable for human consumption. However, the Bible does not specify what other animals, such as birds or insects, were on the Ark or how many of each kind were taken.

Our popular image of Noah's Ark is that of a small, crowded little boat overflowing with every kind of creature imaginable. Whatever it may have carried, the Ark certainly was not small. According to the Bible (Genesis 6:15), the Ark was 300 cubits, or 450 feet, in length, which was no small feat of construction for just Noah and his three sons. In comparison, Columbus's *Santa Maria* was 75 feet long, the *Mayflower* 90 feet, and the largest known wooden ship, built in the 1800s, was 377 feet in overall length.

Armor suits

Contrary to our image of the fallen knight helplessly incapable of standing up in his clanging suit of armor, armor suits were not clumsy and awkward, and weighed much less than most people would expect.

Protective armor suits first appeared in Bronze Age Greece and, through thousands of years of development and use, were perfected into very protective and practical equipment. Although earlier Roman shields, plates, and helmets often weighed up to a hundred pounds, by the time armor suits had reached their peak during the fifteenth and sixteenth centuries, they usually weighed between fifty and sixty pounds. This is about as much weight as a modern infantryman in the U.S. Army carries.

The weight of an armor suit was comfortably distributed over the entire body, and its wearer could run, climb, and lie or fall down and easily stand up again. The suit consisted of small, separate units strapped together which provided both flexibility and protection. Suits intended only for jousting were cumbersome for any other purpose, and it is this type of armor suit that is often displayed in museums.

Armored suits reflected great metallurgical skill in creating beauty of form while providing the utmost in utility. However, the advent of firearms and the need for faster cavalry made them obsolete by the seventeenth century. The only piece of armored equipment still regularly worn by soldiers is the modern military helmet.

Assault and battery

Assault and battery are not the same thing. Contrary to popular belief, assault is not the physical act of attacking another person.

Assault is simply the threat to do bodily harm by someone whose ability to carry out the threat is such that the victim fears he is in imminent danger. Physical contact is not necessary for assault to occur.

Battery is the actual contact by a person, or something he uses, against someone else. It must be intentional and without the consent of the victim. Injury is not required for battery to take place.

Thus, shaking your fist in someone's face during an argument can be considered assault, while actually striking them is battery.

Atlas

Atlas did not hold up the world on his shoulders as is usually depicted in art and mythology. As one of the original Greek gods, Atlas was condemned by Zeus to support the heavens on his shoulders as punishment for taking part in the war against Uranus.

Atomic bomb casualties

The belief that the atomic bombs dropped on Hiroshima and Nagasaki in Japan caused more loss of life and destruction than any other single event in warfare is not true. This misconception underestimates the destructive capability of conventional weapons. Air attacks on Tokyo and the German city of Dresden in World War II resulted in more deaths and devastation than was evident at either Hiroshima or Nagasaki.

The atomic bomb dropped on Hiroshima on August 9, 1945, killed about seventy-five thousand people and destroyed nearly a third of the city. The second bomb dropped on Nagasaki resulted in the deaths of about thirty-five thousand Japanese.

The German city of Dresden was the target of a conventional, combined American and British bombing attack mostly during the night of February 13–14, 1945. It is regarded as the most controversial example of aerial overkill, as both explosive and incendiary bombs obliterated the city of nearly a million. About one hundred thirty-five thousand people, mostly civilians, were killed as the greatest firestorm ever known destroyed nearly the entire city of Dresden.

In another conventional attack more devastating than Hiroshima, a one-night attack on Tokyo on March 9–10, 1945 by 279 B-29 bombers dropped 1,665 tons of napalm on the population center of the city. About eighty-five thousand people were killed.

The causes of death in the Tokyo attack were direct incineration, with many victims actually roasted in their beds, suffocation, and scalding when people were forced into boiling rivers and canals. The resulting firestorm leveled much of the densely populated city within six hours, and killed more Japanese than did the Hiroshima blast.

Automobile, invention of

Contrary to what most car-loving Americans think, the automobile was not invented by Henry Ford, or by any other American for that matter. It was Germany that became the birthplace of the automobile, France its nursery, and later, it was the United States that became the automobile's playground.

While primitive steam mobiles were put together as early as 1769, usable steam automobiles were in existence in Europe by the 1870s. But, these vehicles were nothing more than cumbersome novelties. A practical horseless carriage needed a smaller, lighter, and more efficient power source.

This was provided by two German engineers, Nikolaus Otto and Gottlieb Daimler, who invented, patented, and produced the internal combustion engine in 1876. By 1885, another German, Karl Benz, used his version of this engine to produce, along with Daimler, the first motorized automobiles that are considered the forerunner of the modern car. In France, by the end of the nineteenth century, the Duryeas, and numerous other producers, were also manufacturing their own autos on a large scale.

The American credited with developing the first U.S. auto was Elwood Haynea, who, in 1894, drove his machine into history, and later, into the National Museum in Washington, as the first American-made automobile. But before Haynea and the other Americans, such as Henry Ford, who made the automobile practical for the average person, it was the Europeans, following a tradition of a hundred years of tinkering, who actually first invented the automobile.

B

"Everybody is ignorant,
only on different subjects."

Will Rogers

Baby Ruth

There is no connection between the popular Baby Ruth candy bar and the famous baseball player Babe Ruth. In fact, the association between the two is so common that most people usually incorrectly call the candy bar "Babe Ruth."

However, the Baby Ruth candy bar was named after the White House baby and first daughter of President and Mrs. Grover Cleveland, Ruth Cleveland. Shortly after Ruth's birth, the press began referring to her as Baby Ruth. Thirty years later in 1921, the name was still popular with the American people, and was used by the Curtis Candy Company as the name for their new candy bar.

Bacteria

Bacteria are not always the harmful little bugs that most people think they are. While a very few are pathogens, the vast majority are quite harmless. Many are not only beneficial, but essential for life on earth. These one-celled organisms are found everywhere on, in, and above the earth and constitute a vital

21

group in the biological community. In fact, without bacteria, there would be no life as we know it.

The most important role of bacteria is in decomposing dead plant and animal tissues. Bacteria also significantly contribute to the digestive systems of animals, including man, and provide a protective defense around the human body to destroy intruding viruses. In addition, we even regularly eat untold numbers of bacteria or foods produced from bacterial action, such as cheese, yogurt, and sour cream.

Bad Breath

Contrary to what the manufacturers of mouthwashes would like us to believe, bad breath is not usually the result of food odors or bacteria in the mouth. Mouthwashes are largely cosmetic and do not affect the principal cause of ordinary bad breath.

The normal mouth is supposed to contain protective and useful microbes. One drop of saliva is swarming with over ten million bacteria, most of which live where mouthwashes cannot reach. Even if they did, the microbes would reappear almost immediately after mouth rinsing.

Odors from foods such as onions and garlic do not actually originate in the mouth. These foods contain volatile oils that are absorbed by the digestive system into the bloodstream, where they are then transported to the lungs. The oils are then mixed with the exhaled carbon dioxide, producing the offending mouth odor. Thus, bad breath emanates from the lungs and not the mouth itself.

True halitosis is a symptom of poor oral hygiene, tooth decay, gum problems, or infection and should be professionally treated.

Bagpipe

Although it is the official national instrument of Scotland, the bagpipe is not of Scottish origin. The bagpipe (it is singular and not, as is commonly spoken, bagpipes) has been popular throughout history in many parts of the world.

The bagpipe is mentioned in the Bible, was played by the ancient Romans and Greeks, and coins from Nero's time depict the bagpipe. It spread from the Mediterranean and was well known all over Europe for fifteen hundred years.

In the thirteenth century, the bagpipe appeared in Britain, Ireland, and finally Scotland. It is still found throughout the world, especially among mountain tribes, but is now most popular in Scotland.

Bald eagle

The bald eagle, America's national bird and the only eagle native to North America, is not bald. The name originated from the bird's characteristic slicked-down white feathers covering its head.

A Middle English word, *balded*, meaning "white" or "having white fur or feathers," was still in common use when the English first settled America. After encountering this unique American bird, they called it the *balded* eagle. However, after the word *balded* disappeared from everyday use, the name became transformed to the bald eagle.

Baltimore Oriole

The familiar black and orange bird found throughout the eastern United States called the Baltimore Oriole was not named after the city of Baltimore as one might assume. The bird acquired its name long before the town of Baltimore was first settled.

George Calvert, who established the colony of Maryland in 1632, had assumed the title of Lord Baltimore and adopted black and orange as the family's colors. The Baltimore Oriole derived its popular name because its colors were the same as those of the Baltimore family. The bird was already known as the Baltimore bird by 1669, whereas the city was not even founded until 1729.

Bamboo

Bamboo is not a tree. Although woody and treelike in appearance, it is actually a grass. Growing in tropical regions in thick, grasslike clumps, some types of bamboo can grow a foot a day to heights of 100 to 120 feet in just three months, making it the fastest growing plant in the world.

Bananas

The banana is a very common and popular fruit. However, like most things that surround us, very little is actually known about this fruit, and much that is generally thought to be true about the banana is not.

The banana does not grow on a tree. Although the plant may look like a tree, it is actually considered a very large herb. Having no roots, the plant produces rhizomes, which spread out to generate new plants. The so-called trunk of the banana plant does not contain any wood, but is really a false stem made up of large leaf sheaths tightly wrapped together in a tubular configuration. In fact, the banana "tree" is the largest known plant without a woody stem or trunk.

The fruit of the banana is actually classified by botanists as a berry. It is picked green, not to preserve them longer during shipment, but because they become almost inedible if allowed to ripen on the plant. Unless removed before ripe, the starches will not convert to sugar, the banana will lack taste, the skin will break open, and the fruit will quickly rot. A banana that is flecked with brown specks, known as sugar specks, is at its best for eating.

Each plant produces just one fruit bearing stem, which takes fifiteen to eighteen months to develop, and it will do so just one time. The fruit forms on a long stalk which emerges from the center of the leafy trunk. The "fingers," as the individual bananas are called, hang down as they develop on the stalk. But, as their weight increases, the stalk invariably bends over and the bananas spend most of their time on the plant growing upside down.

The single stalk from a plant contains clusters of thirty to seventy bananas growing in clumps, or "hands." These clumps grow in a ring around the stalk, with the familiar supermarket bunch being only a portion of each clump which has been sliced off.

In the wild, uncultivated state, bananas are practically inedible, being leathery and full of seeds. The part of the banana that is eaten is not a seed. It is a fleshy pulp that formerly contained seeds. Commercially grown bananas have been developed in a seedless form so that the crop is now virtually sterile. Bananas can now reproduce only through human intervention.

Pound for pound, bananas are the most popular fruit sold in

the United States, even ahead of the all-American apple in per-capita consumption, and close to the combined production of all citrus fruits. But surprisingly, about 35 percent of a banana's weight consists of the peel.

Bananas are also more than just monkey food. They are an excellent source of nutrition, and are ideal for providing quick energy and potassium as the most easily digested natural food for humans.

Bank checks

It is popularly believed that bank checks are formal documents valid only if written on the standard, preprinted forms provided by banks. This is not true.

In most states, a check is simply a written order directing a bank to pay on demand a specified amount of money from the account of the person writing the check, payable only to the person named on it. It can be written on anything for any amount, and not just on a form specified by a bank. It can be written and dated on a Sunday, since a check is not a contract.

The rules for check writing are few and simple. The amount to be paid must be written in both numbers and words, and the name of the payee and of the bank must also be written.

A check written in pencil is usually legal. It can be written on an ordinary piece of paper or on anything else that can be reasonably handled.

For example, Cornelius Vanderbilt, one of the richest men who ever lived, never used a regular bank checkbook. His checks were all written on half sheets of plain writing paper. Checks have been written in anger and jest on anything from rocks to shirts, all of which are acceptable forms of payment.

Baseball bats

It is a common misconception among most people who have ever played baseball that the trademark on a wooden baseball bat should be on the opposite side of the bat from where the ball is hit. This is not true. The position of the trademark should actually be pointing straight up when the bat strikes the ball.

The strongest part of a wooden bat is "against the grain," which are the lines of growth in the wood. The weakest part is the "top of the grain." All wooden baseball bats are branded when made with the trademark of the manufacturer on "top of the grain," so that either the trademark side or its opposite is identified as the weakest part of the bat.

Consequently, when hitting a baseball with a wooden bat, the bat should be held with the trademark facing straight up, 90° to the oncoming ball, thereby exposing the strongest part of the bat to the pitch. If the ball is hit with the trademark opposite the ball's point of contact, the weakest part of the bat will be struck.

Baseball, invention of

The popular belief that baseball was invented by Abner Doubleday in Cooperstown, New York, in 1839, is commonly accepted as fact. Although this legend makes a delightful story to explain the origins of America's pastime, it is not true.

The idea that Doubleday invented the game of baseball began with the report issued by the Special Baseball Commission of 1906–07. This commission was formed by A. G. Spalding, president of the sporting goods company that bears his name.

Spalding created the commission in an attempt to establish the fact that baseball was an American game free from all foreign influence. He felt it would benefit the image of baseball, as well as his sporting goods business, to authenticate the sport as the all-American pastime. With this purpose in mind, the commission became a rubber stamp for Spalding's views.

Spalding selected as the commission chairman a friend who had also gone to high school with Doubleday. The commission was a farce, being composed of politicians, Spalding's business friends, and ex-athletes. No serious research was ever conducted to support their findings. According to the commission, Doubleday, a popular Union general, sportsman, and writer, was proclaimed the inventor of baseball, and the game was to be forever known as an American sport.

However, baseball clearly derived from the English game of rounders. A baseball-like game, rounders had been a popular English sport which was also played in colonial America. The first use of the word baseball appeared in a 1744 book depicting a rounders-like game referred to as "base-ball." An 1829 London book describes a similar game, as does a Boston book in 1834.

The person now generally credited by historians for having

the most to do with the creation of modern baseball is Alexander J. Cartwright, who devised a baseball-like game in 1840 and prescribed official rules and diagrams in 1845. Cartwright did not invent the sport, but he did formalize and structure the commonly played rounders-like game of the period.

Cartwright's contributions are documented, while absolutely no support exists for the Doubleday theory. It is strange that even Doubleday himself, who had been a writer, never wrote a single word about the game he supposedly invented.

Basketball

Basketball is the only major sport played in the United States that is totally American in origin. Every other sport evolved or was basically copied from a game played in another country.

The game of basketball was invented by James Naismith on December 1, 1891. As an instructor at the YMCA Training School, now Springfield College, in Springfield, Massachusetts, Naismith responded to his students' complaints about the boring gymnasium classes, which consisted of marching and calisthenics. After some trial and error, he devised a game with two closed-bottomed peach baskets and a soccer ball.

To say that the game's popularity spread rapidly would be an understatement. During the Christmas break that December, word quickly spread of Naismith's new game, and by the next month he hurriedly printed rules in the campus newspaper.

In a short time, the basic principles of basketball were established, including the use of closed-bottom nets instead of baskets by 1893. However, surprisingly, no one figured out until 1912 that using bottomless nets would greatly increase the game's speed. Nevertheless, despite this shortcoming, the only sport truly American had already become widely established.

Basketball rim

Contrary to what anyone who has ever played basketball might think, a metal basketball rim is more than twice the diameter of a regulation basketball. The rim is nineteen inches in diameter, while a basketball has a diameter of nine inches.

Bats

Bats are not blind. All bats have well developed, functional eyes and can see, although their eyesight is not as acute as other mammals, and they do not see colors. Fruit-eating bats have large eyes suited for keen night vision, while insect-eating bats have smaller eyes that combine with the bat's sense of hearing for detecting objects. Many species seek food only in weak light and require good vision.

In addition to sight, most bats rely on sound reflection, or echolocation, to locate objects. This form of sonar uses the reflected audible and ultrasonic sounds emitted by the bat to find its way in the dark. Because of this unique ability to use sound, the vision of bats has been generally underestimated by most people.

Bear hug

The tight embrace known as a bear hug, in which one person wraps their arms around and squeezes another, is not done by bears. At no time in their everyday behavior, as a means of obtaining food, for attacking, or to protect their young, is there any gesture or movement that can be characterized as a hug.

The mistaken idea that a bear hugs stems from the notion that a bear's pawing behavior is an attempt to grab and hold its intended victim. But because of its anatomical structure, a bear will attack only by striking a rounded blow with its strong paws. It will powerfully drive its claws into the body, and then the bear will tear the victim with its teeth. But it will never grab, hold, and hug its victim.

Bears hibernating

Contrary to popular belief, bears do not really hibernate. Although they do sleep through most of the winter, their winter sleep is not true hibernation. In fact, animals that do hibernate are actually few in number.

Hibernation is a state of greatly reduced metabolic activity including a significantly lowered body temperature with a barely perceptible heartbeat. It is a state close to death. True hibernators usually cannot be woken up, even when placed in a warm environment.

Most mammals, including bears, return to an underground

burrow or den for the winter and lapse into a long, but fairly normal, sleep. The body temperature of a bear drops only a few degrees during their sleep, and they can easily be awakened in a few minutes. In fact, most of their normal body functions continue during the winter sleep, and bears will often move around or go out to eat in mild weather. Females will even have their cubs in their winter den.

Bees as social insects

Our popular image of the bee as a social insect living in crowded, but highly organized, societies is not entirely correct. Contrary to popular opinion, not all bees are social. In fact, most are solitary.

In the United States, only two kinds of bees are social—honey and bumble bees. The majority, such as leaf cutters, carpenter bees, and mining bees, are actually solitary insects.

Solitary bees build individual nests, usually by burrowing into the ground, wood, or moist clay. There are no queens responsible for all egg production. Individual female bees simply deposit eggs into their nests and leave. Bees that are solitary do not engage in social behavior, except in connection with mating, do not build hives, and lack the division of labor and specialization typical of the more familiar social bees.

Bees collecting honey

Bees do not collect honey. Instead, they gather nectar from the flower, which is then converted into honey by other bees in the hive.

After the female bee extracts the nectar, it is stored in a special stomach not used for digestion while the bee transports it to the hive. Other worker bees then dry this watery liquid and convert it into honey. In order to produce one pound of honey, the bees in a hive must travel a combined distance of twice around the world collecting nectar from about two million flowers.

Bell, Alexander Graham

Alexander Graham Bell was not solely responsible for the invention of the telephone. Bell is famous because he improved upon the ideas and apparatus of others, made the telephone a practical device, recognized its potential for commercial success, and, probably most important, because he just beat another inventor to the patent office.

The fact that others had already contributed much to the development of crude telephones is well documented. Several inventors were devising similar instruments at the same time as Bell, and later, many claims were made for the telephone's invention.

The telephone was actually a device just waiting to be invented. The mechanics of sound vibrations were already understood, as were those of electrical transmission. Elisha Gray had been the first to build a receiver, then Bell followed with his own. In 1875, both men lacked a transmitter until, working independently, they each developed a suitable device in 1876.

From this followed one of the great legal contests in patent credit history when Gray and Bell both filed patents for the invention of the telephone. However, Bell arrived at the patent office just two hours before Gray and, after years of litigation, Bell's patent was finally upheld by the U.S. Supreme Court in a divided opinion.

The irony is that Bell's original invention probably would not have worked in a large-scale, long-distance phone system such as the one we have today. Rather, it was Gray's device that is actually closer to our modern telephone. But because Bell had better financial support, he was able to implement and expand his system, and, consequently, has received the popular credit for the telephone's invention.

Bellwether

A bellwether does not have anything to do with meteorology. It is a castrated male sheep (wether) which leads the flock while wearing a bell. A bellwether is, then, any leader or, in a more general sense, anything that forewarns events or trends.

Ben Hur

Ben Hur is not a biblical story as many people believe. He was the main character in an 1880 novel by Lew Wallace.

Ben Hur: A Tale of the Christ was one of the best selling books in American publishing history. It concerns the adventures of Judah Ben Hur, his mother and sister, and their conversion to the Christian faith. *Ben Hur* has been presented on stage many times, and provided the basis for two spectacular films in 1929 and 1959.

Ironically, Lew Wallace was inspired to write the novel after a philosophical argument with an agnostic. His shaken beliefs induced Wallace to write a novel that he believed would reveal the true divinity of Christ.

Between the devil and the deep blue sea

The expression "between the devil and the deep blue sea" does not mean to be between Satan and the bottom of the ocean as a literal, and meaningless, interpretation would suggest.

Devil was an early nautical term for the heavy plank used as a support beam in the hull of a wooden ship. Access around the devil in the ship's interior was usually very difficult. To be between the devil and the deep blue sea simply meant to be in a confined or tight location in the bottom of a ship. The expression now means being between equally harsh alternatives.

Big Ben

The famous clock in the tower of the London House of Parliament is not called Big Ben. It is actually the bell, and not the clock, which is correctly referred to by that name.

The huge bell, nine feet in diameter, weighing over thirteen tons, and having a four hundred pound hammer, entered service in 1859. Big Ben is believed to have been named after Sir Benjamin Hall, the original commissioner of the works.

Billion

According to the system of numeration used in the United States, a billion is a thousand million, or 1,000,000,000. But in Britain, France, and Germany, a billion is a million million, or 1,000,000,000,000, which is called a trillion in the United States. Our billion in those countries is called a milliard.

Birds listening for worms

Birds do not turn and move their heads around in order to listen for worms in the ground as many people believe. Since a bird's eyes are located on each side of its head, there is only a small area directly in front of them where both visual fields overlap. Also, the eyes of most birds do not move around in their sockets very well, whereas the neck of a bird is quite flexible. Consequently, birds will constantly move their heads around in order to place the visual target in this small area of binocular vision. Avian hearing is actually very acute without having to turn their heads in order to improve it.

Birds' wings

It is commonly assumed that birds fly simply by flapping their wings up and down, and that the downward push of the wing moves the bird upward. But if this is true, the question then arises, why doesn't the upstroke of the wing push the bird back down? The answer is because birds do not really fly just by the flapping of their wings up and down. The actual motion of the wing during flight is a roughly circular pattern, but with intricate and elaborately articulated movements.

The wing of a bird is very similar in bone structure to a modified human arm. It has a shoulder, humerus, elbow, forearm, and a ''hand,'' which is fused together to form attachments for the all-important flight feathers.

Wing flapping is a complicated movement that must provide lift, reduce drag, and move the bird forward all at the same time. This is accomplished not only by the wings themselves, but primarily from the feathers attached to the end of the wing. Most flying birds have ten flight feathers on each wing that provide the bird's forward motion, as well as other wing feathers which produce lift. These feathers are more than just a covering, they are absolutely essential for flight.

In order to fly, the flight feathers, which are individually controlled, push backward on the downstroke of the wing and immediately rotate and move forward on the upstroke. Drag is virtually eliminated as the wings and feathers are twisted and reshaped so that the wing tips move backward at whatever speed the bird is moving forward. Most forward thrust is produced on the backward downstroke, while lift is provided by the inner surface of the wing on both strokes. These motions combine so that the wing tips actually form an approximate figure-eight pattern during each cycle, and all within a fraction of a second.

Biweekly, bimonthly, biannually

Although the prefix "bi" means "two," the word *biweekly* can mean both every two weeks or twice a week. Similarly, bimonthly means happening every second month or twice a month. But biannual means twice a year, and biennial means every two years.

To avoid this confusion, the preferred term would be semiweekly, semimonthly, and semiannually to mean twice a week, month, or year. "Semi" means "half," except when used in semiconscious, when it means only "partly," or in semitrailer truck, in which case it does not refer to half a truck, but to a trailer that rests on a tractor instead of riding on its own wheels.

English, a language rich in poetic beauty, ancient in its history, and vast in its scope, is, at times, a bit lacking in precision.

Black widow spiders

The black widow spider derives its name from the erroneous belief that the female invariably kills the male after mating. However, the male usually is not killed, and when he is, reasons other than lover's revenge are responsible for the behavior.

Like most male spiders, mating is a dangerous activity for the black widow. He sometimes runs a considerable risk in approaching his mate, who is usually much larger and may be hungry instead of ready to mate. Intricate behavior is required to approach the female to signal a mating response, and some males do not signal properly. They are then mistaken for an intruder and are killed and eaten.

After mating, the male must quickly leave before the normal predatory instincts return to the female. If the delay is too long, the female may regard the male as an intruder and kill him. On other occasions, the male, who usually fasts before mating, often is weakened, and he then becomes an easy victim for the female. However, a fatal outcome is not usually the rule, and only occasionally does the female live up to her reputation.

Blackboard chalk

The common chalk used in schoolrooms is not really chalk at all, but a manufactured substance that contains none of the actual material.

Naturally occurring chalk is usually a sedimentary, limestone rock composed of soft, fine granules that vary in color from pure white to gray. It is a marine deposit and has many agricultural and industrial uses, including cement production and as a stomach antacid.

Man-made chalk is of two types. The older variety is molded from simple plaster of paris, consisting of calcium sulfate made from gypsum, and is very soft and dusty. Newer types of chalk are extruded forms of plaster of paris, but are also mixed with clay and calcium carbonate, making them somewhat harder. These additives weigh down the dust particles from the chalk causing them to fall instead of floating through the air. It is the extruded plaster-of-paris "chalk" that is now most common in classrooms.

Blackheads

The little dark spots in the skin known as blackheads are not globs of dirt as is generally believed. Blackheads are dried plugs of fatty material in the ducts, or sebaceous follicle, of the oil-secreting glands of the skin.

At times, these glands fail to release their fatty secretions in the correct manner, causing them to enlarge. The resulting oily clumps darken at the skin's surface and produce the familiar dark, pimplelike spot. Albinos, who lack the skin pigmentation melanin, have light-colored "blackheads."

Blood

Blood is not always red. Actually, human blood is only red half the time and throughout half the body. Otherwise, it is usually a purplish blue.

Blood is red only in the arteries after it has left the heart when it is laden with oxygen. However, once the oxygen has been released throughout the body, blood picks up carbon dioxide and other wastes from the body's cells. It then takes on a purplish, almost blue, color in the veins as it is returned to the heart. In fact, half the heart itself is colored purplish blue from the deoxygenated blood. When cut, though, this blood in the veins immediately turns red when exposed to the oxygen in the air.

Blood, sweat, and tears

"Blood, sweat, and tears" were not the words used by Winston Churchill in describing conditions during World War II. What he actually said was, "Blood, toil, tears, and sweat."

The expression also had a long tradition before it was made famous by Churchill. John Donne in 1611, Lord Byron in 1823, and Lord Alfred Douglas in 1919 expressed similar phrases. However, Churchill's use of the phrase made it so familiar that he is usually credited with originating it.

Blue laws

Puritan blue laws and current Sunday blue laws were not named so because they made people sad, although many of them could have had that effect. These laws derived their name simply because they were originally printed on blue paper.

Laws regulating conduct on Sunday are sixteen centuries old and in England date to the thirteenth century. Early colonists brought these traditions to America and made them even more prohibitive because of their religious zeal.

In 1665, the governor of the New Haven Colony and clergymen drew up a strict legal code that regulated personal conduct, particularly on Sunday. Since these laws were written on blue paper, they commonly became known as blue laws. Puritan blue laws included the forbidding of cooking, shaving, travel, routine housework, or even sexual intercourse on Sunday.

Blue laws, now referred to as Sunday laws, have continued to exist in American society. Ostensibly, not to impose religious beliefs, but to protect public health or to enhance the idea of a day of rest, Sunday laws forbid conducting business on Sunday, selling alcohol, or signing contracts.

In the United States, early blue laws were clearly motivated by religious purposes. However, courts have interpreted them as secular attempts to establish a day of rest. In recent years, Sunday laws have generally been rescinded pertaining to most retail business activity.

Boa constrictors

Contrary to popular belief, boa constrictors do not crush their prey to death. After pouncing on their victims, constrictors, which range in length from four to thirty-seven feet, usually place two or three coils of their body around the chest of the victim. Then, as breath is exhaled, the constrictor takes up the slack by tightening the coil. The prey quickly suffocates after only a few breaths.

Boats and ships

There is a difference between a boat and a ship, although the two words are often used interchangeably. Ships are larger, navigate in oceans, and travel on regular sea lanes. They include ocean liners, tankers, and aircraft carriers.

Boats are smaller, usually cruise rivers and lakes, and, most importantly, can be carried on a ship. Almost all yachts and pleasure craft, motorboats, ferries, and tugs are considered boats.

Bobcat

Generally assumed to be a large, tigerlike cat, the bobcat is only about twice the size of the average house cat. Bobcats, which range over most of North America, are about thirty-one to thirty-five inches long, including the tail. The average male weighs about twenty pounds, and the female is even smaller.

The name "bobcat" comes from its short, stumpy tail which is uncharacteristic for a cat. It is not particularly dangerous, as it feeds mainly on small birds and rodents.

Body hair

It is generally assumed that body hair somehow knows when it has been cut so that it can resume growing. But since hair is dead tissue, it does not really know much of anything. "Knowing" when to grow is actually dependent on factors other than hair intelligence.

There are two types of hair on the human body—hair that grows continuously on the scalp and the face of men, and hair of definite length that appears over the rest of the body of both sexes.

The second type—body hair—actually alternates between a growth cycle and dormancy. The hair follicle in the skin produces a hair of a certain length and then stops and rests. It later repeats the cycle, growing a new hair which then pushes out the old one, causing it to fall out.

Fortunately, this process does not occur in unison over the whole body, or we would shed like dogs. Shaving or cutting body hair simply cuts off hairs that are in various stages of this growth cycle. Hairs that reappear as stubble the next day are only those hairs that were in the growth cycle when cut.

Dormant follicles remain unaffected by the cutting and do not produce a new hair until possibly weeks later. Thus, hairs do not "know" when to grow after being cut, but only certain ones continue growing which create that impression.

Bogart, Humphrey

Although commonly used by Bogart impersonators to characterize him, Humphrey Bogart never says, "Play it again, Sam," in the film *Casablanca*.

Boiling point

The boiling point of water is not an absolute, specific temperature. Although most people think that water boils at 212°F, this only occurs at sea level and at mean atmospheric pressure. At higher elevations or under lower air pressure, water boils at lower temperatures.

As water is heated, internal bubbles of vapor pressure form in the liquid. The boiling point is reached when the internal vapor pressure of these bubbles equals the external atmospheric pressure on the surface of the liquid, allowing the vapor bubbles to break free and evaporate into the atmosphere.

However, contrary to popular belief, the little bubbles visible in boiling water are not air bubbles. They are actually steam—pockets of pure, invisible water vapor—being forced out of the liquid by the heating. When the boiling point is reached, all additional heat is absorbed without any accompanying increase in the temperature of a liquid so that at sea level, water cannot be heated higher than 212°F no matter how much heat is applied.

Since the boiling point depends on the external pressure of a liquid's surface, and since air is less dense at higher elevations, the air pressure exerted on a liquid decreases as altitude increases. The effect of this is to lower the boiling point as altitude increases. This difference amounts to a decrease of one degree in the boiling point of water for every 538 feet of altitude. Similarly, the boiling point is raised by increasing surface pressure on a liquid, as occurs in a pressure cooker.

On Pikes Peak, the boiling point of water is 187°F. An egg could be boiled, but it would take considerably longer. On Mt. Everest, it would be very difficult, if not impossible, to hardboil eggs because the water would boil at such a low temperature.

Bones

It is not true that human bones are solid, dry, brittle, and white. Bones are extremely porous, pulsating, blood-soaked living tissues. They are soft, relatively lightweight, and actually have a spongelike interior. In fact, if bones were solid, movement would be very difficult because of the tremendous weight they would have.

Human bone is made up of four distinct layers. The center is a core of marrow where white blood cells are produced. Next is a fairly large area of thick, spongy, and very porous bonelike material full of blood vessels and cells. This layer is surrounded by a wall of hard, calcified material. It is this hard layer that conforms to our popular image of bone. Finally, a thin layer of skinlike tissue covers the bone.

Bones are not white, either, but actually range in color from beige to light brown. The white, sterile skeleton bones seen in displays have been carefully boiled and cleaned. In fact, the word skeleton comes from a Greek word meaning ''dried up.''

Boomerangs

It is commonly believed that boomerangs are uniquely Australian and that they are aboriginal throwing sticks designed to return to the thrower. Both of these notions are untrue.

Throwing sticks and clubs used as hunting tools and weapons of warfare have been known in all areas of the world throughout history. The word boomerang is simply the Australian aborigines' term for their version of the throwing stick. Most Australian boomerangs, like those elsewhere, are intended to follow a straight line toward the target and can be extremely accurate and deadly.

Throughout history the returning boomerang has been unknown among hunting tribes outside Australia. It is also unknown among many tribes within Australia. The Australian aborigines regard the returning boomerang simply as a toy or recreational throwing stick. In fact, the returning boomerang is not, and never has been, considered a serious weapon and is rarely used by Australian natives. But it captured the attention and interest of foreigners, and the popular image of the boomerang now erroneously consists of just this type of throwing stick.

Boston Tea Party

Every school child learns that the Boston Tea Party was a protest by colonial Americans against higher taxes on imported British tea. However, this is incorrect. The truth is, the price of tea was actually lowered by the British, and the colonists reacted by dumping some of it into the Boston harbor.

Under the Townshend Act, many goods brought into the colonies were heavily taxed by the British. To appease the disgruntled Americans, these tariffs were repealed, with the exception of tea. However, Americans were generally unconcerned by this event since most of their tea supply came from less expensive, smuggled Dutch tea, much of it by John Hancock.

As a result, British tea manufacturers accumulated seventeen million pounds of surplus tea. In an attempt to sell it, the Tea Act was passed by Parliament, eliminating all duties on British tea and pricing it below the cost of smuggled Dutch tea.

To demonstrate their resistance to British interference in what was increasingly seen as an American, and not British, economy, the colonists refused to allow the unloading of the cheaper tea. On December 16, 1773, about sixty men dressed as Indians, with several thousand onlookers, dumped the cargo of cheap tea from three British ships into Boston Harbor in what became known as the Boston Tea Party.

Bowie knife

The bowie knife was not invented by James Bowie. The credit for its invention belongs to his brother, Rezin Pleasant Bowie, in the early 1820s.

Although Rezin Bowie designed the knife, he did not actually make it. The first bowie knife was made by a blacksmith named Jesse Cliffe. The knife was made famous by the success James

Bowie had with it in the Sandbar Duel, and it became standard equipment for the American frontiersman.

Boxing Day

As a legal holiday in Britain and Canada, Boxing Day has nothing to do with fighting. It refers to the custom of giving gift boxes to faithful employees and servants on the day after Christmas. Originally, it was the day all Christmas presents were given in England.

Bucking bronco

Bucking broncos in the rodeo do not buck and rear because there is an unfamiliar rider on them, because of any bucking instincts they may have, or because of their natural talents for showmanship. They buck because a strap, called a flank girth, is tightly tied around the animal's midsection and across the sensitive side flanks while it is in the chute. This technique is used in bareback and saddle-bronc riding to create the impression that the bronco is a wild, uncontrolled, and untamed animal when, in fact, it is only reacting to the discomfort of the strap.

Buffalo

If a person were to abide by the words of the popular old western song, "Oh, give me a home, where the buffalo roam," they would be living in Africa or Asia. The term buffalo is commonly, but erroneously, applied to the North American animals that are correctly called bison.

Buffalo is the popular name for various species of cattle native to Africa and Asia. The African varieties have a smooth black coat and resemble cattle more than do the familiar water buffalo of Asia.

The American bison is a cattlelike animal with a low-slung head, horns that curve inward, and the characteristic dark, shaggy fur covering the head, neck, and hump. The European bison, or wisent, is smaller and less shaggy than the American bison and is now found only in zoos.

There are two types of American bison—a plains and a woodlands bison. The plains bison was formerly known for its large herds throughout the Midwest. But by 1900, their numbers had been reduced by about fifty million from recreational hunting.

The native American herd is now nearly extinct with only a few hundred animals left alive.

Buffalo, New York

New York's second largest city, Buffalo, was not named after the animal called the buffalo. The name of the city actually derives from an Indian mispronunciation of a French word for the river where the town was established.

French trappers, who first settled the area in the late 1700s, built a trading post along what is now the Niagara River. It is believed that an early French missionary named a small creek at the site of this settlement the *belle fleume*, meaning beautiful river.

Local Indians, who were familiar with the white man's word "buffalo," failed to distinguish *belle fleume* from the word "buffalo" and began calling the town "boof-flo." Although the town was officially named New Amsterdam in 1803, it was still commonly called Buffalo Creek by most people. The name remained in popular use, and was later shortened to Buffalo and made official.

Bug

The word "bug," in the slang expression, "Don't bug me," has nothing to do with insects and never did. Bug, meaning to annoy or upset, derives as slang from Black English which, in turn, acquired it from the West African word *bagu*, meaning to annoy.

Bulldog

The bulldog does not derive its name because its unique appearance resembles a bull. The name was acquired in medieval England when the sport of bullbaiting was popular.

Bullbaiting consisted of having trained dogs attack bulls. The dogs would grab onto the bull's snout with its powerful jaws and hang on as long as possible. Dogs were bred with strong neck and jaw muscles and with short, flat faces to facilitate their task.

Bullbaiting was outlawed in England in 1835. Further breeding since then has produced the gentle disposition of the modern bulldog, although its appearance remains much the same.

Bullet-proof glass

Technically, there really is no such thing as bullet-proof glass. To be correct, the material is actually called bullet-resistant laminated glass, and although it will stop bullets, it is not really the glass that provides the protection.

The bullet-stopping ingredient in this type of glass is extremely strong but clear plastic sheets that are sandwiched between layers of fairly common tempered glass. Although tempered glass is somewhat stronger than ordinary glass, by itself it cannot stop or significantly slow down a bullet. Most bullet-resistant glass contains at least three to five layers of these protective plastic sheets between layers of tempered glass and is quite thick.

Bullet-resistant glass actually originated as airplanes, particularly jets, reached such high speeds that cockpit windows were often smashed by birds. By adding additional plastic layers to the type of glass developed, it was found that this material would also stop bullets. However, since each protective layer is weakened as it is struck, repeated projectiles can eventually penetrate bullet-resistant glass.

Bulls seeing red

Although in bullfights the matador waves a red cape in front of the bull, bulls cannot see red—or any other color, for that matter. Like many animals, including dogs, bulls see only in various shades of light and dark.

In most animals, colors are irrelevant and distant vision is usually poor, but the perception of motion is very acute. It is actually the movement of the cape by the matador, rather than its color, that attracts the bull's attention. Similar results could be achieved with a cape of any color as long as it was moved to attract the bull.

Bumper-to-bumper traffic

When in the middle of a freeway traffic jam, most people assume that an accident, breakdown, or some other obstruction ahead is causing the bumper-to-bumper traffic. However, traffic experts agree that quite often there is no real reason for a backup.

Highway drivers usually operate efficiently down to speeds of about 35 mph. When the volume of traffic increases to reduce speeds below 35 mph, a "shock-wave effect" is produced.

At this point, drivers begin to react irrationally when close together, and overreact to the slightest stimuli to slow down. Even the brief flash of a brake light ahead will initiate other drivers to slam on their brakes and begin the backup. As speeds get slower and distances between cars shorten, the shock-wave effect increases and jam-ups worsen, and often for no apparent reason.

Bunker Hill

The famous Revolutionary War conflict known as the Battle of Bunker Hill was actually fought on nearby Breeds Hill. The site of the battle is even commemorated by a 221-foot-high granite obelisk that stands on Breeds Hill.

The Battle of Bunker Hill was the first major engagement of the Revolutionary War and was fought for the control of Boston. The Americans, under the command of Colonel William Prescott, were ordered to fortify Bunker Hill. For some reason still unexplained, Prescott went beyond Bunker and established his position on Breeds Hill. The original battle reports ignored the error, which was never corrected, and it has been known ever since as the Battle of Bunker Hill.

Bunsen burner

The familiar chemistry laboratory device called the Bunsen burner was not invented by its namesake. Robert Wilhelm Bunsen merely introduced the burner and popularized it in 1855. Its true inventor is not known for certain. However, it is believed that either Peter Desdega or Michael Farady invented the instrument.

By controlling the amount of air that combines with a flammable gas, the Bunsen burner produces a hotter flame than could be possible by using just the surrounding air and gas alone.

A Bunsen burner's flame typically burns at about 2,700° F. Not merely limited to the laboratory as most people think, the principle involved in the operation of this seemingly simple device was also the forerunner of the modern gas stove and gas furnace.

Buried bodies

Buried human bodies are not under the control of the family of the deceased or of the cemetery in which they are buried. Although laws vary from state to state, generally after burial, the body is considered to be in the custody of the law and under the control of a court.

No individuals, including relatives, are entitled to view or disinter a body once it is buried. Although a change of burial place is frequently permitted by court approval, it is usually done only to move the burial place closer to other deceased relatives. Exhumations are strictly controlled and only infrequently permitted.

Buttermilk

Contrary to popular belief, buttermilk does not contain a higher fat content than does regular milk. Actually, it is a nutritious liquid made from milk that has had most of the fat removed.

Buttermilk is produced as a by-product of churning cream into butter. Fat granules float to the surface during the process, are removed to make the butter, and the remaining liquid is the buttermilk. Buttermilk is a healthy beverage containing water, milk sugar, casein (a protein), and much less fat than does regular milk.

True buttermilk is generally not sold directly for human consumption in the United States, although its composition is similar to skim milk. Buttermilk, because of its sour taste, is usually condensed, dried, and used in baking and packaged cake mixes.

Usually, it is cultured buttermilk that is sold as a beverage in the United States. Cultured buttermilk is made by adding certain bacteria to skim milk to produce fermentation. The resulting liquid is thicker than natural buttermilk, less sour, but otherwise similar to true buttermilk in that it is relatively low in fat content.

Butterscotch and hopscotch

The familiar candy named butterscotch and the children's hopping game called hopscotch have nothing to do with Scotland as their names might suggest. Both words are derived from an earlier form of the word *scotch* which commonly meant "to score, mark, or cut'' something. Butterscotch is cut, or scotched, into little pieces, while in hopscotch the playing area is marked, or scotched, into small squares.

C

"The little I know
I owe to my ignorance."

Sacha Guitry

CCCP

In the Russian abbreviation CCCP, none of the C's stand for communism or communist. The letters simply represent the name of the country as it is written in the Russian alphabet.

Russian script is based on the Cyrillic alphabet, which does not contain the English letters S and R. The equivalent for these letters in Russian is C and P. The name of the country, the Union of Soviet Socialist Republics, in Russian, but using the English alphabet, is Soyuz Sovetskykh Sotsialisticheskikh Respublik. Written in the Russian alphabet, which is very dissimilar to English, the first letters of each word form the abbreviation CCCP.

Cabinet

There is no provision in the U.S. Constitution that either requires or refers to the fact that a President should appoint a cabinet. It is an unofficial institution that has simply developed through time and is now considered an "official" part of the executive office.

The executive powers of the President are set forth in Article

II of the U.S. Constitution. Section 2 states that the President ". . . may require the opinion, in writing, of the principal officer in each of the executive departments, upon any subject relating to the duties of their respective offices . . ."

George Washington interpreted this section to provide the authority to organize the heads of his three executive departments into an advisory committee. Within a few years, by 1793, the name "cabinet" had been applied to this group, and the practice had become an unofficial part of the executive office.

Through history, the cabinet has served by custom as an advisory council to the President. Because the framers of the Constitution apparently intended that the Senate advise the President, it has also become custom for the Senate to confirm cabinet appointments.

Currently, the cabinet is now, in effect, an administrative and bureaucratic rather than advisory group. Presidents now rely more on an informal group of private advisers, which do not depend on Senate confirmation.

Caesar, Julius

Julius Caesar was not an emperor of Rome as most people think. There were no Roman emperors until after his death in 44 B.C. when his successor, Augustus, became the first Roman emperor.

Julius Caesar, though, was a renowned Roman general, statesman, politician, orator, and writer who was appointed dictator of Rome. After his death, the first five Roman emperors retained the title "Caesar" as a symbol of respect, admiration, and authority, but Julius himself was never an emperor.

Caesar salad

The Caesar salad is not named after Julius Caesar. The popular cold dish was named for its creator, Caesar Gardini, who first prepared the salad in his Caesar's Place Restaurant in Tijuana, Mexico. It was made popular when it was also later served in Mike Romanoff's famous Hollywood restaurant.

Cagney, James

Although the popular image of James Cagney includes the famous line "You dirty rat," Cagney never said these words in any of his films. The expression was simply invented and made famous by impersonators of Cagney.

California sliding into the ocean

It is a popular misconception that California will someday break off from the American continent and slide into the Pacific Ocean. This belief, however, reflects an incorrect idea of what is really happening geologically in California. The truth is, the western portion of California is actually sliding north, and is in no danger of suddenly disappearing into the sea.

It is now known that the major landmass areas of the world are drifting and floating around on the earth's surface—a concept referred to as plate tectonics. Western California, which is part of the Pacific continental plate, is moving north against the rest of California and the North American continent. The line along which these two continental plates is drifting is the San Andreas fault. The all-too-familiar California earthquakes are the result of tension that is built up in the underlying rock from this movement suddenly being released as the ground springs another few inches northward.

Los Angeles and the western portion of California are sliding along this fault line toward Alaska averaging two inches per year. At this rate, Los Angeles will be in the vicinity of Fairbanks, Alaska, in about ten to fifteen million years.

Camels

Contrary to common belief, camels do not store water in their humps, stomachs, or anywhere else. However, the humps do contribute to the unique ability of the camel to conserve water for a considerable length of time under harsh conditions.

A camel can exist without drinking water for up to eight days in desert, summer heat, and for as long as eight weeks in the winter. Although the humps do not contain water, the secret of the camel's ability to conserve water is found in its humps, combined with other characteristics of its physiology.

The hump of the camel actually contains fat. The hydrogen molecules in this fat react with oxygen molecules from inhaled air to form water. The fatty hump, then, is really part of a water-producing machine inside the camel. For every pound of fat in the hump, one pint of water is produced.

The concentrated fat in the hump also means that very little fat is deposited under the camel's skin. This allows body heat to be rapidly dissipated. The camel also sweats very little, has a low rate of urine flow, can tolerate low levels of body fluids, and is thought to be able to recycle waste water. In addition, a camel can consume enormous amounts of water at one drinking, which it then conserves far more efficiently than any other animal.

Canary Islands

The name for the Canary Islands has nothing to do with the small, yellow songbird. The Islands were originally named *insulae canariae* by the Romans, meaning "island of dogs" in reference to the numerous wild dogs that inhabited the islands. The name eventually became "Canary" in the mistaken belief that it originally referred to the bird.

Candelabra

A large, branched candlestick or holder for lights, such as the type made popular by Liberace, is properly called a candelabrum, which is the singular form of the word. Two or more candelabrum are candelabra.

Captain of a ship

Contrary to popular belief, the captain of a ship cannot perform a marriage ceremony on board his ship unless he is legally authorized to marry people on land. In order for the marriage to be recognized, any person who performs the ceremony must be legally empowered to do so, such as a religious authority or authorized civil servant.

Although the maritime authority vested in a ship's captain entails certain powers, it does not include matters of civil jurisdiction such as marriage ceremonies. This includes the Merchant Marine; U.S. Navy regulations, which specifically forbid commanding officers from performing marriages; and the masters of British, Soviet, and other ships.

Also, the popular adage that a captain must go down with a

sinking ship is completely false. There is no law, provision, or custom dictating such self-sacrifice. A ship's master, as senior officer aboard, by tradition would be expected to direct the evacuation of passengers and crew before abandoning his ship.

However, a captain is often the last one off a sinking ship. But the reason this occurs on a damaged or sinking vessel usually has nothing to do with chivalry. Often, the senior officers of a ship elect to stay aboard to prevent the abandoned ship from being claimed as a salvage prize by another vessel.

Carat and karat

The words *carat* and *karat* are not interchangeable nor are they simply different spellings of the same word. Although they do have different meanings, the terms are, at least, measures of valuable commodities.

A carat is a unit of weight used for the measurement of precious stones and gems. The international standard, or metric, carat is .2 grams. Therefore, a six-carat ruby would weigh 1.2 grams.

Karat, on the other hand, is used to express the purity of gold, but does not refer to its weight. Pure gold is assumed to have twenty-four parts, or karats, of gold. The amount of gold in an object is measured as a proportion of these twenty-four parts. For example, eighteen-karat gold contains eighteen parts gold and six parts alloy.

Cashews

Have you ever wondered why cashews are never sold while still in their shells? The reason is simple. Cashews do not have shells. They do not have shells because they are not nuts as most people believe.

Cashews are botanically classified as the seed of a tropical and semitropical fruit called the cashew apple. These apples grow on the cashew tree and are edible, pear-shaped, sour fruits about the same size as a large ordinary apple. Hanging exposed from the lower end of the cashew apples are several comma-shaped, nutlike pods. Within these pods are the seeds, or "nuts," of the apple, which are commonly known as cashews.

The cashew seedpod hanging from the apple has a two-layered, leathery covering between which is contained a blackish, irritating oil called cardol. This oil is extremely caustic and produces severe skin irritation. Cardol is also used as an insecticide.

The outer covering of the cashew seedpod is difficult to remove, and it must be taken off without touching the cardol. However, mechanical procedures and the roasting process effectively remove all traces of the oil. For these reasons, cashews are not sold in their natural form.

Catgut

Catgut is not, and probably never was, made from the intestines of cats. It comes from sheep entrails treated with chromic acid.

Catgut is a tough cord that is generally used for stringing musical instruments and provides the material for about half the surgical sutures used in medicine in the United States. Although tennis and badminton rackets were once strung with catgut, nylon is now regularly used.

Even though it is doubtful that cat guts were ever used in catgut, since they do not produce a very strong cord, no one really knows how the name came into existence. One theory of questionable validity, but containing a certain amount of rationale, is that it was called catgut because the sound produced from a violin strung with this material resembles the sound of a wailing cat.

Cathedral

A cathedral is not necessarily a large or magnificent church. Size or splendor alone do not determine which churches are called cathedrals.

A cathedral is defined as an edifice in which a residential bishop has his official seat or throne—the cathedra. It is the principal home church of a bishop's diocese, or territory.

Many large and beautiful churches are not cathedrals, and some cathedrals are rather unpretentious little churches. But by virtue of the importance of bishops in episcopal church government, most cathedrals are large and architecturally splendid. However, size alone does not make a church a cathedral.

Celibacy

The general belief that celibacy refers to an abstinence from sexual intercourse is incorrect. Celibacy simply means the state of being unmarried, usually because of religious motives. It has nothing to do with refraining from sex, except as an indirect consequence of being unmarried.

Celibacy is common among many religious orders including Roman Catholics, Hindus, and Buddhists. In Christian ideology, it is a voluntary renunciation of marriage for the purpose of practicing perfect chastity to support the priest in his choice of his supreme love for Christ.

Cellophane

Cellophane, which has been around longer than most people realize, is not made from plastic, but from shredded and aged plant fibers. This tough, flexible, and transparent film is prepared from wood pulp and is actually a pure form of cellulose.

Cellophane was invented in 1908 by a Swiss chemist named Jacques Brandenberger while he was trying to produce a stain-proof tablecloth. However, cellophane was a product whose time had not yet come. In order to use it in its most popular, modern application, cellophane had to wait for the refrigerator and the ubiquitous leftovers from modern meals before it appeared in common use. Although still manufactured, cellophane is in increasing competition with various synthetic polymer plastic products such as Saran Wrap.

Cement and concrete

The terms *cement* and *concrete* are usually used interchangeably by most people. However, they are not the same thing. Cars do not drive on cement; they drive on concrete.

Cement is one of the ingredients in concrete and consists of a powdered mixture of calcium silicate and aluminates. Concrete is a mixture of sand, gravel, and water that is hardened by the addition of cement.

The term *cement* may actually be correctly used to refer to any bonding agent such as glue, putty, or solder. What is normally thought of as cement for construction purposes is specifically referred to as hydraulic cement.

There are three types of hydraulic cement of which the most

common is Portland. Although most people believe that Portland cement is a brand name having some connection with Portland, Oregon, it is neither. The name for this type of cement derives from its discovery in 1824 by a British stonemason who noticed that it resembled stone quarried near Portland, England, and hence the name.

Center of the earth

It is a fallacy that the center of the earth is molten rock. The inner core of the earth, with a diameter of about sixteen hundred miles, is actually a dense region of solid, magnetic, and probably iron metallic rocklike material. This solidified core is surrounded by an outer layer of molten iron about twenty-three hundred miles thick. Thus, although there is molten rock inside the earth, it is not located at the earth's center.

The solid, inner core of the earth is actually about 2,000°F hotter than is the molten material around it. The enormous pressure at the center of the earth of over fifty million pounds per square inch prevents the core from liquefying despite its higher temperature. However, even though the center is solid, its temperature is about the same as that of the surface of the sun.

Centipedes

Although the name *centipede* literally means one hundred feet, centipedes actually have from 28 to 354 legs depending on the species, of which there are about twenty-eight hundred. Centipedes, which are not insects, move rapidly on 14 to 177 pairs of legs with each pair attached to a separate body segment.

The common house centipede, the only species able to live in dwellings, is the fastest centipede, but it has only fifteen pairs of very long legs. The largest centipedes, which are burrowing tropical varieties, grow up to eleven inches long.

Chameleons

The popular belief that chameleons have the ability to change colors to match their surroundings is much exaggerated, if not untrue. Many other lizards can change colors just as well, and some fish such as the sea horse, flounder, squid, and octopus can actually change colors to match their surroundings better than chameleons.

The name chameleon is commonly misapplied to the iguanid lizard of the United States and Central America. This new world lizard is correctly known as the anole. It is the anole that is usually sold in pet stores in the United States, but under the name *chameleon*. True chameleons are found only in Africa, Asia, and some areas of the Middle East.

Although chameleons do change colors, this adaptation is limited to various hues and patterns that only resemble the general tone of their surroundings. But it is only a coincidence if the color change matches the background of the lizard.

The color change of the chameleon is, in reality, a behavioral response involving the direct reaction of the skin to light, temperature, and mood. In fact, it is now recognized that moods, such as fright and anger, are more important factors in stimulating color change than is camouflage. However, what change does occur is usually limited to slight modifications of hue or lightness and darkness, and is independent of the background.

Color change is just one of the more interesting features of these unusual lizards. Chameleons have large, bulging eyes that can individually rotate, an insect-capturing tongue that can extend twice the length of the chameleon's body, and some even have helmet-shaped heads, horns, spikes, skinflats, and plates reminiscent of dinosaurs.

Chamois

Chamois leather does not come from the goatlike animal called the chamois. Although the chamois, native to the mountains of southern Europe and Asia, was the original source of "shammey" leather, modern commercial chamois now is made from the skins of domestic sheep and goats.

More chamois leather is ruined by too much attention than by a lack of care. Chamois should be washed in clean, lukewarm water and hung to dry. It should never be washed with detergents, which strip the tanning oils from the leather, eventually drying and hardening the chamois.

Chauvinism

To label someone as a chauvinist is not really the epithet that most people think it is. Chauvinism simply means an unreasoning, boastful devotion to one's country in the form of extreme patriotism. The term originated from Nicholas Chauvin, a French soldier in the Napoleonic wars, whose mindless and vociferous loyalty to his leaders and the lost imperial cause led to his name becoming synonymous with blind devotion.

During the civil rights movement, the term *white chauvinist* appeared to describe a racist devoted to white supremacy. In the 1960s, with the rise of feminism, *male chauvinist* was invented to refer to a man blindly committed to male superiority, and the term now has generally acquired this new meaning. But *chauvinist* alone means quite a different thing.

Chef

It is commonly, but erroneously, believed that a chef is a cook. While chefs do occasionally prepare meals and dishes, and although they are trained in the culinary arts, most chefs usually do not cook.

A chef is one who supervises and coordinates the activities of cooking in larger restaurants, cafeterias, hotels, and other eating places. Chefs plan and prepare menus, develop recipes, and make food purchases. They also direct and instruct cooks, determine food requirements and supplies for quality, and even maintain payrolls. Their training includes all of these activities in overseeing the kitchen cooks in an establishment.

Cheshire cat

The Cheshire cat has no existence anywhere except in the expression, "to grin like a Cheshire cat." The term refers to a forced or sneering smile that reveals the teeth and gums. Although the term is usually thought to have originated in Lewis Carroll's *Alice's Adventures in Wonderland*, Carroll himself was merely using a previously existing and familiar proverbial expression in his story.

The fact is, no one really knows the true origin of the phrase *Cheshire cat*. What is known for certain is that there is no such breed of cat called a Cheshire and never has been.

Signboards in Cheshire, England, often contained grinning cats, and Cheshire cheese reportedly was once made in the shape of cats. But how these symbols arose or what connection Cheshire County ever had with cats is unknown.

Chicago Fire

Despite the popular legends, the Great Chicago Fire of October 8, 1871, was not started by Mrs. O'Leary's cow kicking over a lantern while being milked. Even though an official board of inquiry was conducted by the Chicago Fire Department, the real cause of the fire was never determined.

It is true that the fire started somewhere behind the house of Patrick and Catherine O'Leary. However, it was much too late at night for anyone to be out milking a cow. It is also known that when a neighbor first discovered the blaze, the O'Learys were already asleep.

The familiar story about the cow kicking over a lantern first appeared in a newspaper account written by Michael Aherns shortly after the fire. However, Aherns later admitted just before his death that he had actually fabricated the story in order to create interest in his original account.

Few buildings survived the inferno, which killed about 250 people and destroyed over seventeen thousand buildings in a five-mile-long path of destruction. One building that was left standing was the home of Pat and Kate O'Leary.

Chief Justice

In the United States, there is no Chief Justice of the Supreme Court. The correct title is simply Chief Justice of the United States. The Chief Justice is one of the nine members of the Supreme Court with no significant judicial powers beyond any other judge of the court.

Appointed by the President and confirmed by the Senate, as are the other Associate Justices, the Chief Justice has the power of the presiding officer of the court. However, the term *chief justice* is also applied to the presiding judge of the highest appellate court of any jurisdiction. Although it usually refers to the chief of the U.S. Supreme Court, it also is accorded to the presiding officer of many of the highest state courts.

The only mention of a Chief Justice in the U.S. Constitution regards impeachment proceedings of the President. The Judicial Act of 1789, which established the Supreme Court, provides for a Chief Justice, but does not specify any duties or authority. The Chief Justice has by tradition acquired many duties as the symbolic head of the federal judiciary. However, the prestige and reputation of the office has been created mainly from the strength of the men who have held it and not from the position itself.

Chinese checkers

Chinese checkers, the game played with colored marbles on a star-shaped board, is not Chinese and never was. It is a modern version of a nineteenth-century English game called Halma which became popular in the United States during the 1930s.

Although Chinese checkers is now played in China, it was introduced there from England via the United States and Japan. The name Chinese checkers for the American version of Halma most likely derives from the similarity between the star-shaped playing board used in the game and the star on the national flag of China.

Chocolate and tooth decay

It is not true that milk chocolate causes cavities. In fact, research tends to indicate that not only is milk chocolate's potential for cavity causing much lower than might be expected, but that this type of chocolate may actually contribute to the reduction of tooth decay rather than be a cause of it.

According to the American Dental Association, the calcium, phosphate, lipids, and protein content of milk chocolate seem to modify the acid production in the mouth which leads to cavities. This is also true for dairy products in general and aged cheeses in particular. Also, the simple sugars contained in milk chocolate are less harmful than the complex sugars found in other foods and are quickly dissolved from the tooth surface. Although research is continuing, it is certain that milk chocolate is one of the few foods with a very low cavity-causing potential. Evidence now tends to support the notion that some of the oils contained in milk chocolate may actually even prevent tooth decay.

Cholesterol

It has currently become popular to attack cholesterol as one of the great evils of the twentieth century. However, cholesterol is an indispensable component of all cells and is vital to cell growth and survival. Without it, we would not be alive.

Cholesterol is an odorless, tasteless, white fatty alcohol found in all animal tissues. All steroid hormones, such as the stress hormone cortisol and the male and female sex hormones testosterone and estradiol, are derived from cholesterol. About one-seventh of the brain is made of cholesterol. It is an essential biochemical necessity for many physiological functions, including the solubility of absorbed fats from foods.

Although excessive levels are now believed to be associated with coronary heart disease, the human body manufactures its own cholesterol in order to survive and adapt to the environment. Natural checks on cholesterol levels are usually maintained by receptors in the liver. Although excessive dietary intake of cholesterol can overload this system, its vital role should not be ignored.

Chop suey

Chop suey was not originally a native Chinese food, nor is it entirely an American concoction either. It was first prepared by a Chinese chef in America for both Chinese and American diplomats.

The personal cook of the Chinese ambassador to the United States was instructed to prepare a meal at a New York dinner party honoring the ambassador, Li Hung-Chang, on August 29, 1896. For the main course, a new dish was made up which he called *tsa sui*, which is Mandaran for "odds and ends." The name for this new dish was phonetically translated by Americans as chop suey. Following the dinner, the recipe for chop suey was printed in a New York newspaper, and it soon became popular throughout the country.

Chopsticks

The song "Chopsticks" was not named after the Chinese eating utensil. Instead the quick little waltz takes its name from the chopping motion of the hands traditionally required to play it.

"Chopsticks" was written by a sixteen-year-old British girl, Euphemia Allen, as "The Celebrated Chopsticks Waltz." Instructions were to play it "with both hands turned sideways" in order to "imitate the chopping from which this waltz gets its name."

Christ as Jesus' last name

It is usually assumed by most people that Christ is the sur-
name of Jesus. This is not true. Christ is not a name; it is simply
a title accorded to Jesus.

Last names were virtually unknown during the time that Jesus
lived. In fact, surnames did not appear as a regular custom until
the tenth century after the Normans conquered England. Prior
to that, second "names" were not really names at all. If anything followed a person's name, it was usually an indication of
the geographic origin or description of the person. Thus, Jesus
was frequently referred to as Jesus of Nazareth.

Christ is an early Hebrew word used as a title and means "the
anointed one." The use of this term was first applied as "Jesus
the Christ." However, the New Testament makes no mention
of the word Christ, since this term developed in early Christianity well after the lifetime of Jesus.

Eventually, the name Jesus or Jesus of Nazareth was ordinarily supplemented by the title Christ, and finally it became
simply Jesus Christ. However, Paul sometimes even reversed
the order using the title Christ Jesus. But in any event, Christ
was never specifically used as the last name of Jesus.

Christmas

Traditional December 25 Christmas celebrations in the United
States have little or nothing to do with Jesus or Christianity. Our
customs are an amalgamation of traditions from numerous cultures accumulated over many centuries, while December 25 itself is largely a date without significance.

For over two hundred years after the birth of Christ, no one
knew, and few really cared, when Jesus was born. Until the
fourth century, it simply was not customary to recognize or
celebrate as we do the birth date of a notable or common person.
Instead, if any date was remembered at all, the person's death
date was usually observed and commemorated. Thus, the exact
date of Jesus' birth, like that of many other people in early
history, has been lost.

It was pure speculation and historical circumstance that December 25 is now celebrated as the day of Jesus' birth. Ancient
pagan rituals often included some type of ceremony or celebration to accompany the winter solstice on December 21 or 22.

Also, a popular Roman religion competing with Christianity observed December 25 as a day of feasting and celebration.

To enhance the appeal of Christianity among the pagans and to unify the various customs and rituals throughout the Christian world, Roman Bishop Liberius, in 354, chose December 25 as the date for the birth of Jesus. No real evidence existed then to support his choice and little basis exists for it today. In fact, according to various events referred to in the Bible, modern historians and theologians now believe that Jesus was probably born in October or November. Some authorities place the date as early as July.

Many current customs associated with Christmas also have nothing to do with the birth or life of Jesus. Decorated Christmas trees, for example, originated with the practice of tree worship by druids and primitive Scandinavians several hundred years before the birth of Christ. The custom spread to Germany during the medieval ages as ''paradise trees,'' usually firs decorated with apples, and were used in ceremonies associated with the birth of Adam and Eve.

Our current custom of decorating Christmas trees derived from Queen Victoria in England who, in 1840, first decorated an evergreen at Christmas. This practice gained immediate popularity throughout Europe. Pennsylvania Germans later introduced the Christmas tree into the United States where it also became a favorite tradition.

Santa Claus, as one might expect, also has little to do with Christianity. However, contrary to popular belief, Santa's gift giving has nothing to do with the gifts given to Jesus by the wise men. Based upon a real person, Saint Nicholas was a fourth-century bishop in what is now Turkey. As the patron saint of young schoolboys, his generosity and gift giving became well known. Many myths of gift bearing characters at Christmas evolved from his legend.

Among them was the Dutch Sinter Klass, a fir-trimmed, robed, pipe-smoking, children's gift giver. The Dutch brought this tradition to America where the familiar Santa Claus emerged, primarily through Clement C. Moore's *A Visit from St. Nicholas.* This 1822 story added the sleigh and reindeer and nearly completed our modern picture of Santa Claus.

Festive Christmas customs were generally adopted much later

in the United States than in other countries. Christmas celebrations were strongly discouraged in colonial America. Regarded as sacred by the Pilgrims, observances other than a simple church service were severely punished. However, this piety changed as the influx of other nationalities increased and undermined the Puritan legacy. By the 1880s, the many separate ethnic and religious customs had blended into our present familiar and largely secular Christmas traditions in the United States.

Churchill, Winston

Winston Churchill is usually credited with originating the term *iron curtain* in his 1946 speech in which he said, "From Stetlin in the Baltic to Trieste in the Atlantic, an iron curtain has descended across the Continent." However, the term had been used by others for forty years before Churchill, yet it is still popularly believed that he introduced the expression.

In 1914, during World War I, the queen of Belgium said, "Between them [Germany] and me there is now a bloody iron curtain which has descended forever." The infamous German Joseph Goebbels also used this phrase in 1945 to express concern over the Russian encirclement of Germany, and several others have also used the expression prior to Churchill.

Cinderella

Cinderella is a traditional European fairy tale with over five hundred extant versions, some going back to the ninth century. However, Cinderella never had glass slippers until a translation error changed them from fur to glass in the late 1600s.

In most earlier versions, Cinderella's slippers were usually made of some rare metal or valuable covering. But a popular French story using slippers of white squirrel fur was incorrectly translated by Charles Perrault in his 1697 anthology of fairy tales subtitled *Tales of Mother Goose.* An older French word for fur was confused with a newer word for glass, and Cinderella acquired slippers of glass in the mistranslation. No versions of the tale had glass slippers until this error, and all subsequent popular versions have used glass for the slippers.

Circumstantial evidence

It is commonly believed that circumstantial evidence is merely a suspicion without proof, or the unproven coincidence of two events, and that it is not considered acceptable evidence in court. None of these ideas are true.

In law, there are only two types of evidence—direct and circumstantial. Direct evidence is based on personal observation and proves a fact without the need for other evidence. Circumstantial evidence involves facts that tend to indirectly establish an issue or question. All evidence except direct witness testimony is circumstantial.

The law gives equal weight to both direct and circumstantial evidence. In fact, without indirect facts, no legal system would work, since direct witness is usually not available in all situations. Circumstantial evidence is fully admissible in court and often essential in establishing fact.

Cleopatra

The famous Ptolemaic ruler of Egypt, Cleopatra, was not an Egyptian. Actually, there were seven women who reigned under the name Cleopatra, and none of them were Egyptians.

The Ptolemys, who ruled Egypt for two hundred fifty years, were Macedonians, native to an area north of the Aegean Sea in what is now Greece, Yugoslavia, and Bulgaria. The Cleopatra immortalized in Hollywood film was Cleopatra VII, a Macedonian, who was also part Greek and Iranian.

Born Philopator in 69 B.C., she killed herself forty years later to end the degenerating Ptolemy dynasty. Cleopatra was not nearly as historically important as Hollywood has led us to believe. Her fame comes largely from the West and from her marriage to Mark Antony, who played a decisive role in the course of Roman and European history.

Cocoons

Butterflies do not change from the caterpillar stage into an adult insect in a cocoon as most people think. Only moths undergo metamorphosis in a cocoon. A butterfly usually forms from an unenclosed structure called a chrysalis.

There are few real distinctions between butterflies and moths. One of the more apparent differences is the type of structure in which the insect pupates. Butterfly larva form a chrysalis, which is contained within a sheathlike covering, from which it changes into the adult insect. A chrysalis is not just an enclosure, it is the mummylike structure itself with only a thin covering and a rough, angular shape. The chrysalis is actually the transforming state of the caterpillar itself.

Most moth larva spin the familiar rounded, smooth, protective covering, often of silk, around themselves before they, too, develop their chrysalis. This wrapping is called a cocoon. The butterfly chrysalis is rarely enclosed in a cocoon, and the term chrysalis is never applied to the pupating stage of a moth.

Coffee beans

Coffee beans are not beans at all. They are actually the seeds, or pits, of a red, cherrylike fruit. True beans are the seeds or pods of certain leguminous plants used mainly for food.

Growing on treelike tropical shrubs, these small, red berries contain a fleshy pulp within which are the green seeds called coffee beans. Each berry contains just two beans, while each plant produces less than two pounds of beans annually.

Coffee, sobering effects of

It is a dangerous myth that drinking coffee can sober up an intoxicated person. This misconception has undoubtedly put thousands of drunks on the road behind the wheel of a car thinking they have been detoxified by a cup of coffee.

There is no known way to sober up a person who is drunk. Time and rest are the only remedies to remove alcohol from the blood. Alcohol is eliminated from the circulatory system by the liver at the rate of about one half-ounce per hour and there is no way to speed up the process. All that can be done is to slow down the rate of absorption in the first place by drinking alcohol while food is in the stomach.

Drinking coffee, or any other liquid, might be helpful to relieve the symptoms of a hangover, since dehydration is one of the usual effects of alcohol on the body. But it serves no purpose in lowering blood alcohol levels.

Coins as legal tender

It is commonly believed by many people that large numbers of pennies, nickels, dimes, and quarters can be used in all transactions as legal tender in the United States. It is also believed by others that the use of large numbers of coins is not always acceptable as legal tender. The truth is, the use of coins as unlimited legal tender is a complex issue on which even the U.S. Department of Treasury is unsure.

In the past, various laws have limited the use of coins as legal tender. The Coinage Acts of 1873 and 1879 provided that pennies and nickels are legal tender for debts not exceeding twenty-five cents, and that dimes, quarters, and half dollars are legal tender up to amounts of ten dollars. However, a 1933 law states that "all coins" shall be legal tender for "all debts."

In 1982, coinage laws were codified and all sections pertaining to legal tender were combined into one provision. The statute states, "U.S. coins and currency . . . are legal tender for all debts, public charges, taxes, and dues." Under this new language, it appears that all coins could be used to pay any amount of debt.

However, legal history is unclear on whether the earlier Coinage Acts are still in force. The rules of statutory interpretation indicate that all coinage acts are still in effect, since the earlier, more specific statutes may prevail over later more general laws.

Until the conflicting laws are interpreted by the courts, no one, including the Treasury Department, is sure whether large numbers of coins are legal tender. Since no real legal or financial problem seems to exist for the use of coins in unlimited amounts, the question still remains concerning the legality of their use.

Cold-blooded animals

Animals referred to as cold-blooded do not really have cold blood. All the term actually means is that their body temperature varies with the temperature of their surroundings. The term *cold-blooded* is simply used to contrast with *warm-blooded*, which refers to animals that maintain a constant body temperature. Although their temperatures can vary greatly, many so-called cold-blooded animals in warm regions may actually have higher body temperatures than do most warm-blooded animals.

Coldness of outer space

Outer space is usually thought to be extremely cold. However, space is not cold. In fact, it has no temperature at all.

Temperature refers to the average kinetic heat content per atom of matter. Thus, only matter can have a temperature. Cold, in particular, pertains to the very slow movement of molecules. Since in space the molecules are so very far apart, the concept of temperature, for all practical purposes, is meaningless.

Although space has no temperature, it is nevertheless considered a "temperature sink," which drains the heat out of anything in it. This transfer of heat, largely through radiation, is a significant problem for space craft and satellites. For example, one side of the space shuttle away from the sun may become -180° to -250° F, while the other side facing the sun is quite warm.

Columbus, Christopher

Nearly everyone knows that Christopher Columbus discovered America in 1492 and proved that the earth was round. Unfortunately, nearly everyone would be wrong, because much of what is commonly believed about Columbus is not true.

In the first place, Columbus never even saw the North American continent. During his four expeditions to the New World, all of his explorations were to islands in the Caribbean or to South America. His celebrated "discovery" of America was actually of a small island near San Salvador. Also, to the day of his death in 1506, Columbus refused to take credit for the discovery of a new continent. Columbus persisted in his belief that he had reached his intended destination of India.

The first Europeans to actually arrive in North America were Norwegian Vikings, probably Leif Eriksson, around A.D. 1000. The first sixteenth century explorer to set foot on what is now the United States was Juan Ponce de León in 1513.

Contrary to popular belief, the first land sighting in the New World was not made by Columbus himself. It was actually a crewman aboard the *Nina*, Roderigo de Triana, who first saw land. Columbus later took credit for the sighting in his journal.

It is also a popular misconception that Columbus' voyage proved that the earth was round. This belief is untrue. Most geographers and scientists since the time of the early Greeks knew the earth was not flat, as did Columbus. This misbelief proves to be one of the oldest and most enduring in history despite considerable evidence to the contrary. In fact, Columbus is known to have studied maps and a crude globe, prior to his voyage, which depicted a round earth.

Columbus had difficulty obtaining financial support for his voyage to Asia, not because people thought he would sail off the end of the earth, but because most learned men believed that the Orient was simply too far to reach by sailing west. His crew's greatest concern was that supplies would be exhausted on the long voyage to Asia.

But by precipitous miscalculation, Columbus figured the distance to the Orient by sailing west was just two thousand four hundred miles. As a result, Queen Isabella agreed to finance the expedition. It would have been a disastrous mistake had he not bumped into an unknown continent on the way.

It is now known that Columbus never used the name Christopher Columbus. The name Columbus is actually an English equivalent of his original Italian name, Cristoforo Colombo. However, he never wrote in Italian and, so far as is known, all surviving writings of Columbus are in Castilian. In this form of Spanish, he used the name Cristóbal Colón, and was referred to in this manner during his lifetime.

Despite numerous paintings and portraits depicting the appearance of Columbus, most of which are different, all existing pictures of him were made from written or spoken descriptions, many after his death, or copied from such drawings. There were no drawings, sketches, or paintings ever made of Columbus while he was alive, and we cannot be sure what he really looked like.

Common cold

Contrary to what most people think, the common cold is not usually caused by being chilled, from wet feet, or from the coughs and sneezes of other people. Few colds are actually transmitted through the air. Rather, they are usually carried and spread by the hands.

Current research has determined that there is a very low concentration of cold viruses in the saliva and mouth, and that cold germs can survive for only a few minutes after being expelled into the air from a cough or sneeze. Air, it turns out, is a very hostile environment for the cold virus.

Studies have also shown that the hands are seventy percent effective in spreading colds, compared to only ten percent for the sneeze. The durable little cold viruses, and there are several hundred different kinds, can survive for an hour on a handkerchief or tissue, two hours on hands, and up to seventy-two hours on a hard surface, such as a door handle. Consequently, it is now accepted that hand contact with the virus on a hard surface followed by contact with the mouth or nose is the most likely way the virus enters the body.

The best prevention, then, is good ventilation, regular washing of the hands, using disposable tissues instead of handkerchiefs, and keeping the hands from the mouth, nose, and eyes.

Compass pointing to the North Pole

Contrary to what most people believe, a compass needle does not point to the geographic North Pole. It does not usually point to the magnetic North Pole either. In fact, a compass needle does not really point to anything, but merely aligns itself with the earth's magnetic lines of force at a given location.

The earth's magnetic field is a complex phenomenon. The geographic North Pole is that familiar spot where the earth's axis of rotation ends at the top of the earth. It is not to be confused with the magnetic North Pole, which is the northern pole of the earth's geomagnetic axis where the magnetic lines of force converge at the earth's surface.

The magnetic lines of force that encompass the earth and converge at both the North and South geomagnetic poles are not straight. They are quite irregular, with numerous anomalies produced by compression from solar wind and from the geographic and geologic features of a particular location. These lines of force vary from place to place and even from time to time at the same place. In addition, the magnetic pole itself wanders in a roughly circular path about one hundred miles in diameter.

A compass needle simply aligns itself with these lines of magnetic force wherever it is located, but does not necessarily point to the North Pole in the process. Using a compass and following the needle to the magnetic North Pole, one would traverse an irregular path along the earth's surface ending up about five hundred miles from the geographic North Pole at 76° N. latitude and 101° W. longitude near Thule, Greenland.

Consistency is the hobgoblin of little minds

Ralph Waldon Emerson did not write, "Consistency is the hobgoblin of little minds." Instead, his actual words were, "A foolish consistency is the hobgoblin of little minds adored by little statesmen and philosophers and divines." The correct use of the word foolish in Emerson's quotation makes his idea more understandable than the usually misquoted version.

Corpus delicti

The *corpus delicti* is not just the dead body in a murder case. Derived from Latin, the term means "body of a crime," or the material evidence that a crime has been committed, such as a body, a stolen automobile, or the bank records of embezzled funds.

Corpus delicti are also the facts that prove that a crime has been committed. It is the first thing to establish in court in order to achieve a conviction. The second thing that must be proven is that the defendant is the person who committed the crime.

In a murder case, the *corpus delicti* may include a dead body. However, only a few jurisdictions require the actual production of a corpse to convict a person of murder.

Cotton gin

When Eli Whitney invented his mechanical cotton picker in 1792, he did not name it the cotton gin in reference to the alcoholic beverage. Whitney, who was a northerner, used the word gin simply as a shortened form of the word engine. He felt that it sounded more colloquially appealing to the southern cotton growers.

While the cotton gin dramatically changed the South's economy, it did little to benefit Whitney. His machine was so efficient and amazingly simple that any country handyman could copy it—and they did. By 1797, his company was out of business.

Despite his fame associated with this invention, Eli Whitney's most important contribution was not the cotton gin. He is also credited with inventing the system of mass production based on interchangeable parts. This was first applied to the gun-manufacturing industry, and led to the greatest change ever seen in economic history—mass production and the assembly line.

Cowboys

Nothing in American folklore is so well established as is the image of the cowboy. However, as a cattle-driving trailhand, the cowboy flourished for only a short twenty-year period in the American west.

The name *cowboy* did not even originate in the western United States. Along the Atlantic Piedmont in the eighteenth century, cattle were herded by cow boys, pronounced then as two words. During Revolutionary times, the cowboy was used to refer to Tories operating with cowbells in New York to lure patriots into an ambush. By the 1820s the Spanish *vaquero* and the English *buckaroo* gave way to the term *cowboy* in the American west.

Primarily just ranch hands, the cowboy took on his more familiar and legendary role in 1867. It was then that a livestock trader named Joe McCoy—the original real McCoy—hired some ranch hands to bring longhorn cattle from Texas along the Chisholm Trail to the railhead in Abilene, Kansas. It was on these grueling and often rowdy journeys that the cowboy acquired his popular image.

But by 1887, bad weather, the spread of homesteaders' barbed wire, and the extension of the rail line ended the reign of the cowboy as the cattle-driving vagabond of the west. Their legendary role on the trail lasted just twenty years, after which they returned to their more sedentary duties as ranch hands. From this brief period, novels and other popular fiction enabled the cowboy to attain immortality as the self-reliant, silent hero of the west, an image later perpetuated by movies and television.

Crickets

It is not true, as most people think, that crickets chirp by rubbing their legs together. The sounds are made as the cricket rubs a scraper, located on one forewing, along a row of 50 to 250 teeth on an opposite forewing. The number of chirps depend on the number of teeth struck per second. Chirping is done only by the male cricket to produce different songs for calling a mate and fighting. Both sexes have highly sensitive organs for sound reception on their forelegs.

It is true that there is a direct relationship between chirping and the temperature. By counting the number of chirps in fifteen seconds and adding forty, the chirping little cricket will be giving the Fahrenheit temperature.

Crocker, Betty

The well-known "writer" of cookbooks, Betty Crocker, is not a real person and never was. An advertising man invented the name for the author of cookbooks that were published by the large food company General Mills. Betty was chosen simply as a popular first name, while Crocker came from William G. Crocker, who was then director of General Mills.

Cross

The traditional Christian cross used as a symbol commemorating the crucifixion of Jesus is not the same shape as the cross used by the Romans to crucify Christ. Although the historical record is incomplete, it seems likely that the most familiar of all Christian symbols is historically incorrect.

Many different forms of crosses have been used by civilizations throughout history. The ancient Egyptians, Phoenicians, and the Aztecs used the T-shaped cross as a symbol of life and eternity. A cross with four equal arms was commonly used by the Hindus, Buddhists, and Babylonians representing the elements of life. Various shapes of crosses are common symbols in the art and symbolism of many cultures throughout history.

It is known that the cross used by the Romans between the sixth century B.C. and the fourth century A.D., when crucifixion was common, was the T-shaped (tau) cross, and there is no reason to believe that this cross was not used in the crucifixion of Jesus. Since early Christians forbade the use of images to allow any representation of the Crucifixion, no pictorial record exists indicating the actual shape of the cross used to crucify Jesus. The Bible mentions the cross of Christ only once (Matthew 27:37), but no inference regarding its shape can be made from this reference.

It is now believed that the shape for the Christian cross probably evolved from the first two letters, *XP*, of the Greek word for Christ. These letters were commonly used in early Christian symbolism to represent Christ by a largely illiterate population.

The shape of these Greek letters eventually appeared as a cross-like design in the shape of what now is called the traditional (Latin) Christian cross.

There are now more than four hundred different forms of the cross employed in modern heraldry. The one most familiar to Western Christians is the Latin, or long, cross popularized by European art. Other Christian religions use different forms of the cross as symbols for Christ's death, such as the T-shaped (tau) cross of St. Anthony, the X-shaped cross of St. Andrew, and the Greek cross with arms of equal length. Other, more elaborate, forms include the Russian, Maltese, and Papal cross. In all cases, they must be regarded as religious symbols and not as historically authentic representations.

Currency

The largest denomination of U.S. currency now being issued is only the one hundred dollar bill. The issuance of currency in denominations of five hundred dollars, one thousand dollars, five thousand dollars, and ten thousand dollars was discontinued in 1969 because of declining use. The one hundred thousand dollar bill was never in circulation, but was only used for trans-actions between the Federal Reserve System and the Treasury Department. Large-denomination bills are still considered legal tender if in use, but these bills are now removed from circulation as they reach Federal Reserve Banks.

Large-denomination bills are no longer considered necessary since paper money has been substantially replaced by check-book money in daily business life. More recently, the credit card and computer transactions have provided the basis for most large-scale monetary exchanges.

Curveball

The baseball pitch known as a curve does not really curve sideways as most people think it does. The direction in which the ball moves is essentially downward. A curveball should ac-tually be called a dropball. In fact, during baseball's early days, the curve was actually called the "out drop" pitch.

If correctly thrown, the hand will snap the ball over the index finger as it is released. The ball spins from top to bottom, aero-dynamically causing it to curve downward. In fact, if a pitcher were theoretically suspended in midair and properly threw a curve with sufficient velocity, the ball would follow a circular path around and below the pitcher finally hitting him in the back of the head.

Some pitches do curve sideways. However these are sliders, roundhouses, or improperly thrown curveballs.

Custer, George Armstrong

Usually referred to at the Battle of the Little Big Horn as General George Armstrong Custer, he was, in fact, not a general at the time of the famous battle. It is true that Custer had once been a brigadier general, the nation's youngest at twenty-three, and elevated to major general during the Civil War. But after the war when Civil War officers lost their prewar volunteer ranks in an army reorganization, Custer became a captain. He was later promoted to lieutenant colonel, which was his actual rank when killed at the Little Big Horn.

Cyclones

It is a popular misconception that a cyclone is a Pacific hurricane or some other kind of large, violent storm. It is not.

Cyclone is a meteorological term that simply means a wide pattern of winds circulating around a low-pressure area. These winds rotate counterclockwise in the Northern Hemisphere and clockwise in the Southern Hemisphere. Tornadoes, hurricanes, storms, and weak low-pressure systems are all cyclones of different sizes and intensities.

Tropical cyclones are larger and more intense, and are known as hurricanes in the Atlantic Ocean and typhoons in the Pacific. Anti-cyclones, which are regions of high atmospheric pressure and circulate clockwise in the Northern Hemisphere, are larger, but usually contain lower wind velocities than cyclones.

D

"Nothing is so ignorant
as the ignorance of certainty."

Aldous Huxley

Dachshund

The name of the low, long dog is not pronounced "dash hound." Its correct name is dachshund, and is pronounced "doks-hund." Bred and used in Germany to hunt rabbits, badgers, and other burrowing animals, the name derives from the German *dachs* for badger and *hund* for dog.

Daddy longlegs

It comes as a surprise to most people to learn that a daddy longlegs is not a spider. In fact, it is not even an insect.

The daddy longlegs, or harvestman as it is also called, may look like a spider, and may even have eight legs like one, but these similarities are only a coincidence. Classified along with scorpians, ticks, mites, and spiders in the class Arachnida, the daddy longlegs belongs to the separate order Phalangida, while spiders are of the order Araneida. The difference between the two is more than a technical one.

The daddy longlegs has only one oval-shaped body segment and eats by chewing both animal and soft plant foods. It also has two eyes—one facing forward and one looking backward.

The eight long, delicate legs provide more than just a handy method of locomotion over obstacles on the ground. Most of the daddy longleg's senses are located along its legs.

In contrast, spiders have two body segments and obtain nourishment by sucking, not chewing, liquid juices from animal prey. An insect, unlike a daddy longlegs or spider, has six legs, three body segments, antennae, and compound eyes.

Dandelions

Dandelions are often jokingly referred to, especially by children, as "dandy lions." However, the remark is not as facetious as it appears to be. The name *dandelion* does, in fact, refer to lions. The word is from the French *dent de lion*, meaning "lion's tooth," in reference to the jagged, toothed edges of the plant's leaves.

Dangerous jobs

According to the National Safety Council, the job of garbageman is more dangerous, in terms of injuries, than either a policeman or fireman. In fact, garbagemen have the highest injury rate with more lost workdays than any other major category of job classification. In addition, statistics indicate that taxicab drivers have a greater chance of being shot on the job than do policemen.

Darwin, Charles

The expression most commonly associated with Charles Darwin, survival of the fittest, did not actually originate with Darwin. Although Darwin later used the term, it was first introduced by Herbert Spencer. Darwin credited Spencer with the concept and admitted that the term was more accurate and appropriate than his own expression of natural selection.

Nor was Darwin's evolutionary theory an original idea. Ancient Greeks had suggested a theory of natural adaptation. Newton's idea of mutating links in the chain of being, Linnaeus's immutability of species, and Geoffroy's original use of the term *evolution* in 1831 provided the theoretical basis of Darwin's work. The significant contribution of Darwin was the expansion of these evolutionary ideas in a scientific work supported by a monumental body of physical evidence. It was the proof provided by Darwin that subsequently led to the widespread acceptance of evolutionary theory.

Declaration of Independence

The Declaration of Independence was not signed on July 4, 1776, nor was independence from England proclaimed on that date. The truth is, Independence Day could just as well be celebrated anytime between July 2 and August 2 and have just as much historical validity as does the July 4th celebration.

The Continental Congress approved a resolution calling for independence from England on July 2, 1776. This resolution was the formal legislative act that severed ties with England and expressed the intent of colonial America to become independent.

The vote for the principle of independence on that date prompted John Adams, in a letter to his wife written the next day, July 3, to write,

> "Yesterday . . . a resolution was passed . . . that these United Colonies are, and of right ought to be, free and independent States. . . . The Second day of July . . . ought to be commenorated. . . . It ought to be solemnized with pomp and parade, with shows, games, sports, guns, bells, bonfires, and illuminations— from this time forward for everyone."

On July 3, 1776, newspapers printed accounts of the vote for independence. By July 4, Jefferson had completed the first draft of the document that declared independence. This Declaration, the one now cherished as symbolizing American independence, was intended to explain to England's King George the reasons for the July 2nd independence vote. Jefferson's document was approved on July 4. However, only John Hancock signed it on that date. Copies were sent to printers and it took several weeks to prepare the final versions.

In the meantime, on July 8, public proclamations were posted of the Declaration. On July 19, a resolution was passed that members of Congress sign the Declaration when official copies were prepared.

Finally, on August 2, 1776, an engrossed parchment copy was available. Fifty members of Congress who were present at that time signed the Declaration. All who voted for independence on July 2 did not sign the final copy, and all who signed on August 2 did not originally vote for independence in July. But the copy signed on August 2, 1776, is generally referred to as the original Declaration of Independence and is now displayed in the National Archives. Other signatures were affixed at later dates, with the last one not added until 1781.

Democracy and republic

A democracy and a republic are not the same thing, although many people do not realize that they actually refer to different forms of government. A democracy simply means a government that is responsible to the rule of the people or, at least, their elected representatives. A republic is any form of government, including a dictatorship, without a hereditary ruler or monarch, such as a king.

Thus, the United States is both a democracy and a republic. England, one of the world's oldest democracies, is not a republic, while the Soviet Union is a republic but not a democracy.

Deserts

There are two common misconceptions usually associated with deserts. One is that deserts are limited to just hot and dry places, and the second is that deserts consist of vast areas of rolling sand and dunes. Both these ideas are incorrect.

The term desert applies to both hot, dry regions and to cold, ice-covered, inhospitable areas. They are characterized as having little potential for human habitation because of dryness, unpredictable precipitation, or cold.

Both deserts of cold and deserts of dryness have an annual precipitation of less than one or two inches. Deserts of dryness comprise about 18 percent of the earth's land area, while deserts of cold make up about 16 percent in tundras, ice fields, and polar regions.

Contrary to our usual image of desert terrain, largely created by Hollywood, arid deserts actually contain only small areas of rolling sand dunes. Sharp, angular rock formations, raised plateaus of rock, and large flat stone and gravel areas are the rule in deserts of dryness.

For example, the Sahara Desert is only 20 percent sand with

the rest barren rock, rocky plateaus, and gravel-covered plains. The Kalahari, Gobi, and Great Australian Deserts are mostly rock. In fact, the sand is there only because it has been produced by wind erosion from these large, rocky areas.

Dew

The moisture seen on the ground in the morning which is often called dew does not always fall, or condense, downward as most people think it does. Many times, what is thought to be dew is actually moisture that has risen out of the ground rather than falling on it.

True dew is a surprisingly complex phenomenon. It usually forms when warm, moist air cools at night, contacts a cool surface, and condenses as visible moisture on that surface. Factors such as relative humidity, dew point, and temperature determine dew formation.

But most, if not all, moisture on plants and grass in the morning is not dew at all, but comes from the plant itself through the pores of the leaves. When cooler air covers the warmer ground, the evaporation of water from the plant causes it to condense as "rising dew." It is a continuation of the plant's normal process of supplying the leaves with water, but is not actually dew.

Diamonds

Because gem-quality diamonds seen in jewelry are usually colorless, it is generally assumed that all diamonds are clear and glasslike in appearance. This is not so. In nature, diamonds can vary greatly, with color ranging from colorless to brown and even black. Diamonds may also be transparent, translucent, or opaque.

Gem-quality diamonds that are colorless, or nearly so, are by far the most precious of all diamonds. But these are very rare and very expensive. Other so-called "fancy" gems exhibit red, blue, green, orange, and yellow tints.

More common are industrial-quality diamonds which are usually gray, brown, or black. Their dark appearance greatly reduces their value, yet does not affect their characteristic strength and durability. The fact that these darker gems are more common and less expensive makes their widespread industrial use possible.

Dinosaurs

Most people believe that dinosaurs were large, vicious, meat-eating lizards that proved to be unsuccessfully adapted to their environment. None of these are true. In fact, the name *dinosaur* itself, meaning "terrible lizard," reflects these misconceptions.

Dinosaurs were not lizards as their name suggests. Although they are usually referred to as reptiles, they were unlike any reptile alive today. Dinosaurs had a skeletal system different from any other known reptile, and they were the only "reptiles" that ever lived that could walk like a mammal. Many are also now thought to have been warm-blooded creatures.

Most dinosaurs were peaceful plant eaters who rarely hunted anything except a bush or tree. Many of the largest dinosaurs were plant eaters, while some meat eaters were no bigger than a present-day chicken. In all, most were actually quite small, fairly agile, and some could even swim or fly.

Dinosaurs were also a very successful form of life on earth. Existing for over one hundred fifty million years, dinosaurs were the dominant species on the planet as they constantly changed, progressed, and evolved. This is a long time by any standard. In comparison, humans, even in our most primitive forms, have existed for about only fifty thousand years.

Contrary to the impression created by Hollywood films, cavemen, or any other form of human, never lived while dinosaurs existed. The fact is, dinosaurs preceded *Homo sapiens* by about sixty million years.

During their reign, dinosaurs lived on every continent except Antarctica. They dominated all other life-forms, including mammals, and probably disappeared only after the earth's climate drastically and suddenly changed.

Disney, Walt

Walt Disney did not draw the original Mickey Mouse in his first short cartoon, never drew him in later animated films, and, in fact, always had trouble trying to sketch the little mouse that made him famous.

Disney had actually abandoned his dream to become an animator early in his career. After realizing that he did not have the talent for animation, he concentrated on the production and commercial side of the business. Although Disney created the idea for Mickey, established his personality, and supplied the voice in Mickey's early cartoons, all of the sketching and animation was done by Ub Iwerks, who was Disney's chief animator in the early days of the studio.

Dixie

Dixie, the term most commonly associated with the South, did not originally refer to a geographic region nor did it come from the Mason and Dixon line.

The exact beginning of the term Dixie is not known for certain; however, there are two likely sources. One explanation derives from the ten-dollar notes issued by the Citizens Bank of New Orleans prior to the Civil War. These bills were printed bilingually in English and French and bore the French word *dix* for ten. They became known as dixies and, eventually, New Orleans, Louisiana, and the entire South were known as the land of dixie.

Another explanation is that the name became popular following the success of an 1859 New York minstrel show. The curtain call finale contained the song, "I Wish I was in Dixie's Land." Dixie referred to Dixie Lane, the name given to the Manhattan farm of John Dixie in the show. The song became popular in both the North and South, was Abraham Lincoln's favorite, and was adopted as the unofficial national anthem of the Confederacy.

It is likely that both of these events together contributed to the popularization of the term *dixie*. However, in neither case was the term originally used to refer to the South.

Dock, pier, and wharf

The words *dock*, *pier*, and *wharf* are often used interchangeably, but these words are quite different in meaning.

A dock is not a man-made facility where ships are moored. Rather, a dock is actually an enclosed body of water, usually artificial, for the mooring, loading, unloading, or repair of a ship. It is not the built-up area around the water where people stand alongside a boat, but the body of water itself. This is reflected in the term *dry dock*, which is an area (dock) emptied of water in order to build or repair ships.

A pier and a wharf are similar, except that a pier extends out into the water, usually at right angles to the shore, whereas a wharf runs along the shoreline. Both are used as mooring locations and for the loading and unloading of ships. However, a wharf normally contains buildings for the storage of the shipped goods.

Dog days of summer

Hot, lazy days in summer are not called dog days because of any connection with dogs or their tendency to lie around in the heat. The expression *dog days* acquired its name in ancient times when the rising of the star Sirius, known as the Dog Star, was in conjunction with the rising sun, originally between July 3 and August 11. This forty-day period, first noticed around 2770 B.C., was associated with the hottest days of summer and became popularly known as the dog days.

Owing to the precession of the equinoxes, this celestial event occurred one day later every four years, so that now, the hottest time of the year no longer coincides with the conjunction of the Dog Star and the sun. But July and August are still commonly referred to as the dog days of summer for this reason.

Dogs aging

It is an old wives' tale that dogs age at the rate of seven dog years for one human year. This popular misconception completely misconstrues the true nature of a dog's life cycle.

Dogs mature at a much faster rate in their early years than do humans. During the first three weeks, birth weight is nearly doubled, and a dog will usually reach its adult size in about six months. Nearly all of a dog's growth and development occurs during the first two years, after which the rate is much slower, or has even ceased.

The first three months of a dog's life are similar to about five human years. At six months, a dog is at the level of a ten to twelve year old child, while a one-year-old dog and a sixteen-year-old human are at a similar stage of development and nearly at sexual maturity.

A dog at two is considered well into adulthood, already sexually mature, and about equal to a twenty-four to twenty-five year old human. By the time a dog is five or six, it is in middle age. When a dog reaches age ten, the old adage does apply, as a single dog year equals six or eight human years.

Dogs barking

Dogs in the wild seldom, if ever, bark. Only those dogs who have come into contact with humans or other domesticated dogs exhibit this behavior. Wolves, foxes, wild dogs, and other canines only howl, growl, snarl, yelp, or whine, but do not bark. Although the reason for this is not known for certain, it is believed that the barking sounds of domesticated dogs are an attempt to imitate human sounds.

A barking dog is not usually a sign of aggressive behavior. Evolving from wolves about twelve thousand years ago, all breeds of domestic dogs retain their wolflike brain and social instincts. Barking is the domesticated dogs' alarm to others in his pack—canine or human—that something is wrong or that an intruder is present. It is the silent, snarling, or growling dog that is actually most dangerous.

Dogs sweating

Dogs do not sweat with their tongues as most people believe. They do have some sweat glands, but the ones of most importance are on the pads, or soles, of their feet. There are no sweat glands near the muzzle.

Dogs are cooled mainly by rapid breathing, which is the reason why they pant. A wet tongue hanging out is not evidence of a dog sweating, but is simply an increased saliva flow used by the dog to speed up evaporation and cooling.

Dolphins and porpoises

A great deal of confusion exists concerning the difference between dolphins and porpoises, and for good reason. The terms apply to three distinct types of animals—two mammals and one fish—all three of which are popularly referred to as *dolphins*, while the name *porpoise* is often used for two of them.

Dolphins are true mammals of the whale family. They are warm-blooded, breathe air, and nurse their young. The common, or bottle-nose, dolphin, is slender and possesses the long beak-like snout with the characteristic natural smile of the aquarium star. It is playful, can be well trained and is extremely intelligent. These dolphins are often mistaken for, and incorrectly called, porpoises.

Another dolphin is a true fish. It possesses a squarish head, a long dorsal fin, and is usually bluish with luminous shades of other colors. This dolphin is also referred to as a dorado.

The porpoise is shorter than the dolphin and has a heavier body, smaller dorsal fin, and a blunt, rounded snout with no beak. It is also a mammal, and its name is often extended to the dolphins, especially the bottle-nosed dolphin.

Donkeys, mules, jackasses, and asses

The differences between a donkey, mule, jackass, and ass are usually not clearly understood, and the names are often incorrectly used interchangeably. However, they are different animals, but all have their origin in the wild ass.

Known as the Old World horse, the ass is an African and Asian wild horse midway between the zebra and the true wild horse. Asses are small, about eighty inches long, are fast running, and have the characteristic long ears.

A donkey is simply a domesticated descendent of the wild ass. It is only slightly larger, has large ears, and, like the ass, is a good pack and draft animal but not suited for riding. The burro is a small donkey known in the Southwest and Mexico by its Spanish name. A male donkey is referred to as a jackass. A female donkey is called a jenny.

Mules are the offspring of a male donkey (jackass) and a female horse (mare). A type of mule produced from a female donkey (jenny) and a male horse (stallion) is a hinny. Both mules and hinnies are usually sterile.

Mules are more desirable than horses and donkeys because of their size and strength. They also have an advantage in hot weather, can be fed more cheaply, accept hard work, and make excellent pack animals due to their surefootedness and endurance.

Don't give up the ship

Commander James Lawrence did not say, "Don't give up the ship," while in battle on the U.S. frigate *Chesapeake*. As he was carried below mortally wounded he actually said, "Tell the men to fire faster and not give up the ship; fight her till she sinks." His words were ineffective, as the *Chesapeake* was captured by the British.

Double jeopardy

The sacred principle in criminal law known as double jeopardy, which holds that a person may not be tried or prosecuted twice for the same offense, is not always true. Although guaranteed in the Fifth Amendment to the U.S. Constitution, and extended to the states through the due process clause of the Fourteenth Amendment, it does not apply when an act is an offense against both federal and state laws.

This is known as the dual sovereignty doctrine and allows each jurisdiction, the federal and state sovereignties, to punish a person if its separate laws were broken. It is not regarded as a violation of the guarantee against double jeopardy.

However, some states have enacted laws prohibiting prosecution for the same act once the federal government has prosecuted. Also, it has been the policy of the federal government since 1959 not to prosecute if a state has already done so for the same offense, but they are not required to refrain from prosecuting a second time.

Also, double jeopardy does not apply in cases involving new trials resulting from appeals, motions for retrial, or cases with hung juries or other jury irregularities where a second trial is considered to be in the best interests of justice.

Drink like a fish

To say that a person drinks like a fish means that they drink a great deal or nothing at all. It all depends on whether the remark refers to saltwater or freshwater fish.

A significant problem for fish is the need to maintain their internal water balance. Saltwater fish lose body fluids to the outside seawater through the process of osmosis, because the body fluid of the fish is less concentrated than is seawater and tends to flow outward. To counter this drying-out, the kidneys of saltwater fish retain as much water as possible, and these fish drink water copiously.

Freshwater species live in an environment of low osmotic pressure relative to their body fluids and face the danger of becoming waterlogged. Their kidneys release large volumes of diluted urine and they do not drink water. Water enters their mouth and gills for breathing, but the gullet constricts tightly to keep water out of the body.

For this reason, only a few fish can live in both types of water. The salmon and eel, for example, slowly adjust to different water types with unique, specialized body parts during spawning migrations.

Thus, to be correct when saying that someone drinks like a fish when referring to their excessive drinking habits, it should be made clear that they drink like a saltwater fish. Otherwise, it is more of a compliment than an insult.

Drinking straws

When drinking through a straw, the liquid is not sucked up the straw as one might think. The action of a drinking straw is actually produced by the liquid being pushed up by the air pressure on the liquid's surface outside of the straw.

This happens because air has weight. When removing the air from the straw by sucking, the air pressure on the liquid inside the straw is reduced relative to the air pressure on the liquid's surface outside the straw. The greater pressure, or weight, on the outside pushes the liquid up into the straw.

There is a limit to the height that the weight of air will push liquid up a straw. A straw longer than thirty-three feet at sea level will not work no matter how powerfully the air is sucked out of it. Similarly, a straw will not work in space since there is no air pressure to push on the liquid's surface.

E

"History is a lie agreed upon."

Voltaire

Ears

The two flaps of skin attached to the sides of the head are not ears. The ear is an internal organ of hearing that consists of an inner, middle, and outer, or external, ear. The portion known as the external ear is specifically made up of just the ear canal and the eardrum, but not the flexible appendages that are usually called ears.

These fibrous, skin-covered pieces of cartilage on the side of the head are called pinnas, sometimes also referred to as auricles. They are more related to the muscle and skin configuration of the head than to the actual organ of hearing known as the ear.

In humans, pinnas are relatively useless remnants of the movable external flaps typical of most other vertebrates that can be turned in different directions to locate sounds. Human pinnas still contain muscles for this purpose, but during our evolutionary development, most people have lost the ability to voluntarily move their pinnas, although there are some individuals who do have this control.

The value of the pinna in directing sound into the ear canal is generally overrated in humans. For pinna size to give any real

85

advantage in hearing, it would have to be as large as a hand. Elephants, which have the largest ear flaps of any animal, have very poor hearing. In actuality, the only extra sound produced by a large pinna is an occasional wisecrack.

Earth is round

The earth is not really round. It is an oblate spheroid, which means it is slightly flattened at the poles and bulges at the equator.

The polar diameter of the earth is about twenty-six miles less than is the equatorial diameter. As a result, the equator is about thirteen miles farther from the center of the earth than are the North and South Poles. This fact was predicted in 1687 by Isaac Newton, based on the effects of centrifugal forces resulting from the rotation of the earth. While this difference may seem significant, it really has little practical consequence, since this flattening, as reported by astronauts from space, is not even visible.

Eat like a bird

The popular expression "to eat like a bird" is somewhat misleading. Although birds may not appear to eat much simply in terms of quantity, they eat far more in relation to their size than do humans.

Eating, like most aspects of a bird's existence, is related to the difficulties associated with flying. Birds require a constant supply of lightweight, high-energy foods to fuel their fast-running metabolism. Digestion operates at a fantastic rate. In some, a berry can be completely digested in twenty minutes. To reduce weight, there is practically no system for the storage of wastes, and this high-speed processing plant must be refilled constantly.

Adult birds of many species will commonly eat one-fourth to one-half of their own body weight each day. An American robin can eat about seventy worms or insects per day. This is the equivalent of an average man eating nine or ten pounds of food daily, whereas the average person actually consumes about two pounds a day. Food consumption among birds is even greater with younger birds. If food is available, some baby birds will eat their own weight every day.

Edison, Thomas

The electric light bulb was not invented by Thomas Edison. His most significant contribution was actually the improvement of the incandescent lamp in 1879 and the development of a commercially successful public lighting system.

The history of the incandescent light is long and includes the names of many scientists and inventors. Sir Humphrey Davy, said to be the true inventor of the electric light, caused an arc lamp to glow as early as 1802 when he passed electricity through a platinum wire. However, Davy did not pursue the discovery as a means of illumination.

By the 1840s, arc lamps strong enough to light halls were in use. In the 1860s light bulbs with filaments had been developed, although their use was fairly limited because of their short life span. By 1867, even the fluorescent light had been invented.

In 1845, J. W. Starr applied for an English patent for a light consisting of a carbon conductor in an evacuated tube which was very similar to Edison's later device. However, Starr died the next year at the age of twenty-five. His ideas were pursued by Joseph Swan, but until the 1870s, he could not make the light practical.

Edison began work on developing a long-lasting filament light in 1877, and made his famous breakthrough on October 21, 1879. After trying thousands of filaments, he placed a carbonized cotton thread in a bulb whose air had been pumped out, and produced the world's first long-lasting light bulb.

However, Swan had made independent and similar progress on an incandescent light and filed a patent infringement action against Edison, which Swan won. Their settlement led to the Edison and Swan United Electric Company. Edison later bought out Swan's interest in the company, and on his own established the first large-scale commercial lighting system.

However, both men, improving on the achievement of others, were responsible for devising a practical incandescent lamp. But, Edison alone can be credited for his enterprise in the development of public lighting, establishing an electrical distribution system that could be operated economically, and for promoting the general use of electricity.

Eggshell color

Contrary to popular belief, eggshell color has nothing to do with the quality or nutritional content of an egg, or the diet of the hen that laid it. Brown and white eggs are nutritionally identical, have the same composition, and possess similar cooking characteristics.

The color of an egg is produced by pigments in the outermost layer of the shell and ranges from white to deep brown. However, the color of the shell reflects only the ancestry of the chicken. Brown eggs are produced from hens with an Asiatic lineage and white eggs come from birds originating in the Mediterranean area.

To predict eggshell color, this formula may be applied: chicken breeds with white earlobes lay white eggs, while breeds with red earlobes lay brown eggs.

Egyptian embalming

It is a popular misconception that the ancient Egyptians possessed some mysterious secret for embalming. However, the ''secret'' to the success of Egyptian embalming was actually no secret at all. The fact that mummies, and other less familiar remains, were preserved so well for thousands of years is found anywhere and everywhere in Egypt—the hot, dry sand and climate.

No special embalming material or substance acted to preserve the bodies. Rather, loosely wrapping the remains in animal skins or linens, and then placing them in a sandy, shallow, temporary grave was, in fact, the key to preservation. After drying in this manner, the body was then prepared for a permanent burial.

By the fifth century B.C., all internal organs, except the heart and brain, were removed from the body. The resulting cavities were filled with myrrh and spices, although this, in reality, had little effect on preservation.

Pre-dynasty burials were thus preserved from putrefaction through contact with the hot, dry sand. However, later burials in more elaborate tombs, with tightly wrapped bodies, but without exposure to the dry sand, did not last well.

Einstein, Albert

When Albert Einstein was awarded the Nobel Prize for physics in 1921, he was not honored for his famous and profound theory of relativity, which was published sixteen years earlier. Instead, the award was for his much lesser known work on the photoelectric effect of light. It is believed that the selection committee wanted to honor Einstein, but for a less controversial subject than his relativity theory.

Electoral College

Americans do not ever really vote for the President of the United States. The President and Vice President are the only elective federal officials who are not elected by a direct vote of the people. They are actually chosen by members of the Electoral College. It is these electors, as they are called, who receive the votes in a presidential election.

The Electoral College is an institution that has been in existence since the founding of the country. On presidential election day, each state chooses as many electors as it has senators and representatives in Congress. Political parties usually nominate these electors at state conventions who are committed, but not obliged, to a certain candidate. Although their names do not usually appear on the ballot, they are the ones who actually receive the votes in a presidential election.

The chosen electors meet in December following a presidential election in their respective states and vote for their party's nominees. However, the Constitution does not require that electors vote for their nominees, and they may vote for anyone they prefer. Occasionally, they have done just that. These results are sent to the U.S. Senate where, on January 6, the winning candidate is declared the President-elect.

This system has, on three occasions, produced a President who did not win the popular vote, yet received a majority of electoral votes. John Adams (1824), Rutherford B. Hayes (1876), and Benjamin Harrison (1888) were elected while receiving fewer votes than did their opponents.

Electric eel

The electric eel is not an eel. It is an eel-shaped, South American freshwater fish also called the knifefish. The name eel has been misapplied to many other fishes that are shaped like eels but are quite distinct, are not true eels, and are not related to one another.

Nor is the electric eel the only electric fish. There are actually about five hundred species of electric fish, with the electric eel being the most potent and well known. Electric eels can produce up to six hundred fifty volts, enough to kill prey or to stun a human.

Elephants

The popular image of the elephant as a circus performer, combined with the many unusual attributes of these animals, has led to the existence of many common misconceptions about elephants.

For example, elephants do not drink water through their trunks as is often believed. The trunk, or proboscis, is analogous to the nose and upper lip of other mammals. To drink, an elephant fills its trunk and then squirts the water into its mouth. Drinking through its trunk would be like a human drinking through his or her nose.

The trunk is also not the awkward appendage that it seems to be. Although six feet long and weighing three hundred pounds, it is powerful, yet agile and sensitive. An elephant's trunk can pull a tree out by the roots, or it can pick up an object as small as a single blade of grass.

It is not true that elephants are afraid of mice. Mice are frequently found in the straw quarters around elephants, and elephants show little concern. In studies done to test this question, mice released near elephants did not produce any noticeable response from the elephants. In part, this is because an elephant's eyesight is so poor that it probably cannot even see an animal as small as a mouse.

Although the largest land animal, and appearing slow and ponderous, elephants are actually quite fast and very agile. In short distances, they can run faster than humans, and they can move through various terrains silently and quickly. They also possess an extraordinary sense of balance and touch, but are one of the few animals lacking the leg muscles to get all four feet off the ground simultaneously in any kind of jumping motion.

Most people do not believe that elephants can swim. In fact, they enjoy the water and swim readily and efficiently. To swim, an elephant will completely submerge itself with just the trunk sticking above the water like a snorkel and paddle around with its feet.

It is a popular misconception that elephants never forget. Their memory, although good, is not exceptional. What is often mistaken to be a keen memory is really part of the elephant's high level of intelligence. But its memory is no better than many other mammals.

There is also no such thing as an elephant graveyard. Elephants have been extensively hunted in the past for their ivory tusks and, since they live in family-like herds, large groups were often killed together within a small area. After large numbers of elephant bones had been found in one place, the erroneous myth of an elephant graveyard appeared to explain them.

Emancipation Proclamation

Contrary to popular belief, the Emancipation Proclamation issued by Abraham Lincoln did not free any slaves. This proclamation stands as one of the most commonly misunderstood presidential acts in American history.

The Emancipation Proclamation, issued on January 1, 1863, specifically proclaimed the freedom of all slaves, but only in regions then under Confederate control. It did not apply to northern or border states, Tennessee, or parts of Virginia and Louisiana. Because regions under U.S. control were exempted from its effects, it was completely unenforceable and probably without any constitutional authority.

Its immediate practical result was that the proclamation freed no one. But as Union forces conquered Southern territories, some slaves were later freed as these areas came under U.S. control. However, out of four million slaves in the United States at the time of the proclamation, only about two hundred thousand were ever freed as a direct consequence of the order.

The emancipation was actually more of a political effort by Lincoln rather than a moral one. Lincoln had not been an abolitionist for most of his political career, and he did not denounce slavery in public until 1854. He advocated opposition only to the spread of slavery into new territories and states, refused to free slaves in still-loyal border states, and even established mechanisms to colonize millions of free blacks in Latin America. Lincoln, although privately a compassionate man, was a pragmatist whose main concern in issuing the proclamation was to preserve the Union.

To do this, the emancipation politically served to define the Union cause. It did so as an antislavery crusade in order to mute the growing opposition to the mounting costs and casualties of the war. It also discouraged foreign intervention, especially by England and France, from supporting the Confederate cause.

Despite the emancipation, as the end of the war neared, Lincoln paid little attention to the freed slaves. It was largely left to army field commanders to improvise solutions to the problem, and Congress did not act until 1865 for their rehabilitation. Slavery was officially outlawed, not by the Emancipation Proclamation, but by the Thirteenth Amendment to the Constitution in 1865.

England, Great Britain, British Isles, United Kingdom, and the British Commonwealth

Much to the confusion of Americans, and the consternation of the British, the names England, Great Britain, British Isles, United Kingdom, and the British Commonwealth are not interchangeable. They refer to entirely different political and geographic entities.

England is not a country. It is a political division of the United Kingdom, which is a country. England is located on the island of Great Britain. Great Britain also contains the kingdoms of Scotland and Wales. Like England, neither of these are countries, but are also political divisions within the United Kingdom.

The British Isles are a group of islands consisting of Great Britain, Ireland, the Isle of Man, the Channel Islands, and many adjacent smaller islands. The British Isles, then, refers primarily to a geographic area.

The United Kingdom, or officially, the United Kingdom of Great Britain and Northern Ireland, consists of England, Scot-

land, Wales, and Northern Ireland. Ireland is a sovereign country and is not a part of the United Kingdom. The United Kingdom is a constitutional monarchy with the queen as the head of
state.

The British Commonwealth, now formally named the Commonwealth of Nations, is an association of individual nations
and dependencies linked by a common recognition of the British
monarch as the head of the Commonwealth. It comprises one-
fifth of the world's land surface and includes Canada, Australia,
African nations, and many other countries and British territories.

English horn

The English horn is not English. In fact, it is not even a horn.

Horns are considered lip-vibrated aeophones in which the
sounds are created by the lips vibrating against the mouthpiece,
such as the bugle, cornet, or trumpet. The English horn is not
played in this manner, and is actually a woodwind. Specifically,
it is an oboe pitched a fifth below the standard oboe.

The English horn originated in the Near East, but its name
first appeared in Vienna about 1760 when it was referred to as
the *cor anglais*. *Cor* refers to the curved or hornlike shape it
then had, while the use of *anglais*, or English, remains a mystery.

Exception proves the rule

It is both a popular and logical fallacy to believe that the
exception proves a rule. As a moment's thought will reveal, an
exception can only disprove a rule.

The apparent contradiction created by this expression derives
from the use of the word *prove*. In earlier usage, to prove simply
meant to test or try out. Thus, to say that the exception proves
the rule originally meant that it merely tested it. Because the
word *prove* now more commonly means to establish as fact, the
expression seems meaningless.

Eye for an eye

As measured by modern values, the Old Testament standard
of justice expressed in Exodus 21:24 of an "eye for eye, tooth
for tooth" is popularly believed to justify vindictive, retaliatory

measures. It is commonly used as a rationale for revenge and even as a biblical authority to support capital punishment. Yet when originally framed and set forth by Moses, this code was intended only as an attempt to attain equal and consistent justice and to limit vengeful retaliation.

Under most ancient legal systems, noblemen and higher classes received less punishment than did servants or slaves who committed similar offenses. It was also not at all uncommon for a lower-class person to be killed or seriously injured in retaliation for a very minor injury caused to a person of a privileged class.

As part of the law of retaliation, this ordinance of an "eye for eye" was meant to check passionate vengeance for a slight injury. The standard presented by Moses was meant to limit retaliation only to the extent of the first wrongful act and to provide equal justice for everyone. It was not intended as a justification for revenge as is usually believed.

F

"It is better to know nothing
than to know what ain't so."

Josh Billings

Fahrenheit scale

Most people assume that the zero-degree mark on the Fahrenheit scale has some significance, since both the freezing point of water (32°) and the boiling point (212°) seem somewhat arbitrary. The fact is, there is no real significance to zero degrees on the Fahrenheit scale.

When Daniel Fahrenheit devised his thermometer in 1724, he did not base the gradients on the freezing and boiling points of water. Instead, he designated as zero the temperature he obtained by mixing together equal weights of snow and salt. Fahrenheit believed this was the coldest temperature attainable and a constant value.

Since then, colder temperatures have been observed, and still much colder ones created. Absolute zero is now known to be −459.67° F. The arbitrary nature of the Fahrenheit scale has caused it to lose acceptance, especially among scientists, in favor of the more precise Centigrade scale, or as it is now called, the Celsius scale.

Fetal blood

It is generally believed that during gestation the mother's blood supply and the blood of the fetus are combined and circulated in a single system. This is not true. Maternal and fetal circulation are entirely separate, and at no time is there an exchange of blood between the two.

The organ responsible for the survival of the fetus is the placenta. The fetus is connected to the placenta via the umbilical cord. However, only the blood of the fetus moves through the arteries and veins of this cord.

When the fetus' blood enters the placenta, tiny hairlike growths, called villa, transfer to the fetus molecules of oxygen, protein, carbohydrates, minerals, and vitamins as well as remove the fetal waste products. These essential substances are supplied to the placenta by the mother's blood. However, they are only transferred at the placenta, and the two blood systems do not mix in the process.

Fido

The traditional and popular name for man's best friend, Fido, is not just a cute little word from children's stories, cartoons, or nursery school. It is a fitting title with a long history originating from the Latin word *fidus*, meaning faithful or loyal.

Fields, W. C.

W. C. Fields did not originate the remark usually attributed to him, "Anybody who hates children and dogs can't be all bad." Instead, the statement was actually first made about him during an introduction of Fields by Leo Rosten at a Los Angeles banquet in 1938. It immediately became popular and was often used by Fields himself throughout the rest of his career.

Incidentally, W. C. Fields's tombstone is not inscribed with the words, "I'd rather be in Philadelphia," as is commonly quipped. It simply says, "W. C. Fields, 1880–1946."

Fifty states in the Union

Technically, there are only forty-six states in the United States. The remaining four are not officially referred to as states, but are called commonwealths. These are Kentucky, Massachusetts, Pennsylvania, and Virginia.

The two words actually have about the same meaning. Commonwealth was used in many of the early English royal land charters and originally connoted the idea of more self-government. The terms were preferred and retained by these four states when admitted to the Union.

Finger snapping

The familiar crackling sound made when the thumb and middle finger are snapped together does not come from the thumb and middle finger as one might think. The sound is actually produced when the middle finger strikes the base of the thumb. The snap against the thumb merely provides enough speed to the finger so that its impact with the hand creates the sound.

Fingernails

Although it appears that fingernails grow outward from the ends, this is not true. All growth occurs under the skin at the base of the nail in a continuous process known as accretion, in which living cells cast off nonliving matter accumulated outside the growth cell.

As the nail grows, it secretes a soft, lifeless substance called keratin. This forces the previous growth, killed and hardened by the keratin, out from under the cuticle and forward as it dries into a solid plate. The whole nail, mainly hardened dead skin cells, moves along in one continuous piece. The growth of hair and the horns of animals is a similar process.

All fingernails and toenails do not grow at the same rate. Fingernails grow faster than toenails, and the nails on longer fingers and toes grow faster than on short ones, all of which grow faster in summer than in winter.

Fireside chats

The fireside chats of President Franklin D. Roosevelt were not weekly or regular radio broadcasts. During the twelve years beginning on March 12, 1933, until his death in 1945, there were a total of twenty-seven of these infrequent broadcasts.

Averaging two or three a year, these fireside chats were attempts to update and reassure the nation during the troubling days of the Depression and World War II. However, it was not Roosevelt or the White House who referred to the broadcasts as fireside chats. The quaint name was used only by the press when referring to the President's addresses to the nation.

First U.S. President

George Washington was not the first president of the United States. That position actually belonged to John Hanson. Although Washington was the first president under the U.S. Constitution in 1789, the United States existed as a sovereign nation for thirteen years prior to the adoption of the Constitution. For eight of those years, the government operated under the Articles of Confederation which produced the country's first leaders, including Hanson, but who have generally been ignored by history.

The Articles of Confederation were adopted by Congress in 1777 and ratified by the states in 1781. The Articles had a weak central government with no single executive position. Congress was, in effect, both the legislative and executive branches.

In 1781, this newly formed Congress met and elected John Hanson of Maryland as "President of the U. S. in Congress assembled." Hanson had played a significant role in gaining the adoption of the Articles of Confederation, and Congress recognized his efforts by making him its first President. George Washington wrote Hanson and congratulated him on his "appointment to fill the most important Seat in the United States."

Hanson had limited powers, as did the Congress itself, and occupied a position similar to the current Speaker of the House. He served for one year and resigned because of poor health. However, as "President of the U.S. in Congress assembled," he has been one of history's most forgotten characters.

First word from the moon

It is commonly believed that the first words ever spoken on the moon were, "That's one small step for man, one giant leap for mankind." But, in fact, the first word ever spoken on the moon was, "Houston." Moments after landing on the lunar surface at 4:18 P.M., EDT, on July 20, 1969, Commander Neil Armstrong radioed, "Houston, Tranquility Base here. The *Eagle* has landed."

Flag disposal

Proper maintenance and disposal of the U.S. flag is often misunderstood. An old, discarded flag does not have to be burned for proper disposal. There is also nothing that prohibits washing a dirty flag or mending one when torn.

The Flag Code, which is now public law, has codified the rules and customs pertaining to the use of the flag. Surprisingly, it took nearly 146 years after the Stars and Stripes appeared before any serious attempt was made to establish a code of etiquette for the flag, but it was not until 1976 that it became public law. Under this code, when a flag is in such condition that it is no longer a fitting emblem for display, it should be destroyed in a "dignified way," preferably, but not necessarily, by burning in private.

Flag of the United States

It is a common misconception that the history and design of the United States flag is clearly understood. In fact, very little of the past record surrounding the Stars and Stripes is really known for certain.

Through the first 135 years of our country's history, there was never a standardized flag. The true history of the Stars and Stripes has become so cluttered by myth and tradition that the facts are nearly impossible to establish. Even the many claims made for designing the first flag are all unproven, including the Betsy Ross story.

During the Revolutionary War, each colony and local military unit adopted its own flag. When Washington organized the Continental Army in January, 1777, its first standard was a red-and-white-striped flag with the British Union on it.

Because of great confusion with different flags, on June 14, 1777, the Continental Congress finally adopted a flag with thirteen stars and stripes. However, that original flag law no longer even exists and, judging by the plethora of American flags since then, it was probably quite vague.

Surprisingly, few people following the Revolutionary period bothered to write down anything concerning the flag's origin or design. Later attempts to reconstruct its history produced little precise information.

The "official" flag of thirteen alternating red and white stripes with white stars on a blue field was never formalized. Some displayed vertical stripes, and as new states were admitted, some flags added stripes while others did not. The flag flying over Fort McHenry that inspired Francis Scott Key had fifteen stripes. In 1818, a law returned the number of stripes and stars to thirteen.

The flag continued to change and vary, since only a general design was laid down in the flag law. During the 1800s a white eagle was usually added, while stripes and stars were of various dimensions, shapes, and proportions. During the Civil War, gold stars were also common.

Finally, in 1912, exact standards were set forth with even more precise specifications defining the flag drawn up in 1959. But prior to that time, the history of the Stars and Stripes is surprisingly unclear.

Flame

Contrary to what might seem to be true, a flame is hollow. A flame is essentially a layer of hot gas that surrounds a tapering column of cool, unburned gas. It thus resembles a hollow cone.

The hottest part of a flame is not within the fire itself. Instead, the area just above the tip of the flame produces the highest temperature.

Flammable and inflammable

Although the prefix *in* usually means "not," *flammable* and *inflammable* both mean "easily set on fire." Inflammable can be traced to the Latin *inflammare*, and later to the Old English *enflamen*, meaning to flame or burn.

To avoid possible confusion, especially among persons not familiar with the less-than-logical English language, some warnings on fuel tanks and trucks were changed to *flammable*, which is used technically in preference to *inflammable*. However, most agencies, both international and in the United States, still use *inflammable*, and either form is considered acceptable. The correct word for "not burnable" is *nonflammable*.

Flies

Flies do not have little suction cups on their feet that enable them to cling to walls, windows, and ceilings. As a matter of fact, flies do not even have feet.

Flies, including houseflies, have two claws on each of their six legs similar to the claws of a lobster. Between these claws are a pair of hairy pads coated with a sticky liquid.

To hold on, the fly can grasp with its claws or stick to the smooth surfaces with its pads. However, the sticky substance, along with the claws, provides just enough holding power to permit the fly to also take off quickly.

Flying animals

Although named flying squirrels, flying fish, flying frogs, and flying lizards, none can actually fly. These animals possess membranes that are attached to their bodies usually, but not always, connected to the legs. Since they do not have wings, these attachments permit gliding, but no actual flying.

This gliding behavior is often extremely well developed. For example, a species of giant flying squirrels has been observed to glide over two miles, although the North American species is limited to distances of about one hundred fifty feet. Some flying lemurs can also glide up to four hundred feet. Most other so-called flying animals can glide effectively from trees and bushes over shorter distances.

Fortune cookies

Most Americans consider fortune cookies to be a typically Chinese food and custom. They are not. Fortune cookies are an American creation.

Fortune cookie dough is actually similar to a traditional Chinese flat wafer cookie. There is even a precedent in Chinese custom for written messages inside of cakes, especially birth announcements.

However, the fortune cookie, as we know it, was invented in the United States. In 1918, a Chinese immigrant named George Jung devised the curled little cookie. He placed messages inside them to amuse diners in Chinese restaurants while waiting for their meals. Early versions simply contained verses from the Bible. However, Jung quickly became more creative and included messages, proverbs, and predictions.

Foul line in baseball

Despite its name, the foul line and foul pole in baseball are in fair territory. The lines, which extend from home plate at right angles to the outfield, mark the boundaries of the field. But in baseball, the lines are part of the playing field, and any ball hitting the foul line or foul pole is actually a fair ball.

Fractures, simple and compound

Simple and compound fractures have nothing to do with the number of places in which the bone is broken as is commonly believed.

A simple fracture means that though the bone may be broken in one or more places, the skin is not cut or perforated by the bone. A compound fracture is one in which the bone may also be broken in one or more places, but the skin and protective tissues around the bone are lacerated by the broken bone itself. Since the skin is opened, there is contact between the injury and the air in a compound fracture.

Thus, a bone broken in one place may be a compound fracture, while a bone broken in several places may be a simple fracture.

Frankenstein

Frankenstein was not the name of the monster in Mary Shelley's famous novel. The monster never even had a name.

Frankenstein was really Victor Frankenstein, the man who created the monster. He was not a doctor or a medical student, either. Victor was just a young scientist whose desire to create life inadvertently led him to the making of the monster.

Mary Shelley wrote *Frankenstein* when she was eighteen years old. Shelley and three friends wiled away a rainy night writing scary stories for each other and *Frankenstein* was born. Shelly later expanded her original story into the famous novel.

French and Indian War

The French and Indian War was not a conflict between France and the Indians in North America. The struggle for empire on the American continent from 1754–1763 was between France, its Canadian colonies, and their American Indian allies on one side against Britain and its American colonies on the other side.

The British victory won French Canada and opened up the frontier west of the Alleghenies for American expansion.

French fries

France has little to do with the name for the french fry. The term actually refers to the method of preparing and cooking the potatoes rather than to the country of its origin.

Although the exact beginnings of the name *french fry* are not precisely known, it most likely derives from the technique of frenching—cutting up meats and vegetables into thin strips—or french-frying—frying in very hot, deep fat until crisp. Both cooking methods are used in making french fries, and the name apparently derived from these techniques.

It is known that french fries acquired their name and originated in Belgium in the nineteenth century, and were served by street vendors in waxed paper cones. French-fried potatoes then became popular in England, France, and the United States.

French poodle

The French poodle did not originate in France, but in Germany, as a water hunting dog. It was bred and trained to jump into the water to retrieve ducks. These water dogs were called, in German, *puddel* dogs, meaning "splash." This later became pronounced as "poodle" in English.

Because these dogs later achieved great popularity in France, they became known as the French poodle. However, the term *French* is not even an official name or type of poodle. There are only three recognized varieties: the standard, miniature, and toy poodles, which differ only in size.

Frozen food

Cold temperatures do not kill the bacteria in frozen foods as most people believe. The organisms responsible for decaying food can survive temperatures much lower than a typical food freezer can attain. Freezing merely inhibits their growth and activity, and makes the bacteria so inactive that storage is possible for long periods of time. However, the fungi and bacteria return to their normal work once the food is unfrozen.

For this reason, when freezing food it should be frozen as rapidly as possible to reduce the formation of large, undesirable ice crystals. Since ice does not get colder than 32° F, organisms will be more active in and around these crystals than elsewhere. The ideal temperature for frozen foods is 0° F or below.

Fruits and vegetables

The question of what constitutes a fruit or a vegetable is not as simple as one might imagine. There are both popular and botanical definitions which, in many cases, are not the same.

In popular usage, a fruit is the fleshy, succulent, and sweet part of a plant, usually eaten raw and often as a dessert. It is distinguished from a vegetable that is commonly understood to mean any plant cultivated for human food and generally eaten with a meal.

A vegetable can include the roots (carrots), tubers (potatoes), stems (celery), leaves (lettuce), flowers (cauliflower), fruit (tomato), and seeds (corn). These everyday groupings are largely based on custom, tradition, and use, but have little to do with botanical considerations, which are often quite different.

Botanically, a fruit is the ripened ovary of a flower, its contents, and any related parts. There is no botanical classification called a vegetable, so many plants that we normally think of as vegetables are, in fact, actually fruits.

According to the botanical definition, fruits include olives, tomatoes, squash, cashews, kernels of wheat, corn, rice, and anything else growing from a plant's flower. However, other vegetables, such as beans and peas, are not fruits, but like the peanut, which is really not even a nut, are legumes.

Some plants, although fruits, are not the kind we think they are. Tomatoes and grapes are fruits with fleshy pericarps and a soft skin and are actually considered berries. Watermelons and cucumbers are, in fact, also berries, but with a harder skin, or rind. Oranges, lemons, and bananas, too, are berries only with a thicker leathery skin. Yet plants commonly referred to as berries, such as strawberries, raspberries, and blackberries, are not berries at all, but are brambles containing aggregate compound fruits.

Plants producing fruits with an inedible core, such as apples and pears, are called pomes. However, it is the core that is actually the true fruit of pomes and not the part usually eaten, since just the core derives from the ovarian parts of the flower.

Fulton, Robert, and the steamboat

Despite the prevailing lesson from most schoolbooks, Robert Fulton did not invent the steamboat. The history of the steamboat is well documented, and the honor for its invention belongs to John Fitch.

In 1786, Fitch built a simple steamboat and unsuccessfully attempted to demonstrate its value to the Continental Congress in Philadelphia. Later, in 1790, he placed an improved vessel in service, but could not make it profitable. By the 1800s, numerous steamboats had been built and put into use, yet none proved to be a financial success.

Robert Fulton did what no one else had previously been able to do. He made a commercial success out of steamboat service. In 1807, he placed his steamboat in use on the Hudson River and provided regular service between New York and Albany. It became a profitable venture for Fulton and made the steamboat commercially viable and, just as important, popular with the public.

Fulton's first steamboat was not called the *Clermont* as is usually believed. It was named the *North River Steamboat*. Since the first port of call on the trip was Clermont, the name was later changed by Fulton to appeal to the local passengers in the area.

Funny bone

The spot on the elbow which, when bumped, produces the familiar twinge up the arm is not a bone at all. This so-called funny bone, below the elbow and at the end of the humerus bone, is actually where the ulnar nerve passes through a shallow unprotected area near the surface and is partially exposed to external contact.

Bumping the elbow on the funny bone creates sudden pressure on the nerve causing an unpleasant, sharp, stinging sensation through the arm. The phenomenon is technically referred to as the olecranon process.

This area is called the funny bone in witty reference to the humerus bone, which is only indirectly involved in the phenomenon. Recently, it has also been called the crazy bone. In either case, the funniest part of it is when it happens to somebody else.

G

"An ignorant person is one who doesn't know
what you have just found out."

Will Rogers

Galileo and the telescope

Contrary to popular belief, the telescope was not invented by
Galileo. The honor for that invention belongs to Hans Lippershey, who first devised a telescope in 1608.

Lippershey was a Dutch lens grinder and spectacle maker
who created an instrument that made distant objects appear much
closer. Although the Dutch government tried to keep the invention a secret, Galileo heard of the new telescope and set out to
duplicate the device.

Not only did he do so within one year, but Galileo's telescope
was three times more powerful than Lippershey's. This enabled
Galileo to make the many important astronomical discoveries
that led to his popular association with the telescope.

Gas rationing

Gas rationing during World War II was not implemented to
conserve gasoline as most people think. Its purpose was really
to conserve rubber and tires.

At the beginning of the war, the Allies had control of about
85 percent of the world's oil production. However, after its in-

cursion into Indochina, Japan controlled about 97 percent of the world's natural rubber supply. The United States had only a one-year civilian supply of rubber in reserve, which was considered inadequate to meet the huge anticipated military demand for the war.

Gasoline rationing was imposed in 1942 to reduce tire use and conserve rubber until a synthetic product could be developed. Rationing tires alone would not have had the effect of immediately reducing driving and tire wear. A critical shortage of rubber would have occurred within a few years anyway. Gas rationing was seen as the only effective way to accomplish an immediate reduction in driving in order to conserve the limited supply of rubber.

Geography

Hawaii is not the westernmost point of the United States. It is Cape Wrangell, Attu Island, Aleutian Islands, Alaska, that is actually across the International Date Line and only about two miles from the easternmost islands of the Soviet Union.

Berlin, Germany, and Warsaw, Poland, are farther north than are parts of Alaska.

Canada's southermost point, Pelee Island in Lake Erie, is farther south than are parts of twenty-seven states. Pelee Island actually lies more to the south than do parts of Nevada and California.

The southernmost point in the United States is not Florida or Texas, but Ka Lae Island, Hawaii.

In square miles, Jacksonville, Florida, and not Los Angeles, is the largest city in the United States.

Excluding Alaska, the northernmost state is Minnesota, which extends 130 miles farther north than does Maine.

North America is not actually directly north of South America. All of Alaska, 85 percent of Canada, 90 percent of the 48 states, all of Mexico, and all of Central America except Panama lie west of South America. The two continents could just as easily have been called East and West America.

Pensacola, Florida, is farther west than Washington Island, Wisconson.

Reno, Nevada, is farther west than Los Angeles, California.

Virginia extends ninety-five miles farther west than does West

Virginia. It was not named solely for its geographic location, but for when some western counties of Virginia refused to secede from the Union in 1863 with the rest of Virginia.

The West Indies are nowhere near India, although Columbus named it in the mistaken belief that he had arrived in the Orient. The island chain is in the Caribbean Sea.

Germ

A germ is not necessarily a bad little microscopic bug that can make you sick. It is, more correctly, any small, rudimentary piece of living organism capable of reproducing, such as a seed, pod, or cell. That is why the small bit of living protoplasm in a wheat kernel is called wheat germ. However, various small bacteria and viruses have popularly become known as germs despite the fact that the meaning of the word is more general and benign.

Gettysburg Address

Abraham Lincoln did not write the Gettysburg Address on the back of an envelope while riding the train to Gettysburg. This enduring myth in American history is as persistent as it is false.

Recognized as Lincoln's best known and most quoted speech, the address was given to dedicate the Soldiers National Cemetery at Gettysburg, Pennsylvania, on November 19, 1862. Lincoln began the first draft for the speech on November 8, two weeks before the event. There were five written drafts, all on White House stationery. The Associated Press had even been given an advance copy of the speech for reproduction in newspapers.

Lincoln probably did not take a casual approach to the address at Gettysburg following his previous embarrassment at another Civil War battlefield cemetery. Several months earlier, while visiting Antietam shortly after the battle, he was criticized for his informal and inappropriate remarks made there. The opposition press reported Lincoln's behavior as if he had desecrated a sacred spot. Lincoln saw the Gettysburg speech as a chance to express his true reverence, and prepared it well in advance.

Giraffes

Even though the giraffe has the longest neck of any other animal, usually ten to twelve feet, its bone structure contains the same number of cervical vertebrae as all other mammals, including humans and whales. In the giraffe's neck, the seven vertebrae are simply farther apart. Other than length, there is no real difference between the neck of a giraffe and the human neck.

Gladiators

The popular belief that gladiator fights in ancient Rome usually pitted hapless Christians against Roman warriors in the Coliseum is another misconception created by Hollywood.

Gladiator fights began as a form of human sacrifice used at Roman funerals to commemorate the dead. However, by the first century B.C., they became more popular than the funerals themselves, and were instituted at various holiday celebrations during the Roman Empire.

Although Christians were used at times for this purpose, they were not normally the chief attraction at these spectacles. Most participants were prisoners of war and convicted criminals. Some were also volunteers who served because of the prestige attached to participation in the events.

It is also highly unlikely that Christians were even thrown to the lions in the Coliseum or anywhere else. This idea also appears to have been a creation of Hollywood films, as little historical or biblical evidence exists to support the myth.

Glass

Despite the fact that glass feels like a solid and certainly breaks like one, the physical properties of glass really make it more similar to a liquid than anything else. In fact, being more liquid than solid is what allows us to see through glass.

Technically, glass is considered to be a highly viscous liquid. It possesses a hard noncrystalline structure with random molecular orientation similar to a fluid. At room temperature, glass flows like any other liquid. However, its viscosity is so high that its movement is not apparent.

Glass is perfectly elastic up to its fracture point and has no freezing or melting point as do other solids. Instead, it gradually stiffens as cooled and softens as heated. Glass is molecularly a liquid, but with all of the properties of a solid except that light can pass through it.

For example, the glass in eyeglasses is continuously in the process of oozing out of the frames. However, it would take thousands of years to actually drip out. But in very old homes, glass is often thicker at the bottom of windowpanes than at the top due to the downward flow of the glass from gravity.

Go west, young man

Horace Greeley is usually attributed with originating the remark, "Go west, young man, go west." However, Greeley did not first use this expression. His role was simply to reprint in an 1851 edition of his *New York Tribune* an article by John L. Soule in which Soule wrote, "Go west, young man, and grow up with the country."

The expression caught on with the public and, because it first appeared in Greeley's newspaper, it became popularly associated with him. Despite repeated attempts by Greeley to disclaim credit for the remark, most people still believe he originated it.

Golf balls

The little dimples on a golf ball are not there simply for appearance. A dimpled golf ball actually travels faster and farther than a perfectly smooth ball of the same size.

The drag of an object traveling through air depends on two things—its size and surface area. Although having greater surface area, a dimpled golf ball produces an airflow in flight that allows the air to slip around the ball in such a way as to create the effect that the ball were smaller and smooth.

However, this advantage from dimples is unique only to small, round objects traveling at certain speeds. If this were not true, modern jet aircraft would also have dimpled surfaces. In fact, it is a peculiar phenomenon occurring mainly at typical golf ball speeds. When golf balls travel extremely fast, dimples have no advantage, while at very slow speeds, they are a disadvantage to flight.

Good Friday

It is ironic that the most solemn and saddest day in the Christian year, which commemorates the death of Jesus, is called Good Friday. However, in its earlier, archaic meaning, the word *good* was synonymous with *holy* and was often used as a euphemism for God. Thus, there was never anything good about Good Friday; it meant simply Holy Friday. Another example of this is found when referring to the Bible as the Good Book.

Gorillas

The gorilla is not a fierce, aggressive, meat-eating, dangerous animal as many people think. It is shy and peaceful, usually slow and docile, and a mostly elusive creature that lacks initiative or force unless threatened.

As the largest primate, with males weighing up to six hundred pounds, the gorilla is a massive animal with powerful arms. However, it is strictly vegetarian, feeding mainly on leaves, bark, roots, and fruits. It spends its day in a continuous cycle of feeding, resting, and sleeping.

The gorilla's aggression is usually limited to symbolic warning gestures. Chest pounding is, in fact, a typical signal warning an intruder or displaying dominance within the troop. But even this behavior is rarely seen, since gorillas normally avoid contact with humans.

Incidentally, the type of warfare characterized by fighting or harassment conducted by small, nonmilitary groups acting independently is not "gorilla," but "guerrilla" warfare. The term originated in Spain in the early 1800s when the first modern example of guerrilla operations on a large scale appeared. It derives from the Spanish word for war, *guerra*, modified to mean "little war."

Government of the people, by the people, for the people

Lincoln's eloquent and memorable 1863 Gettysburg Address is most remembered by its well-known passage, ". . . and that government of the people, by the people, for the people, shall not perish from the earth." However, these words were not originated by Lincoln as is commonly believed.

As early as 1382, John Wycliffe wrote, "This Bible is for the

government of the People, by the People, and for the People."
And in 1830, "The people's government, made for the people,
made by the people, and answerable to the people," was written
by Daniel Webster.

The most convincing evidence that Lincoln did not originate
these now-well-known words is obtained from an 1850 antislavery article by a Boston minister Theodore Parker. He wrote, "A
democracy that is government of all the people, by all the people, for all the people. . . ." William Herndon, Lincoln's former law partner, who collected antislavery material for the
President, included Parker's address in a collection of articles
prepared for Lincoln's reading.

Lincoln was aware of and impressed by Parker's words. Lincoln likely improved and refined the phrase and, since it was
uttered on an historic occasion, it now is credited to Lincoln
simply because he said it last. As Lowell once stated, "Though
old the thought and oft expressed, 'Tis his at last who says it
best."

Grand Central Station

The always-busy railroad depot in the city of New York is not
called Grand Central Station. It is actually named Grand Central
Terminal. The only Grand Central Station in New York is a nearby
subway station for the IRT Lexington Avenue subway line.

Grand Teton Mountains

The Grand Tetons in northwest Wyoming contain some of the
most rugged and beautiful mountain terrain in the Rocky Mountains. Yet the name *Grand Teton* does not refer to the grand
mountains, great peaks, or anything else having to do with sce-
nic splendor. *Teton* is the French word for breast. Thus, Grand
Teton simply means a great, or large breast.

The first recorded discovery of these mountains was made in
1808 by John Colter of the Lewis and Clark expedition. During
the early nineteenth century, this discovery was followed by an
era of explorations by French mountain men and fur traders.

These trappers referred to the South, Middle, and Grand Peaks
as *"los tres tetons,"* or the three breasts. This general area of
mountains later became known as the Grand Tetons from this
imaginative, although inaccurate, description. If nothing else,

the name at least reveals the unusual effects that prolonged, solitary mountain life can have on perception.

Grant, Cary

Except to imitate his impersonators, Cary Grant never said in any of his films, ''Judy, Judy, Judy.'' The expression originated with Larry Storch while doing an impression of Grant. It became so popular, especially among other impersonators, that the expression now is thought to have first come from Grant.

Grant's Tomb

Who is buried in Grant's Tomb? Actually, no one is buried there, and although the remains of Ulysses S. Grant are contained in the tomb, his is not the only body there.

Grant is one of two people in the famous New York City tomb. His wife, Julia Dent Grant, is in a separate, but equally big, coffin. Therefore, it should really be called Grants' Tomb and not Grant's Tomb.

In reality, no one is buried in Grant's Tomb anyway. To bury means to put into the ground, and the Grants were entombed above the ground. The question should really be, then, Who is entombed in Grant's Tomb?

Grant's real name was not Ulysses S. Grant either. He was born Hiram Ulysses Grant. After applying for admission to the U.S. Military Academy at West Point, an error was made on his records and his name was changed. Not wishing to offend anyone, Grant accepted the change and actually came to prefer his newly acquired name.

Great circles

The shortest distance between two points is not always a straight line. On curved surfaces, such as the earth, the shortest distance between any two points is the great circle that passes through those points, and not the straight line drawn between them on a flat map. A great circle is defined as the arc on the surface of a sphere formed when a plane is passed through the center of that sphere.

Great-circle routes are used by airlines and ships on long-distance trips. For example, when flying from New York to Japan, the shortest distance is the northern great-circle route that passes over Alaska. This can be demonstrated by stretching a string on a globe between New York and Tokyo. The string will cross Alaska and appear straight if viewed from directly overhead.

Great Danes

The origin of the name for the Great Dane has nothing to do with Denmark. Great Danes were originally bred in ancient Egypt as large dogs for royalty, and later were used to attack and kill wild boars. Bred to their present stature in Germany as guard dogs, the Great Dane was erroneously named from an old French word for the dog *grand Danois*. It is not known for certain why the French ever associated the dog with Denmark, since the history of the Great Dane has no connection with that country.

Green apples

It is not necessarily true that green apples make people sick. According to the United States Department of Agriculture, both ripe and unripe apples are digestible by the stomach, which does not distinguish between the two. As long as it is chewed sufficiently, a green apple will not cause sickness.

There is a difference, of course, between ripe and unripe fruit. The unripe apple contains more acid and long-chain pectins, which cause the development of gas in the stomach, and people differ in their ability to handle acids and gas in the digestive system. For this reason, some people will have problems eating green apples, but they do not make people sick.

Greenland

Greenland is not green, was not referred to by its discoverers as a green land to attract settlers, was not even a country until 1979, and Greenland is now not even the name of the island.

There is now very little that is green on Greenland. Four-fifths of the island, the largest in the world, is covered by an enormous, permanent ice cap. Greenland has few trees, and only sparse, barren tundra vegetation outside of the ice field. Agriculture is virtually nonexistent with the economy based on fishing and some sheep raising.

A popular misconception is that Erik the Red, an exiled murderer who discovered the island around 982, named the region Greenland in order to mislead and attract settlers. This is not correct. It is now known that for some as-yet-unexplained reason, Greenland has experienced a sudden shift in climate since its discovery and was once slightly warmer. The previous climate, although not greatly different, would have been warm enough to support more vegetation than currently exists there. It is probably true that when Erik the Red made his discovery, Greenland then was much greener than was Erik's homeland of Iceland.

For most of its history, Greenland has not been a country but a part of the Kingdom of Denmark administered by a Danish governor. Since home rule became effective in 1979, Greenland is now an independent nation. With independence, Greenlandic place names were also adopted into official use. Consequently, the correct name for Greenland is now Kalaallit Nunaat.

Grizzly bears

The grizzly bear is a unique and commonly misunderstood animal. It is usually thought to be awkward, aggressive, and a ferocious killer, but in fact, it is none of these.

The name *grizzly* itself has a connotation of something mean and terrible, such as in the phrase ''a grisly murder.'' However, the two words are not spelled the same, and in reference to the bear, *grizzly* simply means ''gray-haired.'' The name is derived from the bear's characteristic silver-tipped fur, although the grizzly's color can vary.

Rather than a blood-thirsty killer, the grizzly bear is primarily a scavenger. About 80 percent of its diet is vegetarian, and much of the rest consists of fish. The grizzly's aggression is usually limited to the protective behavior by the female for her young or by members of both sexes over food. Grizzly bears are usually ambivalent toward humans and generally flee when they contact people. However, it is still considered unwise to approach a grizzly in the wild as they are extremely powerful and will attack.

Although quite large, weighing about twelve hundred pounds and often eight feet in length, the grizzly appears clumsy and slow. However, a grizzly can run as fast as a horse over short distances. They have been timed in a full charge at a speed of forty-four feet per second, while the fastest Olympic sprinter can only run at thirty-three feet per second.

Groundhog Day

Punxsutawney Phil, the meteorological groundhog, does not really come out on February 2 in order to check the weather as folklore would have us believe. Hunger and an interest in acquiring a mate are what really makes the groundhog come out of his burrow. If neither desire is sufficiently strong, the animal will stay in its burrow for more sleep.

The popular legend surrounding the groundhog, also called a woodchuck, developed in Europe with sixteenth-century German farmers. However, in Germany the story originally was based on the badger and not the groundhog. But, when German settlers arrived in Pennsylvania, there were no badgers, so the groundhog, being the closest animal in the area in appearance to the badger, was substituted in the story.

Groundhog Day, February 2, happens to be about the time groundhogs emerge from their burrows after winter in the vicinity of Punxsutawney. But, groundhogs begin to stir in the spring at different dates depending on their geographic latitude and the climate of an area.

According to folklore, if the groundhog sees its shadow, it will be frightened and return to its den, indicating another six weeks of winter. Farmers would then know to delay their spring planting. However, records indicate that the groundhog is right only about 28 percent of the time.

Guillotine

It is true that the beheading machine known as the guillotine was named for Joseph I. Guillotine, a physician and member of the French National Assembly. However, Guillotine did not invent or even design the infamous device which now bears his name.

Dr. Guillotine, in 1789, was dissatisfied with the lack of effectiveness and accuracy of most executioners, and urged the National Assembly to adopt a more swift and humane form of execution. The Assembly commissioned Dr. Antoine Louis to meet Guillotine's requirements for such a machine. It was Dr. Louis who actually designed and built the device.

First used in 1792, the machine was initially called the louis-ette, but with Dr. Guillotine's more prominent position and in-direct association with the apparatus, it soon became known as the guillotine. Upon Guillotine's death, his children changed their names in 1814, as a result of their dubious connection with the guillotine.

The guillotine remains a legal, but rarely used, method of execution in France.

Guinea pigs

It will come as no surprise to anyone that the plump, furry little animal known as the guinea pig is not really a pig at all. However, it is also not from Guinea either. The guinea pig is actually a rodent native to South America and was originally domesticated in pre-Incan times by Peruvian Indians as a food source.

The guinea pig was discovered by Spanish explorers in South America and introduced into Europe during the sixteenth cen-tury by "Guineamen." These were mostly slave traders who traveled with slaves from Guinea, West Africa, to South Amer-ica and then to England. The name apparently derived from the Guineamen who first brought the animal to England. Since these animals grunt and squeal like pigs when hungry, they be-came known as guinea pigs. However, in the wild, a guinea pig is still referred to by its original Indian name of cavy. This is also the preferred term among breeders of the animal.

A guinea pig has become synonymous with a person or thing who is the object of experimentation. However, as an experi-mental animal, the guinea pig is no more than the fifth most popular. Mice, rats, chicks, and rabbits are actually the most common guinea pigs in research.

H

"There is nothing so powerful as truth—
and often nothing so strange."

Daniel Webster

The Hague

The Hague is not a building. It is the name of the capital city of the Netherlands. Although Amsterdam is the legal capital, The Hague is the actual capital since it serves as the seat of the national government and the official residence of the sovereign. The Hague is famous as an international center for conferences, trading, and banking, and contains the International Court of Justice in the Peace Palace.

Incidentally, there are also five cities in the United States whose official names begin with the word *The*. They are The Meadows, Illinois; The Plains, Ohio; The Village of Indian Hill, Ohio; The Village, Oklahoma; and The Dalles, Oregon.

Hail

Raindrops that freeze as they fall through cold air do not produce hail. Frozen precipitation produced in this manner is correctly referred to as sleet. In sleet, the ice pellets are usually much smaller than are hailstones.

Hail originates in convective clouds, usually in warm weather,

118

and develops in strong updrafts of supercooled air of up to 100 mph. These enormous updrafts cause the forming ice particles to rise and permit the hailstone to form by accretion over several minutes as it repeatedly rises and falls. The hailstone ascends through layers of supercooled water vapor and forms in onionlike layers as it passes through the clouds over and over again. As it forms, the water passes directly from its vapor state into the ice of the hailstone in the cloud layers. When the updrafts can no longer support the weight of the ice, it falls as hail.

Hair turning gray

When a person gets older, hair does not turn gray because the body adds gray coloring to the hair. Graying results simply when the normal, life-long pigmentation process of the hair ceases. The typical grayish-white appearance of hair in old age is actually the way it would have always looked in youth if pigments had not been continuously added.

Hair color, whether blond, brown, or black, is produced by varying amounts of a single pigment called melanin, which is added to the hair as it is pushed out of the skin follicle. As each hair is produced, certain amounts of melanin granules, depending on the individual, are attached to the hairs, giving each person their particular hair color.

When the body gets older, both the size of the melanin-producing cells and the number of pigment granules coming from each cell decreases. The coloring of individual hairs ceases, leaving the hair with its original, uncolored, grayish-white appearance. There is no known way to keep these pigmentation cells active through life in order to stop the graying process.

Halos

Despite depictions by generations of biblical artists that Jesus possessed a radiant halo, especially around the head and at manger scenes, the Gospel record nowhere makes a specific reference to an idea that Jesus was ever marked by a visible halo.

Halos, the luminous circle of light usually around the head, clearly developed through history as a symbol for pagan gods. Hindu, Indian, Greek, and Roman art all depicted deities with halos. Christianity, aware of the halo's pagan history, discouraged artists and writers from portraying Jesus in this way for nearly six centuries.

By the seventh century, the Christian church gradually came to adopt the use of the halo as artists and sculptors began to use them in an attempt to glorify the image of Christ. But the use of the halo completely lacks any biblical authority, and the only source for its existence in connection with Jesus is through paintings and sculptures done after the sixth century.

Hanging

Contrary to popular belief, hanging, as a form of execution, does not cause death by strangulation. Death usually occurs by injury to the upper part of the spinal cord from the fracture or dislocation of cervical vertebrae. It is a sudden and usually instantaneous form of death.

For centuries, hanging was one of the commonest means of execution. Until the nineteenth century, the person was simply pushed off a short height with a rope casually placed around the neck. A slow death from strangulation was the usual, and intended, result.

By the latter half of the 1800s, when more humane forms of execution were desired, various types of drops were developed causing, instead, a broken neck. The proper placement of the knot under the left ear meant that during the fall the head was jerked with sufficient force to break the neck.

Hanging is still considered the quickest form of execution in terms of time involved before death results. Although not a pretty sight for spectators, it actually is more speedy than the guillotine, lethal gas, or electrocution, since death occurs before the experience can be felt by the victim.

Hangnail

A hangnail has nothing to do with a hanging fingernail as the word suggests. The term to describe a painful bit of torn cuticle derives from the old Anglo-Saxon words *ang*, meaning pain, and *angnaegl*, for a painful nail.

Hans Brinker

The popular story of the little Dutch boy who plugs a hole in the dike with his finger never really happened. Also, the tale is not even Dutch in origin as is generally believed.

The story comes from the 1865 juvenile classic, *Hans Brinker, or the Silver Skates*. It was written in the United States by Mary Mapes Dodge and, although fiction, provides useful information on the history and social customs of Holland. The story involves fifteen-year-old Hans Brinker, the son of a dike worker in the Netherlands, who saved the town by plugging a leaky dike with his finger.

The story was unknown to the Dutch people until its popularity in the United States eventually spread to Holland. Although it was nothing more than American fiction, there is actually a statue honoring the nonexistent hero at Spaarndam in the Netherlands.

Harlem Globetrotters

The basketball team known as the Harlem Globetrotters did not originate in Harlem, nor were any of the team's first players from New York. Organized in Chicago by Abe Saperstein in 1926, the team began playing in Chicago's Savoy Ballroom until their "home" court was converted into a skating rink. Saperstein then took his team on the road, but never regularly played in New York or any other city.

Saperstein decided to call his team the Harlem Globetrotters "to let people know that they were black and so people would think they had been around." At first, the Globetrotters played serious basketball, but as they improved, no one wanted to play against them. They turned to a clowning style of play with tricky ball handling and achieved world-wide fame. But, they are not based in Harlem, never were, and continue as one of the few professional teams without a home court.

Hay fever

Hay fever is an old folk term for the symptoms produced from seasonal allergic reactions. It has nothing to do with hay, and it is not a fever.

Properly called rhinitis, hay fever refers to the symptoms of sneezing, running nose, and itching eyes as a reaction to inhaled allergens. Hay fever affects about 20 percent of the population in the United States.

In folk history, these symptoms tended to appear when roses bloomed and hay was harvested. Thus, the spring and late summer allergic reactions were popularly referred to as rose and hay fevers. However, they have nothing to do with these plants.

Spring reactions are from tree pollen, mostly maples, poplars, and oaks. Early summer symptoms are produced from grass pollen, while fall allergies are due to weed pollen, usually ragweed.

Headaches

Since the human brain is insensitive to pain, it is a misconception that headaches come directly from the brain. Headache pain generally originates from the nerves, muscles, and tissues outside the skull.

There are three likely sources of headache pain. The most common is the tension, or nervous, headache caused by contractions of muscles of the scalp and back of the neck. Migraine headaches are produced from the dilation and constriction of blood vessels in the scalp, temples and face. The third cause of headaches is congestion and inflammation of the nasal sinuses.

Contrary to popular belief, the eyes and eyestrain seldom cause headaches, except with glaucoma. Headaches actually arising inside the skull, although uncommon, are very important because of the usual seriousness of the cause and should be professionally examined.

Heart

Despite the fact that doctors usually place their stethoscopes on the left side of the chest to listen to the heart and that the heartbeat seems to come from that side of the body, the heart, in fact, is not located on the body's left side. Although the apex of the organ is a little to the left of the body's center line, most of the heart is actually on the right side of the body.

The heart is in a somewhat tilted position so that the left ventricle pushes up slightly toward the surface. This location makes it so easily and misleadingly felt on that side. As the strongest pumping chamber of the heart, the left ventricle makes more sound, creating the impression that the entire organ is positioned on the left side of the chest.

The heart is about the size of two fists placed together and weighs up to one pound. This little lump of muscle beats about one hundred three thousand times in one day. Although the heart is not really heart-shaped, its form resembles the popular Valentine image sufficiently to satisfy most sentimentalists.

Heart attacks

The popular belief that men have more heart attacks than women is not totally supported by the evidence. Although it is true that men do have higher rates of heart attack until the age when women reach menopause, the rates afterward for both sexes are about the same. The significant difference is that the age of onset of higher rates is greater among women.

According to the American Heart Association, the prevalence of coronary heart disease is about the same for men and women in all age groups after the age of sixty-five. While death rates from heart attacks are four times higher for men under fifty-five years of age they are less than one and one-half times greater for men than women sixty-five or older. Of all heart attacks among males, about 45 percent occur in men age sixty-five or older. For all heart attacks among females, about 73 percent strike women sixty-five or older. The mortality rate for heart attacks among women is also 50 percent higher than men, probably due to the higher age of most female victims.

It is thought that the female endocrine system, plus a special composition of lipids in the blood, protects women from heart disease during childbearing years. After menopause, this physiological advantage is not evident, and heart attacks are almost as common and deadly among women as men.

Heartbeat

The characteristic *lub-dub* sound of the human heart is not actually the sound of the heart beating. It is not possible to hear the heart's muscle rhythmically contracting as most people believe. What is really heard is the sound of the valves within the heart slapping shut to prevent the backflow of blood during the contractions of the muscles of the heart.

There are normally two distinct audible sounds referred to as the heartbeat. The first, a low, slightly prolonged *lub* is produced by the closure of the mitral and tricuspid valves. This is followed by a sharper, higher-pitched *dub*, which is the closure of the aortic and pulmonary valves. But the contractions of the heart muscles themselves that pumped the blood are nearly silent.

Heartburn

Although the name suggests something more serious, heartburn has nothing to do with the heart. Technically known as pyrosis, heartburn is the burning sensation felt behind the breastbone, sometimes radiating even into the neck or back.

Heartburn is caused by the presence of gastric secretions, called *reflux*, into the lower portion of the esophagus near the stomach. The reflux, primarily hydrochloric acid, causes pain as it irritates the lining of the esophagus. Generally considered a minor digestive disorder when muscles of the upper stomach fail to contain gastroesophageal reflux, heartburn can also indicate heart disease or a more serious disorder of the digestive tract.

Heinz 57 varieties

The slogan used by Henry J. Heinz, "57 varieties," does not, and never did, refer to the true number of products his company has produced. Heinz always has had more than fifty-seven products, even when the ad was first used.

This slogan was invented by Heinz in 1892 after he noticed a shoe advertisement in a streetcar that claimed twenty-one different styles of shoes. The idea of using a number in advertising appealed to Heinz, and he soon settled on fifty-seven for his marketing slogan. Even in 1892, the Heinz Company was turning out sixty-five different varieties of products, but the number fifty-seven possessed nearly mystical fascination for him.

Today, Heinz produces only two varieties of ketchup, but the entire product line consists of pickles, sauces, soups, baby food, and dozens of other goods that now total over thirteen hundred varieties. But the number fifty-seven retains its hold on the company. The slogan "57 varieties" is still used, the corporate phone number is 237-5757, and its address is P.O. Box 57 in Pittsburgh.

Hemophilia

Hemophilia is not the fatal blood disease most people believe it is. The disease involves only an impairment of clotting, but not actually a complete inability of the blood to clot.

Hemophilia is a comparatively rare, inherited disorder involving a deficiency of a specific clotting factor in the blood. The symptoms, which appear only in males, range from mild to severe. Most hemophiliacs can now lead fairly normal lives, while some are seriously debilitated, and a few may die prematurely. However, the true nature of the disorder contrasts markedly with the popular image of the disease largely derived from its historical association with Europe's royal families in the nineteenth and twentieth centuries.

In hemophilia, coagulation time is relatively normal and bleeding is characteristically a delayed or prolonged oozing or trickling occurring after minor trauma or surgery such as tooth extraction. Even in severe hemophilia, coagulation time ranges from thirty minutes to several hours. Rarely does a hemophiliac have massive bleeding, and never does one bleed to death from a small cut as it is commonly believed.

Joint hemorrhages, gastrointestinal bleeding, and bruising are actually more serious concerns for the hemophiliac than is bleeding to death. However, modern treatment methods have significantly lowered even these risks through the use of new clotting serums.

Hens sitting on their eggs

It is not true that hens actually sit on their eggs in order to hatch them. What really happens is that they more or less squat on their feet, with the legs—and not the eggs—bearing most of the weight of the chicken. The underside of a chicken actually has a V-shaped trough that surrounds the eggs for warmth. By squatting, rather than sitting, the eggs are enveloped in this trough without being crushed.

Hippocratic oath

It is a popular misconception that the Hippocratic oath is routinely taken by doctors, has a specific legal status, or is a required part of a medical degree. The fact is, the Hippocratic oath only serves, at best, as an ideal for professional attitudes and ethics, but is usually regarded by most physician's professional groups, medical schools, and individual doctors to be obsolete.

None of Hippocrates's writings survived his lifetime. All that is known of his teachings has been recorded and passed on by others who lived nearly two hundred years after his death. This is true of the Hippocratic oath. The authorship and historical origin of the oath are so obscure that its date of composition can only be placed between the sixth and first centuries B.C. No one knows how and when the oath was formulated or who really wrote it.

Today, there are no legal obligations involved with the Hippocratic oath. Most professional associations have their own code of ethics, and the oath is considered an issue of individual morality for each physician. Each medical school has its own tradition with respect to the oath, but it is included only as a part of the ceremonies associated with commencement, if at all.

Legally, state licensing boards are responsible for administering tests for licenses to practice medicine within a particular state. But no state board requires the Hippocratic oath or anything similar to it in order to receive a medical license.

Hollywood

Hollywood is not a city in California. Settled in the 1880s and named in 1887, Hollywood did become a city in 1903. However, since 1910 when it was incorporated into the city of Los Angeles, Hollywood has been only a district, or section, within Los Angeles.

Famous as the heart of the motion-picture industry, this district is now mostly a residential community. Although it remains a center for the music recording business, composers, and talent agencies, most of the once-famous movie studios have moved. Most movie stars also now live elsewhere.

The familiar Hollywood trademark—the "Hollywood" sign—was not originally constructed in 1928 to publicize the movie capital. The famous sign, which spells out the name of the city in forty-five foot high white letters, first read "Hollywoodland" as an advertisement for Hollywoodland Realty. But when the "land" part of the sign fell off, the remaining portion soon became recognized as a fitting symbol for the city itself.

Holmes, Sherlock

In none of Sir Arthur Conan Doyle's fifty-six short stories and four novels does Sherlock Holmes ever say, "Elementary, my dear Watson." Holmes frequently does remark, "Elementary," and also says, "My dear Watson," but he never combines the two into the popular expression usually associated with Sherlock Holmes.

Homing pigeons

Contrary to popular belief, there is no instinct to return to any point of origin in a homing pigeon. The homing ability must be taught to the birds through a lengthy process beginning with distances as close as fifty feet.

The migratory movement of some birds is not the same as homing behavior. Migration is a complex, seasonal phenomenon that appears to be instinctual. It is triggered by environmental stimuli and involves flights over great distances returning to relatively specific locations.

Homing is based on the bird's natural urge to return to its nesting area. However, homing pigeons cannot be suddenly taken out of sight and be expected to return over long distances. The birds are gradually moved farther away from their roost until homing is achieved, usually after many successive flights of increasing distance.

Horns and antlers

Horns and antlers may look alike to the casual observer, but they are not the same thing.

Horns are actually part of an animal's skull. They grow out slowly as the animal grows, are attached for life, and are covered by a hard substance tougher than bone known as keratin. Both sexes have horns, and they are found on cows, bison, and mountain sheep.

In contrast, antlers are pure bone and grow quickly out of the top of the head, but are not connected to the skull. In fact, they are one of the fastest growing things in the animal world with some antlers growing as much as one half-inch a day. Antlers, however, drop off each year and are usually grown only on males. Antlers are found on deer, elk, moose, and caribou.

Horses pulling wagons

While most people think that a horse pulls with all four legs, it does not. The propelling and pulling power lies totally in the horse's hindquarters.

The chief function of the front legs of a horse is to hold up the animal. The forelegs share the same physiology as the human shoulder, elbow, and wrist. In the horse, the front legs are connected by muscles that serve as a sort of sling through which the whole body is suspended. But the hind legs are attached to the trunk by powerful ball-and-socket joints and actually do the pulling.

Household appliances

The popular notion that modern household appliances have reduced the time required to do housework is not true. The fact is, according to historical home economists, the modern housewife spends as much time doing housework today, despite modern conveniences, as did colonial women. Although appliances do reduce the amount of physical effort involved in housekeeping and have improved our standard of living, comfort, and health, they have not actually saved time.

The reasons for this paradox are complex and deal with various social, cultural, and technological changes. As each new invention or change appeared, a more complicated social structure was created that tended to increasingly separate the work of women from that of men and children. Whereas many older tasks were family projects, appliances shifted the division of labor onto the woman and freed men and children for other activities.

Many chores were made easier by appliances such as washing machines, ranges, and vacuum cleaners, but they also brought with them more washing and cleaning than was done before. Houses were larger, more clothes were owned, and standards of cleanliness improved so that more time was needed for these chores.

Stores and refrigerators created varied cooking assignments with more time needed for shopping and to fill complex diet and meal routines. Running indoor water meant that bathrooms, toilets, and sinks, which before never existed, had to be cleaned. The result of these and other modern conveniences was simply to create new and bigger jobs which generally became the woman's responsibility and took as much time as ever to complete.

Howe, Elias, and the sewing machine

The sewing machine was not first invented by Elias Howe. However, in 1846 he did improve upon, patent, and successfully manufacture a practical model which led to his being credited with this invention.

By 1830, a French tailor had invented a workable sewing machine. In 1834, twelve years before Howe's machine, Walter Hunt invented a model similar to Howe's, but did not apply for a patent for fear of putting seamstresses out of work. Howe's machine was noteworthy, not for its originality, but for its mechanical improvements and commercial success.

Hudson, Henry

Henry Hudson did not discover the Hudson River, the Hudson Straits, or Hudson Bay. They were all first seen by other Europeans decades before Hudson's first voyage.

In fact, the Hudson River was first discovered eight-four years before Hudson by the Portuguese explorer Estevan Gomez in 1525, although an unsupported claim was also made by Giovanni da Verrazano in 1524. Hudson reached the river now bearing his name in 1609 when it was referred to as the North River to distinguish it from the South (Delaware) River.

Similarly, Portuguese explorers first discovered the Straits and Bay now called Hudson. All of the voyages by Hudson between 1607 and 1611 were for the sole purpose of locating a northwest passage to the Orient, as was much of the early exploration of North America. As a courageous, if not headstrong, explorer, these regions were later named in his honor.

Human longevity

The idea persists that groups of humans exist who are one hundred twenty to one hundred fifty years old. However, the facts do not support these legendary centenarians.

Usually from isolated regions, such as in the Soviet Union or South America, small populations of humans are said to live to great ages. Recipes for their longevity usually include an outdoor existence, hard work, and simple subsistence diets.

However, certain curious factors are evident in these reports of longevity. There is usually an absence in these groups of a proportionate number of elders between the ages of seventy and ninety, there are no birth records, age is a highly venerated status encouraging exaggeration, and the people are illiterate with a poor concept of time. In the case of the Soviets, years have likely been added to their ages in the past to avoid military service under czarist rule.

In addition, cell biologists now believe that there is a definite biological limit to human cell reproduction making the maximum age possible for human life to be about 110 years. No person with a verifiable record of age has ever exceeded this upper limit by more than a few years, let alone a whole group surpassing it by ten to forty years. Such claims for longevity make interesting stories and have been commonly accepted, but are simply untrue.

Humidity

When the humidity is given in a weather report, it does not actually refer to the amount of water in the air. The measure given is, instead, the relative humidity, which is the percent of water in the air in relation to the amount of water the air can hold at a certain temperature. The actual amount of water in a given volume of air is called absolute humidity, and is seldom used in weather reporting.

Even on the muggiest summer day, when the relative humidity may be 60 percent, the actual water content of the air constitutes less than 3 to 5 percent. Because cold air cannot hold as much water as warm air, relative humidity of 30 percent in the winter means that the air actually contains less than one percent water.

Hundred Years War

The Hundred Years War was the popular name given to a series of conflicts between France and England that did not last 100 years. Occurring intermittently from 1337 to 1453, the Hundred Years War lasted 116 years based on the cease-fire, 138 years until the treaty papers were signed, and 216 years until the British totally withdrew from contested French soil.

The name for this war did not become popular until late in

the nineteenth century, by which time most people had forgotten the details or the exact duration of the conflict.

Hunger

The sensation of hunger has little to do with an empty stomach. Hunger begins when certain nutrients are missing in the blood, and a message is sent to the hunger center of the brain. From there, the brain activates the stomach and intestines. Rumbling and growling occur as a consequence of rhythmic contractions and, combined with a psychological reaction to all of these stimuli, the feeling of hunger is experienced.

Conversely, sufficient nutrients in the blood cause the brain to inhibit stomach and intestinal activity, which is supposed to discourage us from eating. However, blood sugar and stomach distention are not the only factors involved in signaling us not to eat. Sensory cues in the mind, such as tastes, smells, and even the sight of food, need also to be satisfied to satiate the urge to eat.

I

"The exact contrary of what is generally believed
is often the truth."

Jean de La Bruyère

Igloos

It is untrue that an igloo is a rounded Eskimo house made
from blocks of ice. Igloo is simply the Eskimo word for house
and is applied to any form of dwelling, not just the icehouse.
The familiar snowhouse, thought to be the Eskimo's principal
shelter, is not even the most common type of igloo.

Eskimo dwellings varied widely in form and type depending
on the building materials available, season of the year, and length
of time to be used. The most common igloo was a semisubter-
ranean house constructed from logs and sod. In summer, tents
from animal hides were often used and, in winter, snowhouses
were built. All of these dwellings are called igloos.

The dwelling popularly thought of as an igloo is properly
referred to as a snowhouse. This kind of igloo is not built from
ice blocks as is usually believed, but from blocks of compacted
snow. Although a once common winter shelter, most Eskimos
today have never even seen a snowhouse.

132

Ignorance is bliss

An often-quoted expression is, "Ignorance is bliss." However, these were not the words originally written by Thomas Gray. What he actually did write was, ". . . where ignorance is bliss, 'tis folly to be wise." Gray never intended to be an advocate of ignorance; only that at times wisdom may not be desirable.

Immaculate Conception

The Immaculate Conception does not refer to the conception of Jesus in his mother, Mary, as is commonly believed. Instead, it pertains to the conception of Mary by her mother. The Immaculate Conception is a complex doctrine of the Church of Rome which is usually confused with the doctrine of the Virgin Birth of Christ.

Pope Pius IX made the Immaculate Conception the official doctrine of the Roman Catholic Church when he declared it as an article of faith in 1854. It was also this same pope who established the doctrine of papal infallibility.

The Immaculate Conception is entirely a spiritual doctrine. It contends that the Virgin Mary was conceived in her mother's womb, Saint Anne, free from all stain of original sin. It views Mary as the first point of contact between historical man and his salvation, Jesus Christ.

This does not connote a virginal birth of Mary. She was conceived and born in the normal human way. The doctrine only implies the grace and holiness of the mother of Jesus, who has been absolved of the eternal burden of original sin which all other men share.

The Immaculate Conception is not the same doctrine as the Virgin Birth of Christ with which it is usually confused. This doctrine refers to the conception of Jesus by his mother, Mary. It holds that he was miraculously begotten and conceived by God and born of the Virgin Mary.

Impeachment

Under Article II of the U.S. Constitution, impeachment does not mean the removal from office of an elected federal official. Impeachment refers simply to the criminal proceeding itself against a public officer.

Impeachment begins with the House of Representatives, drawing up the articles, or charges, of impeachment for and conviction of "Treason, Bribery, or other high Crimes and Misdemeanors." If the articles are passed by a simple majority in the House, they are sent to the Senate where a two-thirds-majority vote is needed for conviction. This process, whether or not resulting in conviction and removal from office, is impeachment.

There is no criminal penalty involved in impeachment, just removal from office. Double jeopardy does not apply and criminal charges may later be brought against the impeached official in federal or state court.

Incest

Although incest taboos have been universally found in all known human societies, popular folk beliefs are untrue that mental defectives, mutants, or other deformed offspring are ordinarily produced from incestuous relations. Most modern geneticists believe that inbreeding does not usually result in defective offspring as is commonly thought. This fact is true even in first-order relations involving father-daughter, mother-son and sister-brother incest.

Anthropologists have never been able to adequately explain what purpose is served by severe and universal prohibitions against incest. One theory has been that biological dangers inevitably result from this type of sexual union. However, harm simply does not occur often enough to be the reason for incest taboos, and this theory has long been discarded.

In fact, inbreeding is known to do no more than intensify whatever traits the inbred population or individuals possessed at the outset. This includes an exaggeration of all genetic traits, both good and bad. It is usually overlooked that inbreeding also magnifies the influence of dominant genes which often leads to what is referred to as the "hybrid vigor" of an inbred group. An example is Cleopatra, often revered for her physical beauty, who was the product of eleven generations of royal sibling marriages in Egypt. Despite incest taboos, the idea that defective offspring are invariably produced from incestuous relations is an erroneous popular misconception.

India ink

India ink, not Indian ink as it is usually called, is not from India and never was. It originated in China and should actually be called Chinese ink which, in fact, is what it is called in France.

This type of ink was developed by the Chinese as early as 2500 B.C. as a suspension of carbon, usually lampblack, gum, and water. Modern India ink is merely a refinement of these early carbon inks.

The name India erroneously appeared for the ink imported from China in a 1665 edition of the Oxford English Dictionary. It has since proven difficult to correct the error in popular usage.

Indian giver

The expression "Indian giver" is commonly applied to a person who gives a gift, and then ungraciously wants it back. This notion does not accurately represent the nature of Indian gift-giving practices, or the origin of the expression itself.

In American Indian culture, as in many other societies, giving a gift meant that a gift of at least equal value was to be returned. In some cultures this practice of reciprocity often became quite intense and competitive. Large gifts would be given in an attempt to humiliate a rival or to establish status in the hope that the returned gift would not be as great.

This did not mean that the gift-giving Indian wanted his own gift back. It simply meant that he expected reciprocity. The failure to return a gift was an affront against the Indian's values.

The white man, at least those not familiar with Indian culture, misinterpreted the Indian's concept of reciprocity to mean that the Indian wanted his own gift back. Hence, the term "Indian giver" came into popular use as an erroneous description of both the American Indian and a person who gives something and then wants it back.

Indians and their decimation

It is a common misconception that the Indian population in the New World was destroyed through years of constant warfare with European settlers. In reality, it was mainly the invisible microorganisms brought from Europe, such as smallpox, measles, cholera, and influenza, that decimated the natives of North, Central, and South America.

The Aztecs and Incas were reduced in numbers from disease nearly 80 percent by the year 1600. Some Indians in South America lost 90 percent of their population from disease within the first fifty years of contact with whites.

In America, the prehistoric Indian population is estimated to have been about 2,500,000. By 1890, this number had fallen to as few as 250,000. Within thirty years after the arrival of Columbus in 1492, nearly all of the native population in the Caribbean had been eliminated by disease. As early as 1640, the Iroquois confederation in the United States had lost nearly half of their people to disease introduced by the white man.

Lacking any racial immunity to the many diseases brought by European settlers and slaves from Africa, Indian populations declined within decades. Those that initially survived the disease faced malnutrition due to depletion of game and other food sources, relocation on unfamiliar land, and armed conflicts.

Innocent verdict

In the American legal system, a jury can only decide that a defendant is guilty or not guilty. Never is an innocent verdict returned.

A decision of not guilty simply means that the jury is unconvinced that the defendant is guilty as accused beyond a reasonable doubt. It does not necessarily imply that the jurors believe the defendant did not commit the crime, only that insufficient evidence was presented for a conviction. Even if a person found not guilty is later known to be guilty, because of double-jeopardy protection provided under the Fifth Amendment, there can be no retrial.

IOU

The abbreviation IOU for a signed paper acknowledging that one owes a sum of money to the holder did not derive from the words "I owe you." Such notes were originally written as "I owe unto," followed by the lender's name. It has since become shortened to IOU with the mistaken presumption that the "U" stands for "you" in the abbreviation.

Iwo Jima

The famous scene of the flag-raising on Mt. Suribachi photographed by Joe Rosenthal won him a Pulitzer Prize and inspired the enormous monument in Arlington National Cemetery. However, the photograph was not taken of the event as it actually happened. The picture is a reenactment of the actual flag-raising. It was staged for Rosenthal by the participants who had captured the hill earlier in the day on February 23, 1945. Nevertheless, the photo symbolized the spirit of the struggle for Iwo Jima, one of the fiercest battles of World War II. The charge up Mt. Suribachi, the small island's highest point, was made by 252 marines, 27 of whom survived the assault.

J

"The only fence against the world
is a thorough knowledge of it."

John Locke

Jellyfish

The jellyfish is not a fish and, of course, it is not made of jelly. It is one of several varieties of marine invertebrates that have no relationship or resemblance at all to fish.

Jellyfish are unique in several ways and little is generally known about them. They are actually 98 percent water in the form of a gelatinous mass for a body and have long, hanging tentacles. The internal composition of a jellyfish is more like pure seawater than is any other living thing. When washed up on shore, jellyfish will virtually disappear as they dry.

Also, the size of a jellyfish depends on how much it eats. However, unlike most other animals, jellyfish can both grow and "degrow." When food supplies are insufficient, jellyfish will actually reduce in size. A twelve-inch jellyfish can de-grow in this way to about the size of a quarter and still remain completely healthy, one of the few living things capable of doing so.

Jesus as a carpenter

No where in the Bible does it mention that Jesus was ever a carpenter as most people think. Although Matthew 13:55 states that he was a carpenter's son, and Mark 6:3 tells that people called him a carpenter, there is no other reference in the Bible indicating the occupation of Jesus.

Jesus, year of birth

Jesus was not born in the year A.D. 1 as is generally assumed from our present calendar system. The selection of this date as the year of Jesus' birth and the decision to begin numbering years from this point was made six hundred years after the death of Christ, and actually reflects an error made by the Roman monk who proposed our present system for dating history.

In 525, Dionysius Exiguus, a monk in the Church of Rome, prepared a plan to revise the method for numbering years. Prior to Dionysius, the Western world followed the Roman calendar. Under this system of dating, year one represented the year in which Rome was supposedly founded. That year is now called 753 B.C., but under the Roman calendar, it was referred to as 1 A.U.C., for *anno urbis conditae*, meaning "the year of the establishment of the city."

Dionysius advocated renumbering the years to conform to the Church's belief that year one should represent the birth year of Jesus. Somehow, since there was then, as now, very little evidence to support his claim, Dionysius determined that Christ was born in 753 A.U.C., which then became A.D. 1 in the Christian-era calendar. (It should be noted that in the Christian-era calendar, there is no year zero.)

The reasons why Dionysius chose this date have never been supported by any convincing evidence. The year of Jesus' birth is only vaguely mentioned in the Gospels, which were written no earlier than sixty-five years after the death of Christ. The Bible, in general, provides no dates in the modern sense of the word. Historical, archaeological, and astronomical data reveal conflicting results. Jews and Romans had used different methods of reckoning time which are now difficult to reconcile. During this period, people paid little attention to the day or year of a person's birth and, despite the significance of Jesus to human history, few people at the time cared when he, or anyone else for that matter, was born. In short, no one really knows the year of Jesus' birth.

However, historians and theologians, largely in accordance with texts relating to King Herod's death, are generally convinced that Dionysius was in error. The year of Jesus' birth was no later than 4 B.C. and possibly as early as 20 B.C. Most agree the date was between 6 and 4 B.C. It is fairly certain, however, that it was not in the year which we now call A.D. 1.

Jones, Casey

The legendary railroad hero Casey Jones was, in fact, not just a legend as most people think. He was a real person whose death is fairly accurately presented in popular song and folklore.

John Luther Jones was born in 1863 near the Kentucky town of Cayce, hence the nickname "Casey" Jones. He really was an engineer on the Illinois Central Cannonball Express who died with his hand on the brake lever trying to deliver on time the eight-hour-late mail. His train smashed into the rear of a freight train on a foggy April day in 1900.

Jordan almonds

The name *jordan almonds* has nothing to do with the country of Jordan. These candy-coated nuts originated in Spain. *Jordan* is a corruption of the French term *jardyne almaunde*, meaning "garden almond."

Jugular vein

The popular expression, "go for the jugular vein," supports the incorrect notion that there exists only a single jugular vein. However, the jugular is actually one of several different veins with this name that take blood from various areas within the head indirectly to the heart.

There are actually five veins in the region of the neck which are known as jugular veins. The external jugular, the posterior external jugular, and the anterior external jugular are smaller veins in the neck. The largest jugulars, and the ones most often referred to as the jugular vein, are the right and left interior jugulars which drain blood from the brain, face, and neck. Despite the name, these veins actually run down the side of the neck, and are the ones most often severed in throat-cutting attacks or injuries.

Juries

Contrary to popular belief, juries do not have to be made up of twelve members, nor are unanimous verdicts required in all cases as most people believe.

Although the Sixth Amendment requires the right to a jury trial, the Supreme Court has indicated that the twelve-member jury was simply an historical accident. The Court found that, in most cases, only a six-member jury was necessary to satisfy the requirements for a trial by jury. However, these rules vary from one jurisdiction to another.

Decisions of juries are not always required to be unanimous, either. In civil cases, in many states, verdicts may be nonunanimous and, in some cases, can even be decided by a simple majority vote.

In addition, a defendant is not even obligated to have his guilt decided by a jury. In either federal or state criminal or civil cases, the defendant may waive his rights to a jury trial altogether and have only a judge hear the case.

K

"That which has always been accepted by everyone,
everywhere, is almost certain to be false."

Paul Valéry

Karate

Karate is usually considered a Japanese martial art. However, it did not begin or even initially become popular there. Originating in India centuries ago, karate made its way to China and other Asian countries, but was not introduced into Japan until much later.

As karate spread, it became enthusiastically practiced in Okinawa in the 1600s as a weaponless form of defense used, ironically, against the Japanese. Japan had prohibited the possession of weapons by the Okinawans, so they perfected karate, as a method of fighting using just bare hands and feet.

Finally, in 1916, an Okinawan, and the founder of modern karate, brought the art to Japan where it became a smashing success. The more formal method of the sport that the Japanese developed was the version of karate that then appeared in the United States.

Kelly, Gene

In the movie musical *Singin' in the Rain*, the sounds in the famous rainy tap-dance scene are not those from the feet of Gene

Kelly. The lesser-known art of foot-dubbing was applied following the filming of Kelly's dancing when it was decided not to subject him again to the foot-soaking ordeal for the soundtrack.

To produce the sounds of the sloshy tapping feet, two young dancing assistants put on their tap shoes and, tapping in puddles of water, matched their sounds to the picture of Kelly tapping on the screen. Both foot dubbers later became Broadway dancing stars.

Kennedy, John F.

The famous words from President John F. Kennedy's 1960 inaugural address, "And so, my fellow Americans, ask not what your country can do for you; ask what you can do for your country," did not originate with John Kennedy. In an 1884 address familiar to many jurists, Oliver Wendell Holmes stated, ". . . to recall what our country has done for each of us, and to ask ourselves what we can do for our country in return." It is considered likely that Kennedy's speech writers were aware of Justice Holmes's remark.

Killer bees

The species of bee spreading north toward the United States from South America popularly known as the killer bee is not really a dangerous threat to human life. These bees, originally brought from Africa to Brazil for study, escaped and became established in South America. However, the Africanized bees are actually very similar to the common U.S. honey bee.

The popular name *killer bee* derives from their tendency to swarm on an intruder in protection of their hive, and to do so over a greater distance from the hive than most other bees. They are also more aggressive than the domestic honey bee. Otherwise, Africanized bees are nearly alike in anatomical structure to the domestic bee. They also possess a barbed stinger that is lost after stinging, preventing multiple attacks, and the venom itself of the "killer" bee is no more potent than that of the common honey bee.

The main concern over Africanized bees comes from beekeepers and agriculturalists. These bees are not very productive honey-makers or pollinators, but are better reproducers than are other bees. The possible effects on these industries, especially the multibillion-dollar agriculture business, which depends on bees for production, are not known. However, it is believed that their effects can be minimized by genetic modification through an inbreeding program with less aggressive domestic bees.

Koala bears

Even though koalas resemble little teddy bears and are often called bears, they are not really bears at all. Koalas are classified as marsupials, as are kangaroos, wombats, and opossums.

Marsupials are considered to be primitive mammals and are found mainly in Australia and New Guinea, except for the North American opossum. Like all marsupials, the koala possesses the familiar pouch for carrying its young.

However, the pouch of the koala and other marsupials is more than just a convenient way for the mother to carry her babies. The pouch essentially serves as an external womb. Marsupial young are born in a virtual embryonic state and are much smaller than one might imagine. At birth, koalas are about three-quarters of an inch long and weigh just an ounce or two. They complete their development by spending months in the pouch of skin on the mother's underbelly.

Koalas are almost totally arboreal and feed exclusively on the young leaves and buds of fewer than twenty of the three hundred fifty species of eucalyptus trees in Australia. Because their diet is so specialized, and since a twenty-four-inch-tall koala will eat about three pounds of leaves a day, few zoos can even attempt to keep them.

Kremlin

There is more than one Kremlin in the Soviet Union. A kremlin is actually the walled, central section of older Russian cities which has a citadel or fortress to protect the center of the town. The Kremlin in Moscow, as the seat of all Soviet government, is the largest and most well known of the many kremlins. But many other cities also have kremlins.

Moscow's Kremlin was first fortified in the twelfth century with its present wall more than seven thousand feet long. It encloses palaces, several cathedrals, tombs, government buildings, halls, as well as the Presidium of the Supreme Soviet.

L

"I am not ashamed to confess
that I am ignorant of what I do not know."

Cicero

"L" sounds in words

Unknown to most people, the letter "l" sound should not be pronounced in the words almond, alms, balm, calm, palm, psalm, qualm, and salmon.

Most dictionaries agree that for correct pronunciation of these words, the letter "l" is silent. Lexicographers point out that people born since World War II are generally more likely to pronounce the letter "l" in these words. This is believed to indicate either an unusually sudden change in acceptable pronunciation or simply an example of increased misuse of the language.

Lacrosse

Most people would probably think that the national sport of Canada is ice hockey. Although hockey is played everywhere in Canada and Canadian players are among the best in the world, lacrosse is actually the official national sport of the country. In 1867, shortly after the birth of Canada, the Canadian Parliament made lacrosse the national game and, as such, it remains popular today in Canada.

Before Europeans came to Canada, lacrosse was regularly played by the Indians of North America. Early French traders saw the game and noted a similarity between the netted sticks used to play and the hooked staff, or crozier, carried by Catholic bishops. They named the game *la crosse*.

Modern lacrosse is rough, but nothing like the game played by the Indians. Matches often were major events with up to one thousand players involved and games lasting for days covering miles of territory. Injuries and even deaths were fairly common.

Largest animal

Dinosaurs were not the largest animals that ever lived on earth. That distinction belongs to the blue whale, which is still found throughout the oceans of the world.

The largest individual animal known to have ever existed was a blue whale found near Antarctica in the early 1900s. It was 124 feet long and weighed about 170 tons, or as much as 2,300 people. In comparison, the largest dinosaurs to have ever lived were the Diplodocus (ninety feet) and Brontosaurus (sixty-five feet). The most famous dinosaur, the Tyrannosaurus, was a mere forty feet in length. At birth, a baby blue is twenty feet long and gains about two hundred pounds a day during its first year. A fully grown blue whale is so large that an elephant could walk into its opened jaw, and a basketball could pass through its largest arteries. Yet, a blue whale's heart beats just nine times a minute. Blue whales often grow to one hundred feet in length.

For its size, the blue whale has no teeth and is the personification of the gentle giant. Although the world's largest animal, it feeds on one of the smallest of all living things, microscopic plankton and krill, by sucking in and straining huge amounts of water containing these organisms.

Because of overhunting in the past, the blue whale is now approaching extinction.

Law of averages

The law of averages is commonly thought to mean that if a coin were tossed ten times, and if it came up heads ten times in a row, then the next toss would be more likely to come up tails. However, such an interpretation involves a prediction about a single event that the mathematical properties of probability theory cannot make. The so-called law of averages can only give a probability for the likelihood of an event to occur, but not a prediction based on prior events.

What has happened to the coin on previous flips is absolutely irrelevant to what follows on future tosses. A coin possesses neither a memory nor a conscience. The law of averages can only predict, in the above example, that on the eleventh toss a tail is likely to occur with a 50 percent probability, and that, after many tosses, the number of heads and tails will be nearly the same.

Lead pencils

The familiar lead pencil does not, and never did, contain any lead. The center core of a pencil is actually treated graphite, or, occasionally, some other material.

When graphite was discovered around 1400, it was referred to as "black lead." This popular but erroneous name was commonly used when wooden pencils were first manufactured in 1662 with graphite cores. Hence, the name *lead pencil* was obtained.

Modern pencils are not made individually as one might assume, but by sandwiching a graphite-clay mixture between sheets of molded wood. These sheets are later cut into individual pencils. The amount of clay mixed with the graphite determines the hardness of the "lead."

Originally, in the United States, pencils were made from red cedar. Now with a diminished cedar supply, cheaper woods are used, but they are dyed to produce the familiar color of old-fashioned pencils.

Leaves turning colors

When the leaves of certain deciduous trees in temperate zones appear to change color in the fall, the tree is not suddenly producing different colors as is often believed. The color change is simply due to the fact that trees cease making green chlorophyll in autumn, and once the usual green pigmentation is no longer present, the colors, which have been in the leaves all summer long, become visible.

This process of autumnal aging, or senescence, is brought

about from decreasing light and temperatures. During summer months, the photosynthesis in the leaf produces green chlorophyll, which comprises about two-thirds of the leaf's pigmentation and determines the green color of the leaf. But other pigments of yellow, brown, and red are also present in varying amounts which we do not see during the summer.

When the leaf begins its autumnal death throes, the production of green pigmentation ceases. The other pigments in the leaf endure longer and, as a result, the leaf takes on a new coloration that had previously been dominated by the green chlorophyll.

Lee, Robert E.

Although Robert E. Lee is best remembered as a commander of the Confederate army during the Civil War, it is not usually known that he was also a distinguished United States career military officer who was not a strong supporter of the Southern cause. In fact, Lee believed that the institution of slavery was a moral curse, and had freed his own family's slaves prior to the start of the war. He also opposed the attempts by Southern states to secede from the Union.

Lee had strong loyalties to both the North and South as hostilities neared. His career included thirty-five years of service to the United States, several of which were as the commander of the West Point Military Academy. However, his family, children, and home were in his beloved Virginia.

Lee's stature and devotion as an American military figure led President Lincoln to offer him command of the Union army when the war began. However, Jefferson Davis had made a similar offer to Lee for command of the Virginia forces. His sentiments prevailed as he sided with Virginia and the South and eventually became general in chief of all Confederate forces.

Having been turned down by one of the nation's most respected military leaders, President Lincoln ordered that the Lee family home be turned into a federal cemetery so that Lee would never wish to return there. The cemetery that now surrounds Lee's Curtis family estate is Arlington National Cemetery.

Lemmings

It is popularly believed the lemmings are suicidal little rodents that once a year trek from their homes to plunge themselves into the sea to die. Although lemmings do undertake mass migration, it is not an annual suicide march.

Lemmings are very prolific, mouselike, Arctic animals that face a constant problem of overpopulation. Every four years, as part of a behavior to alleviate overcrowding, low food supplies trigger the famous mass migration of lemmings. These journeys last for many weeks during which time many die en route. With reduced numbers, the lemmings then can establish new colonies until the cycle is again repeated.

These migrations sometimes take place over water and rocky cliffs. But lemmings can swim and have every intention of trying to complete their journey when encountering water. However, almost nothing in nature will stem the course of a lemming migration and, since the terrain is often hazardous, many die from falls, drowning, and exhaustion. But this is not the same as an intentional suicide. When their numbers have been sufficiently reduced, the urge to migrate ends, and the colony takes up residence at that location.

Leprosy

Leprosy is not the horribly ugly and highly contagious disease most people think it is. In fact, leprosy is actually one of the least contagious of all infectious diseases, has been completely curable since 1950, and with early detection, leaves no deformities.

Biblical references to lepers did not refer to the disease now known as leprosy, but concerned the morally and physically unclean. These negative attitudes continued through history as leprosy was usually regarded as a religious disease dealt with through leper colonies and church organized segregation.

Leprosy, or Hanson's disease as it is now called, is less infectious than the common cold. Among the two types of leprosy, the acute, more mild tuberculoid form is not at all contagious, while the more persistent lepromatic variety is only slightly infectious.

Although the precise way in which leprosy is acquired is not understood, most people outside the 30th parallels of latitude seem to be naturally immune to the disease. Deformities are not as severe or common as are usually imagined, and with early detection can be prevented. Except to facilitate treatment, it is now recognized that the isolation of leprosy patients is unnecessary, and the disease is now curable with medication and early detection.

Libel and slander

Most people usually confuse libel and slander and use the terms interchangeably. Although both refer to a false defamation that injures a person's good name or professional reputation, libel and slander are not the same.

Slander is a defamation that is spoken and heard. Libel is any other false statement, usually written, but also including any physical form that has some permanence, such as motion pictures and television. The spoken words in movies or on television are usually interpreted by courts as libel since their duration is more lasting than the spoken word.

Liberty Bell

The Liberty Bell was not cracked while ringing for independence on July 4, 1776. Much of the history of this famous symbol of American liberty is surrounded by folklore, but the crack did not appear until much later.

Commissioned to hang in the Pennsylvania State House, now named Independence Hall, the bell was first cast in London in 1752. After it was shipped to America, it cracked while being tested on the ground and was recast twice more in Philadelphia.

The bell was rung for special occasions, including the proclaiming of the Declaration of Independence. But it was not rung on the Fourth of July, since public celebrations for independence actually took place several days later. While tolling for the funeral of Chief Justice John Marshall in 1835, it suffered its now famous crack. This fracture became irreparable when further cracked while ringing for the last time in 1846 for George Washington's birthday.

Although originally inscribed with the words, "Proclaim liberty throughout all the land unto all the inhabitants thereof," the bell had little connection with liberty in people's minds until 1839. A pamphlet published during the antislavery movement titled *The Liberty Bell* popularized the bell as a symbol of liberty in America. Since then, a great deal of patriotic folklore has sprung up surrounding the bell, much of it untrue.

Lie-detector tests

A lie-detector test is a popular, but inaccurate, term for the instrument that records various bodily changes that may provide the basis for a reliable diagnosis of truth or deception. The correct term for the device is a polygraph. There is no such thing as a lie-detector test if the term is taken to mean a mechanical or electrical device that will produce a clear indication of lying when verbal statements are made.

The polygraph technique, as it is called, measures respiration, blood pressure, and pulse. A supplemental unit that records the galvanic skin response (GSR) is also part of the procedure. The most valuable indicators are respiration and blood pressure and not, as is commonly believed, the sweating palms measured by the GSR.

The lie-detector test is actually more of a diagnostic procedure than a mechanical operation; the competence of the examiner and skillfully controlled questions produce the most meaningful data. Polygraphs do not simply indicate whether a specific statement is a lie. A pattern of responses compared to various control questions is evaluated by the examiner to determine the truthfulness of the answers. The polygraph usually provides very accurate results, but they are not admissible in court as evidence unless both sides agree in advance to its use.

Lightning

It is a common misconception that a lightning bolt travels downward to the ground. However, the visible bolt actually travels up from the ground with incredible speed and temperature.

Lightning is produced in cumulonimbus clouds in which rising currents of warm air generate huge electrical buildups. These currents produce positive charges in the top of the cloud and negative charges near the bottom. The ground becomes increasingly positive with the air acting as an insulator until the buildup becomes great enough for the stroke to occur.

A lightning bolt is a complex, yet nearly instantaneous event. An invisible fingerlike leader stroke of negatively charged particles zigzags toward the ground in a stop-and-go manner. This invisible ladder of electricity stops about forty feet above the ground. At this instant, the visible, positive discharge stroke rises up to meet the descending leader and flows along its path up into the cloud. This process of an invisible downward leader followed by a visible upward bolt is repeated several times in each stroke of lightning, and all within a few thousandths of a second.

The upward visible stroke travels about sixty thousand miles per second and reaches temperatures of up to 4500°F, five times hotter than the surface of the sun. These high temperatures create a sudden expansion of air producing a sonic boom, which we hear as thunder.

At close range, the color of a lightning bolt is actually an intense blue, but with increasing distance it becomes white or yellowish because of atmospheric absorption or scattering of the light.

Lightning can also occur in a winter snowstorm. The cause of lightning is not directly related to temperature, but to the mixing of different layers of air producing rising currents and electrical buildups. However, air warm enough to sustain this mixing does not usually occur in winter.

The old adage that lightning will not strike twice in the same place is untrue. Like all electric currents or discharges, lightning follows the path of least resistance. Therefore, certain locations, especially tall buildings and trees, are more likely to be struck. In fact, the Empire State Building, as well as many other buildings, is hit by lightning dozens of times a year.

Lightning deaths

It is generally believed that nearly all deaths that result from lightning strikes occur outdoors. This is not only untrue, but creates the illusion of safety when indoors during a thunderstorm.

Statistics refute the belief that lightning is just an outdoor problem. Slightly more than half of all lightning caused deaths in the United States occur indoors. The home, in fact, is the most likely location for a person to be killed by lightning. When combined with commercial-industrial casualties, indoor deaths far outnumber those happening outdoors on open ground, under trees, or during recreational activities on water or beaches.

Lightning also kills more people annually in the United States than do tornadoes, hurricanes, or any other weather force. While houses do provide protection, the simple fact that most people are in their homes during dangerous weather increases the number of possible victims indoors. Home deaths usually result from roof or chimney strikes and the consequent sideflash which kills occupants near plumbing, electrical appliances, fireplaces, televisions, and even telephones.

It is also a myth that being hit by lightning invariably results in death. Of those struck, 70 to 80 percent recover, although some minimal hearing loss, eye damage, or muscular weakness is usually experienced. Burns are also less severe than might be expected, since the charge is so instantaneous that the flesh actually does not have time to burn.

It is also commonly believed that most outdoor lightning deaths take place on golf courses. However, statistics indicate that an average of only about 5 percent of the nation's lightning fatalities and injuries occur on golf courses. Most deaths happen in open fields, such as ballfields, under trees, and in boating and water related incidents.

Limb falling asleep

Contrary to popular belief, when an arm or a leg "falls asleep," the blood supply is not cut off from the affected limb. The sensation of numbness, called neurapraxia, occurs when a major nerve gets compressed against a hard external object or bone. It usually involves the ulnar nerve in the arm or the peroneal nerve in the leg. The pressure results in a temporary and harmless numbness in the limb, but the blood continues to flow normally.

Lincoln–Douglas debates

Popular and historical interest in the dramatic and highly topical Lincoln–Douglas debates for the United States Senate election in 1858 has obscured many of the facts associated with this event. Despite the popular image of these debates, it is not generally known that more people actually heard each candidate in separate speeches than in their joint debates, that the public did not even vote for either candidate anyway, and that Lincoln ended up losing the election.

There were only seven debates conducted between Abraham Lincoln and Senator Stephen A. Douglas in front of relatively small audiences primarily on the territorial slavery issues. By far, each speaker actually made many more appearances making separate speeches before considerably more people.

Regardless of how many people ever heard the debates, the fact remains that in 1858, senators were not even elected by popular vote. The constitutional provisions then in effect stipulated that U.S. senators were elected by state legislatures. This method was used until the passage of the seventeenth amendment in 1913, which allowed for the election of senators by popular vote. Thus, the general population did not directly vote for either Lincoln or Douglas in the election.

The Lincoln–Douglas debates received considerable attention because both parties deviated from then-normal campaign practices and used their candidacies as local referendums on slavery and other national issues. The Republicans and Lincoln won the popular vote, but, through skillful gerrymandering of districts, lost the Illinois Senate race and, thus, the U.S. Senate seat from the state to Douglas.

Lincoln's beard

Abraham Lincoln did not have a beard during most of his public career. Despite our popular image of a bewhiskered Lincoln, he was clean-shaven until he was fifty-one years old.

In 1860, shortly after being elected President, an eleven-year-old girl suggested in a letter to Lincoln that his thin face would look better with whiskers. Lincoln agreed and began growing a beard, which he had for just five years until his death in 1865.

Lincoln's successful career

It is generally believed that the career of a famous person such as Abraham Lincoln was filled with one success after another. Consider the facts.

In 1832, Lincoln lost his job in a failing business partnership. Also in 1832, he was defeated for the state legislature. In 1833, a private business failed. Although elected to the state legislature in 1834, he implemented an internal improvement project that nearly bankrupted the State of Illinois. He also was defeated twice for the house speaker position in 1836 and 1838.

In 1843, Lincoln was defeated for the nomination to the U.S. Congress. Although elected to Congress in 1846, he lost the renomination in 1848. 1849 saw Lincoln run for a land-office position and lose.

In 1854, he was defeated for the U.S. Senate. In 1856, Lincoln was defeated for the nomination for Vice President, and, in 1858, repeated his losing bid for the U.S. Senate. And, in 1860, he was elected U.S. President.

Lindbergh, Charles

Charles Lindbergh was not the first person to fly nonstop across the Atlantic. He was actually the sixty-seventh person to make a nonstop trip. His true claim to fame was that his flight was the first solo nonstop flight across the Atlantic.

Although it made seven stops along the way, the first flight across the Atlantic was actually made in 1919 by a U.S. Navy seaplane. One month later, William Alcock and Arthur Brown made the first nonstop flight across the Atlantic flying from Newfoundland to Ireland. The following month, thirty-one men in a British dirigible made the trip, and in 1924, thirty-three also flew the Atlantic nonstop in a German dirigible.

Lindbergh's solo flight on May 21, 1927, was a thirty-three and one-half hour journey from Long Island, New York, to Le Bourget airfield in Paris. He was awarded the Medal of Honor and twenty-five thousand dollars for his flight and instantly became a national hero. But there were, in fact, sixty-six others who had flown the Atlantic nonstop before Lindbergh.

Lions and tigers

It is not true as most people think that lions and tigers both live in Africa. Lions do, but there are no tigers on the African continent.

The ranges of these two animals do not overlap. Lions are found in western India and Africa, while tigers exist only in the Soviet Far East, Korea, Southeast China, and Northeast India. Tigers once did range over most of Europe, Africa and Asia hundreds of years ago; however, they are now extinct in these areas.

Although lions and tigers do not coexist in the wild, it comes as a surprise to many people to learn that the animals can breed together in captivity producing tigons and ligers. A tigon is a cross between a male tiger and a female lion. The offspring between a male lion and female tiger is known as a liger.

Lloyd's of London

Although it is commonly believed that Lloyd's of London is an insurance company famous for insuring unusual and expensive risks, it is no such thing. It is not possible to obtain an insurance policy of any kind from Lloyd's of London. Lloyd's is actually an association of more than eight thousand individual underwriters which act as separate companies issuing insurance policies.

Lloyd's began as a seventeenth century coffeehouse by Edward L. Lloyd in London. It became a social gathering place, especially for maritime insurance clients, who found it an ideal location to find insurance underwriters.

Lloyd eventually oversaw the policy bidding in his establishment, and Lloyd's became the dominant concern in the insurance business. However, Lloyd's of London itself is only an association that sets the rules for insurance transactions of its members, while assuming no insurance liabilities for losses.

Log cabin

The log cabin was not an original American creation nor was it first used in the frontier West.

Originating in Sweden, the log cabin was brought to America by Swedish settlers in Delaware in 1638. Neither the Dutch at New Amsterdam nor the Pilgrims utilized this type of dwelling.

The log cabin remained in the Delaware Valley until it became popular during the Revolutionary War when it spread south and west. With the expansion and settling of the western lands beyond the tidewater, the log cabin proved to be ideally suited for frontier America. It could be built by only one man with nothing more than an axe, and provided good protection against the weather and attack. Although perfectly suited to the American wilderness, it was, nevertheless, a European import.

Longest day of the year

About ninety-nine people out of a hundred would say that the longest day of the year is June 21. However, in the Northern Hemisphere, the longest day of the year may be either June 21 or June 22. It is usually June 21 except in years preceding a leap year, when the longest day is June 22.

Likewise, the shortest day of the year is either December 21 or December 22. It is usually December 22 in all years except leap years, when it is December 21.

Los Angeles Dodgers

The Los Angeles baseball team is not called the Dodgers because of anything having to do with athletics. Before moving to California, the team played in Brooklyn where the fast-moving and numerous New York streetcars created fear among pedestrians. This prompted local Brooklyn residents to call themselves trolley dodgers, and in the late 1800s, the name "Dodger" was attached to their baseball team. When the Brooklyn Dodgers moved to Los Angeles, they took their familiar nickname with them.

Lost people going in circles

Nearly everyone has heard that people who are lost in a wilderness, desert, or arctic area will unknowingly walk in circles. The reason for this circular movement is assumed to be that one leg is usually shorter than the other, causing an imperceptible turn in that direction. However, this movement is not what usually occurs, nor for this reason.

Experiments have shown that a spiral movement is actually a universal property of living matter in random, disoriented motion. Blindfolded subjects invariably spiral to the left or right as do walkers, swimmers, car drivers, animals, and amoebas. The reason for this is unknown, but it is not because of a shorter leg, since it appears to be evident with motion other than walking.

Lucifer

Lucifer, used as a name for the Devil, is not found in the Bible. There is only one reference to Lucifer in the Bible (Isaiah 14:12), and it does not refer to Satan, but to the king of Babylon.

Lungs

It is a common misconception that the lungs are two empty sacs of air, similar to a bellows, that inflate and deflate like balloons when we breathe. This notion may be functionally descriptive, but physiologically it is totally incorrect.

The lungs are soft, light, and very elastic organs. The interior does not contain a single empty air space, but the lungs are composed of a porous tissue much like a sponge.

The main function of the lungs, of course, is respiration. This exchange of oxygen for carbon dioxide takes place within this porous tissue in tiny air sacs called the alveoli, which comprise most of the lung. Human lungs contain over three hundred million of these tiny air sacs, providing about ninety square yards of surface area for breathing.

Lungs are not pink or red as is generally believed. Although the lungs of a newborn infant are pink, adult lungs are usually white or, at best, a pinkish gray spotted with dark gray or bluish patches. This discoloration is the inevitable consequence of breathing carbon and dust particles in the air as well as other types of pollution.

M

"There's nothing new under the sun,
but there are lots of old things we don't know."

Ambrose Bierce

MacArthur, General Douglas

"Old soldiers never die, they just fade away," is a remark usually attributed to General Douglas MacArthur. It is true that he did close his military career with these words before a joint session of Congress in 1951. However, his speech also referred to the well-known fact that those words were from a British World War I army song and the most popular barracks ballad of that day. The song contained the refrain about old soldiers and was not, even by MacArthur's admission, first said by him.

Mach I

The point at which the velocity of a jet aircraft reaches the speed of sound and produces the familiar sonic boom is commonly referred to as Mach I. However, Mach I is not an absolute, specific speed as is usually believed.

The Mach number, as it is called, is the ratio of the velocity of an object to the speed of sound in the medium in which the object is traveling. Since the speed of sound itself is not a constant, but varies depending on the medium, Mach I does not represent a constant speed either. In air, conditions such as temperature, altitude, and atmospheric pressure affect the speed of sound and, consequently, the Mach number.

For example, the speed of sound at sea level at 0° F is 760 mph, but at thirty-six thousand feet it is only 660 mph. Therefore, Mach I is 760 mph at sea level, and 660 mph at this higher altitude. However, for convenience in nontechnical uses, Mach I is usually assumed to be 660 mph since most supersonic flights are at higher altitudes.

Majority rule

The idea that the election system in the United States operates on the principle of majority rule is pure myth. Elected officials usually receive far less than a majority of votes from the voting age population, since most people simply do not vote. Even when the number of actual votes is considered, candidates often receive less than 50 percent of the votes cast, especially when there are multiple candidates on the ballot.

For example, a voting majority has never elected a U.S. President. Lyndon Johnson came the closest in 1964 when he received 38 percent of the total eligible vote. The smallest share ever recorded was by Martin Van Buren, who obtained votes from just 12 percent of voting age Americans. This occurred prior to women's suffrage. More recently, in 1984, Ronald Reagan was elected president when just 32 percent of the voting-age population cast ballots for him.

This phenomenon is not unique to presidential elections. In fact, it is less apparent on the national level and more obvious in local elections where there are multiple candidates and generally less voter participation.

Instead of majority rule, the American election process is based on a system correctly referred to as plurality, or relative majority. In true majority rule, a candidate must receive more votes than all other candidates combined. A system of plurality exists when one person receives more votes than any other person, which describes elections in the United States.

Plurality, the most common form of election system, often results in the election of persons who have received a minority of votes. The more candidates in a race, the greater likelihood that none will obtain more than 50 percent of the total vote. In fact, fifteen candidates have been elected as U.S. President with a popular vote that was less than 50 percent of the total votes cast.

A few countries do maintain an election system based on majority rule. However, repeated run-off elections are often necessary before one candidate receives a majority vote. In the United States, the only true majority election is in the Electoral College, which constitutionally provides for the selection of the president. However, the electors themselves are elected through a system of plurality.

Mason and Dixon line

When originally drawn, the Mason and Dixon line had nothing to do with the boundary between the North and South during the Civil War. It was, in fact, initially a short 244-mile-long regional border set nearly a hundred years before the Civil War began.

Following a border dispute between a Maryland and Pennsylvania family, two surveyors, Charles Mason and Jeremiah Dixon, laid out a boundary between 1763 and 1767. The line established the Pennsylvania-Maryland border and was extended seventeen years later to the full length of Pennsylvania's southern boundary.

For over fifty years, the Mason and Dixon line had no connection with the slavery issue. In 1819, when the slavery debate began, John Randolph and others began referring to this line as the dividing point between free and slave states. Following the Missouri Compromise in 1820, the line was extended south and west along the Ohio River and across the northern border of Missouri.

It was at this time that the Mason and Dixon line took on its now familiar identity as the dividing line between free and slave states and, during the Civil War, as the border between the North and South. But the Mason and Dixon line had a much more innocuous beginning in American History.

May Day

May Day, the May 1 international celebration of worker solidarity in the Soviet Union and many other socialist countries, actually commemorates the struggle for the eight-hour workday movement in the United States.

Although historically May Day has been an ancient festival celebrating spring and courtship rites, the observances in socialist countries are now mostly political and militarily oriented. But, current celebrations derive from the 1886 Haymarket Riot in Chicago.

The Federation of Organized Trade and Labor Unions in the United States, the forerunner of the AFL–CIO, set May 1, 1886, as the day on which the eight-hour workday was to have begun. On May 4, a large demonstration in Chicago's Haymarket Square supporting this cause turned violent. A bomb was thrown, police were killed, and the crowd was then attacked by the police with many injuries resulting.

To commemorate the event, an international day of labor solidarity was declared on May 1, 1890. The present May Day celebrations in socialist countries, including the Soviet Union, continue this tradition of demonstrating labor unity and the struggle for the eight-hour workday in the United States.

Meat grades

Customers in grocery stores are often confronted with various signs and slogans for meat products, such as "Top grade," "U.S. Finest," "A-1 meat," or "U.S.D.A. Prime." However, these slogans are generally meaningless for the consumer.

The United States Department of Agriculture maintains an inspection service for livestock products which includes two grading systems. One is for quality grades and the other is for yield grades of meat.

Quality grades are the ones most commonly referred to by sellers and indicates leanness. For beef, the eight quality grades are Prime, Choice, Good, Standard, Commercial, Utility, Cutter, and Canner. Veal and calf, lamb and mutton, and sows have similar labels.

Yield grades are indicated by numbers, and range from one to five. They represent the carcass yield in terms of cutability. These grades are based on amount of external, kidney, pelvic, and heart fat, the area of ribeye muscle, and carcass weight.

With either quality or yield, carcass grades indicate the quality of meat and the amount of salable meat the carcass will produce. Contrary to popular opinion, they are not primarily intended for the consumer.

U.S.D.A. grades are meant to provide beef producers, packers, and retailers with indicators to determine sales value, carcass yield, and proportion of trimmed retail cuts available from a carcass. For the consumer, they are merely an indirect means for reflecting preferences for lean meat when making purchases. For the retailer, they provide an array of often misleading advertising slogans.

Medal of Honor

The highest military award for "gallantry and intrepidity at the risk of life above and beyond the call of duty while engaged in an action against an enemy of the United States" is not named the Congressional Medal of Honor. It is officially known simply as the Medal of Honor. Because it was established in 1862 by a joint resolution of Congress, it is often erroneously referred to as the Congressional Medal of Honor.

Midgets and dwarfs

A midget and a dwarf are not the same thing. Midgets are very small people, generally less than 4 feet 4 inches in height, but with normal body and limb proportions. Dwarfs, who are most commonly the result of pituitary hormone deficiencies, are disproportionate in build and generally deformed.

Contrary to popular belief, midgets and dwarfs almost always have normal-sized children even when both parents are midgets and dwarfs. Either word, *midget* or *dwarf*, is now considered inappropriate. The preferred term for both groups is *little people*.

Millipedes

Millipedes, like centipedes, are not insects and the name does not correctly describe the number of their legs. Although the word *millipede* literally means one thousand feet, the total number of legs actually ranges from just twenty to several hundred. The record-setting number of legs on a millipede is known to be 710. However, unlike centipedes, millipedes are slow moving, clumsy, and lack the centipede's poisonous claws.

Miracle on 34th Street

Miracle on 34th Street, one of the most famous Christmas movies of all time, was not even originally intended as a Christmas movie. Neither the producer, Darryl F. Zanuck, or other 20th Century Fox executives thought much about the plot—a little girl who learns to believe in Santa Claus—so the studio released the movie in July 1947. The public loved it, and it has been a Christmas classic ever since.

Mirage

Because our more familiar idea of a mirage includes the ever-receding puddle on the hot highway or the unreachable oasis in the desert, mirages are usually thought to occur in just hot places. However, mirages are also common under conditions of cold as well as heat.

A mirage is an optical illusion created by the bending of light rays from differences in atmospheric density and temperature. The common highway puddle and oasis mirages are known as inferior (lower) mirages in which an object is seen lower than it really is. It is produced under conditions when air temperature decreases with height and light rays are bent downward.

But in colder conditions, especially in polar areas, mirages frequently appear that are known as superior (upper) mirages. In this type, the image is displaced upward from its actual location when air temperature increases with height. In either case, all mirages can be photographed, since the camera lens reacts as does the human eye.

Mona Lisa

Leonardo da Vinci's most famous painting, popularly called the *Mona Lisa*, is actually titled *La Gioconda*. The subject of the portrait was the wife of a merchant named Francesco del Gioconda. The painting was also known for a short time as *Madonna Lisa*, from which the now popular name *Mona Lisa* derives.

La Gioconda is also much smaller than most people imagine it to be. The actual size of the painting is less than two feet on each side. Modern x-ray studies of the canvas have revealed that the famous smiling lady was painted over another portrait which had previously been on the canvas. This was a common practice of artists at the time.

Most observers of the *Mona Lisa* do not realize that despite her well-known smile, she has no eyebrows. This custom of women shaving their eyebrows was a sign of beauty when the portrait was made.

Monarch butterflies

It is a common misconception that monarch butterflies in the eastern United States and Canada migrate several thousand miles to Mexico each winter and return in the spring. This belief is only half true, since the migration for the monarch is a one-way trip. The butterflies that leave in the fall are not the same ones that return in the spring.

Unlike most butterflies, monarchs reproduce after the winter season. They begin their return journey north in the spring, and during the migration, the monarchs stop along the way, reproduce by depositing their eggs, and then die. After hatching, it is the new generation of butterflies that completes the trip North.

Money is the root of all evil

The Bible does not say, "Money is the root of all evil." Instead, it says (Timothy 6:10), "For the love of money is the root of all evil." This difference significantly changes the meaning of the expression, in that it is the love of money and not the money itself that generates the evil.

Monitor and Merrimac

The Civil War naval battle between the *Monitor* and *Merrimac* has become a familiar part of American legend. Unfortunately, as is often the case with folklore, some of our ideas surrounding this event are untrue.

The Confederate ship that the Union *Monitor* engaged was actually named the *Virginia* and not the *Merrimac* as is commonly believed. Lacking time and money, the Confederates were unable to match the Union's ship-building potential, especially for the new iron ships. The Confederates raised the sunken, partially burned, wooden Union frigate *Merrimac* and replaced the upper decks with armor shielded sides, added guns, and renamed it the *Virginia*.

The *Monitor* and *Virginia* fiercely engaged each other for four hours on March 9, 1862. The *Virginia* was badly damaged, and retreated, although both ships ended the battle confident of victory as each made repeated attempts to ram the other. Although it was the first naval battle between ironclads in history, these two ships were not the first iron-sided vessels ever built, as is often believed. A short time after the battle, the *Virginia* was destroyed and scuttled by her own crew, while the *Monitor* sank in a gale the same year.

The brief battle did end the era of wooden fighting ships. However, contrary to popular belief, it had little or no significance on the outcome of the Civil War. But in choosing the incorrect name for the Confederate ship, history has indicated its preference for alliteration over accuracy in naming the engagement the battle of the *Monitor* and *Merrimac*.

Monkey wrench

Frolicking little primates had nothing to do with the invention, design, use, or naming of the monkey wrench. The wrench, with a fixed end and adjustable jaws at right angles to each other, is named after its inventor, Charles Moncky.

Monkeys grooming

The familiar sight of monkeys searching through each other's fur is not because the monkeys are looking for fleas or other parasites. In fact, fleas are not normally even found on healthy monkeys. Although this so-called grooming behavior may provide an occasional insect treat, it is more often loosened skin encrusted with much desired salt for which the monkeys are actually searching.

Moon

The idea that exactly half the surface of the moon, the so-called dark side, is never visible from the earth is untrue.

Although a stabilized position of gravitational forces has been achieved between the earth and the moon, the velocity of the moon's orbit is not uniform. This irregular motion results in the phenomenon known as libration, which enables us to see more than half of the moon's surface in its orbit. From the earth, 59 percent of the surface of the moon is visible at one time or another, while only 41 percent is actually never seen from earth.

Mosquito bites

It is a common fallacy that mosquitoes bite and drink blood for their meals. Mosquitoes do not really bite, and the blood is only used to nourish the female's eggs.

Mosquitoes possess no jaws or biting apparatus of any kind in their mouths with which to bite. Instead, they pierce their victims with a long, hollow, flexible tube called a proboscis, and suck the blood through a nasal tube. Before extracting the blood, the mosquito first injects an anticoagulant to prevent the blood from clotting. It is an allergic reaction to this substance in most people that causes the familiar itchy, little bump.

Only the female mosquito performs this act, and it is done only to obtain blood to nourish its eggs, which develop about two to four days later. But the blood is not a source of food as most people think. Mosquitoes feed only on nectar and other plant juices.

It is estimated that there are over forty thousand mosquitoes for each person in the United States, and that each female mosquito will bite about four times in its life span. Fortunately, they prefer other mammals over humans. However, they are a more dangerous health threat to man than any other insect, not because of their annoying bites, but as potential carriers of malaria, yellow fever, and other serious diseases.

Moss

Moss does not grow on the north side of a tree. It does not grow on the south, east, or west side either. The fuzzy little green plant life often found on the side of a tree is actually liverworts or lichens. They are relatives of mosses, but not true moss.

Although some moss prefers cool and wet locations, many, if not most, grow best in dry, open places. It is the liverworts and lichens that tend to grow in shady retreats away from the sun and often on the north side of a tree.

Moths

Moths do not eat clothes. The damage that is often found in the closet is actually done when the eggs of moths hatch, and the larva begin feeding on clothes, usually wool or fur. After feeding, these larvae eventually form cocoons, change into moths, and fly away to repeat the cycle. Moths themselves live for only a short time, and often do not even eat anything while in the adult stage.

In a natural, outdoor environment, a moth will prefer to lay its eggs in the fur or hair of a dead animal. When the larvae hatch and begin crawling around, they have immediate access to their favorite food—fur.

In houses, the only dead animal furs available are wool sweaters and fur coats, and this is where the moth deposits its eggs. After hatching, the garment becomes the food supply for the larvae just as the animal's fur would be if the moth were outdoors.

Mrs.

Mrs. is not really an abbreviation for anything and cannot be written out as a full word. Originally, it was the abbreviation for mistress, but since the meaning of the word has changed so much, it is no longer used in this way. It simply is the title of respect given to a married woman which has now become a word in itself. The plural of Mrs. is also Mrs.

Murder and homicide

The terms *murder* and *homicide* are often used interchangeably, although there is an important difference between the two. However, there is little difference if you are the victim of either action.

Homicide is any killing of a human being. It may be lawful or unlawful, intentional or accidental, or justifiable or nonjustifiable. Unlawful homicides include murder (intent) and manslaughter (negligence). Lawful homicides involve self-defense (justifiable), legal intervention (law enforcement), accidents without negligence, and combat.

In contrast, murder is the unlawful killing of a human being. Murder is a form of homicide and is considered to be either first-degree, with premeditation, or second-degree, with no premeditation. Manslaughter is a lesser form of murder that is an unlawful killing without malice or intent, but usually involving some degree of negligence.

Muscles

Skeletal muscles, commonly called meat in the butcher shop, do not expand and contract, or push and pull, in order to move parts of the body as most people believe. Muscle tissue has the uniform property of only being able to contract, or shorten, when stimulated by the nervous system.

Muscles of the arms, legs, and any other part of the skeletal system that move are referred to as striated, or voluntary, muscles. They are the only type of muscle in the body that is under voluntary control.

These skeletal muscles are attached at both ends to bones, cartilage, ligaments, skin, or other muscles. When a muscle contracts to move part of the body, the attachments on the other end remain static. But when moving that part back in the opposite direction, this procedure is reversed, with a different set of muscles contracting while the first pulling muscles remain inactive. At no time does any muscle that has just pulled ever push back in the opposite direction.

Mushroom-shaped cloud

It is not true that only a nuclear explosion will produce a mushroom-shaped cloud. Except for the radiation and intensity of the blast, there is nothing unique about the mushroom-shaped cloud produced from an atomic bomb. Any very large above-ground explosion in relatively calm air will result in a cloud having this familiar shape.

A mushroom cloud is produced when a large quantity of air is displaced by the heat and force of a blast. As air rushes back in to fill the void, it collides with itself and rises, along with a considerable amount of smoke and debris, to form the "stem" of the mushroom. The rising column of heated air and particles then billows out as the force dissipates and the air cools to form the "cap" of the mushroom. An example of this type of cloud formation in an explosion that is not nuclear was the awesome mushroom-shaped ash and smoke cloud which rose miles into the air following the 1980 eruption of Mount St. Helens.

Music has charms to soothe a savage beast

William Congreve never wrote, ''Music has charms to soothe a savage beast.'' His actual words were, ''Music has charms to soothe a savage breast.''

Congreve did not believe that a melodious tune would calm a wild animal. Rather, he expressed the notion that the anger and hostility within men could be diminished with music.

N

"I would rather have my ignorance
than another man's knowledge,
because I have got so much more of it."

Mark Twain

National Anthem

Contrary to the role usually attributed to Francis Scott Key, he wrote only the words, but not the music, to "The Star-Spangled Banner." The tune that became our national anthem was actually a popular British and American drinking song to which Key later adapted his short poem.

Francis Scott Key, a lawyer and witness to the British bombardment of Fort McHenry the night of September 13–14, 1814, was so inspired by the sight of the American flag still flying over the fort that he wrote a one-stanza poem on the back of an envelope. He originally entitled it "The Defense of Fort McHenry." The following day, Key's brother-in-law, Judge J. H. Nicholson, suggested that the poem might go well with the popular tune "Anacreon in Heaven." Key adapted his poem to fit this song.

Although the origin of the song is not known for certain, it is believed to have been written by John Stafford Smith, a British composer, in 1780. Anacreon was a Greek poet who was revered as a bard of wine, love, song and revelry. Smith's tune was probably an English drinking ballad, and it became the

171

official song of a London musical society during the 1780s. By 1790, the tune had also become popular in American taverns.

Key later wrote several other stanzas and renamed the song "The Star-Spangled Banner." It was used officially by the army and navy at certain ceremonial occasions in the late 1890s, and was popularly considered, although not officially, the national anthem for many years. Finally, 117 years after Key first wrote the words, Congress made it the official national anthem of the United States on March 3, 1931.

National holidays

Despite what most people seem to think, there are no national holidays in the United States. What does exist is a hodgepodge of federal and state legal holidays with only six days recognized throughout the entire country as the same holiday.

Technically, only states have jurisdiction over legal holidays, which are designated by legislative enactment or executive proclamation. Congress and the President of the United States can legally designate holidays only for the District of Columbia and federal employees. But in practice, most states observe these federal legal public holidays, although often on different days.

There are actually ten federal holidays, but only six of them— New Years Day, the Fourth of July, Labor Day, Veterans Day, Thanksgiving, and Christmas—are officially observed in all fifty states on the same day. Other so-called national holidays are celebrated on different days in various states. In addition, there are over seventy other holidays observed in some states that have the same legal recognition and standing as the more widely observed national holidays.

Nero

Nero did not fiddle while Rome burned, for two reasons. First, the violin, or fiddle, was not invented for fifteen hundred years after the fire. Second, Nero was at his villa, about thirty-five miles from Rome, when the city burned.

It was no secret that Emperor Nero Claudius Caesar wished to rebuild Rome on a more magnificent scale. The nine-day fire, which consumed most of the city in A.D. 64, provided Nero with just that opportunity. But whatever involvement he may have had, the popular adage that he fiddled while the city burned is untrue.

Netherlands, Holland, and the Dutch

The Netherlands, Holland, and the Dutch are not interchangeable names for the same country, region, or population. They refer to completely separate entities—a fact that confuses most people.

The Netherlands is the name of a country in northwestern Europe on the North Sea. It contains several provinces, one of which is Holland. Formerly the chief commercial province of the region, Holland is now largely an administrative unit of the Kingdom of the Netherlands, as the nation is now officially called. Nevertheless, the cultural and historic importance of Holland is reflected in the traditions of the Netherlanders, who commonly still refer to the whole country as Holland.

Dutch is both the official language of the Netherlands and also the common name of its people. Prior to the sixteenth century, the people of the Netherlands called themselves "Diets," meaning simply "the people." The British corrupted the word as "Dutch," and, along with the rest of the world, continued using the name even after the Netherlanders themselves dropped it.

New century

The first day of the new century will not be January 1, 2000, as most people think, but January 1, 2001. Because there is no year zero in the Christian era calendar, the first century lasted from year A.D. 1 to the end of the year 100. The second century began in the year 101. Thus, the first day of the next century will begin on January 1, 2001.

Nightmare

Describing a bad dream as a nightmare has nothing to do with horses. It derives from the Old English word *marra*, meaning a mythical specter or ghost that sat on a sleeping person's chest rendering him incapable of moving or crying out for help.

Nuts

Most people usually refer to any seed with a hard overcoat, or shell, as a nut. However, various fruits popularly referred to as nuts are not true nuts at all in botanical definitions.

Common examples of true nuts are walnuts, pecans, chestnuts, acorns, and filberts. Most true nuts are produced on trees, although this is not a prerequisite. Botanically, the hard shell of a nut does not split open when ripe, but keeps the seed within itself until the embryo sprouts.

Popularly thought of as nuts, but not classified as such by botanists, are other dried fruits and seeds having a hard covering such as the Brazil "nut." Also, the peanut is actually a member of the pea family whose fruits happen to develop underground. Coconuts, pistachios, and cashews are not nuts, but are simply the seeds of ordinary fruits with hard coverings. The almond is the kernel of a stone fruit, or drupe, which is found in the pit of a peachlike fruit.

O

"It's what you learn after you know it all that counts."

John Wooden

Octane rating

Most motorists believe that the octane rating of gasoline is a measure of power or performance of the fuel. However, octane rating has nothing to do with the amount of power or fuel economy that a gasoline can provide.

The octane rating of gasoline is simply a measure of the antiknock resistance of a particular blend of fuel. The higher the octane number, the less tendency it will have to knock.

Knocking refers to the preignition of the fuel-air mixture in high-compression engines. Preignition results when the intense heat within the engine cylinder spontaneously ignites the vaporized fuel before the spark plug fires and maximum compression is achieved. Mild or moderate knocking does not adversely affect performance or cause engine damage.

The octane rating is actually the percentage of isooctane, an antiknock ingredient, needed in a mixture to produce a blend of gas causing a knock of the same intensity as the fuel being measured. For example, if a tested fuel knocks the same as a mixture with 90 percent isooctane, its octane rating is ninety.

175

But it is a measure having nothing to do with the power or performance potential of a fuel.

Old Ironsides

The U.S. frigate *Constitution* did not acquire its nickname "Old Ironsides" because it was made of iron. Constructed in 1797, the forty-four-gun warship was built entirely of wood.

One of the first warships authorized by Congress, the *Constitution* was at sea more often and won more battles than any other warship of its time. It escaped repeated engagements, including those encountered in the War of 1812, with so little damage to its hull that the ship became popularly known as "Old Ironsides."

Olympic marathon

It is a common misconception that Olympic marathon races originated from long-distance foot races of the early Greek Olympics. The fact is, the first Olympics in ancient Greece had no marathon, never did during the duration of the ancient games, and the marathon was included in the modern games only because of a story from Greek mythology.

The first recorded Olympics in 776 B.C. consisted of just one event, a race of about 200 yards. In fact, the first thirteen ancient Olympics had only this one short race. Although longer races were later added, at no time during the nearly 1,200 years of the ancient Olympics was a marathon ever run.

The marathon is based on a story from Greek mythology in which a messenger named Pheidippides reportedly ran 25 miles from the Plain of Marathon to Athens with news of a military event. This legend inspired Olympic officials to include a race of 25 miles in the first modern Olympic games held in 1896. Although the distance has now been increased to 26 miles 385 yards, today's marathon is still based on Greek mythology and not the ancient Olympics.

Opposite side of the earth

Contrary to popular belief, China is not on the opposite side of the earth from the United States. Both the United States and China are in the Northern Hemisphere.

The two points that are on opposite sides of the earth are

called antipodes. The antipode of the geographic center of the United States is in the middle of the Indian Ocean west of Australia. The antipode of China is in the region of Argentina, Chile, and the Pacific Ocean west of Chile.

Oranges

Oranges are not always orange. Depending on the time of the year and the weather, they can be green, yellow, or orange, yet still be ripe. But with a little help from the citrus industry, oranges end up orange.

Oranges are one of the few fruits that do not ripen after they are picked. They will be as ripe as they will ever get when on the tree. Also, oranges will not turn orange even on the tree unless the weather turns slightly cooler. In fact, in cool winter months, orange oranges will frequently turn green as warmer weather returns. In this instance, green oranges will be older and riper than orange ones.

Consequently, at the start of the picking season, oranges are often greenish in color, though ripe. Later, fruit on the tree may become yellow and finally, under favorable conditions, usually turn orange. Much of the early crop is sprayed with a degreening agent, usually ethylene gas, which kills the chlorophyll. The yellow crop is dipped in a red dye to make the oranges orange.

Incidentally, the orange was not named from the color orange, but the word for the color came from the orange fruit. In other words, the fruit was named first, coming from a Sanskrit word. The adjective for the color appeared much later, around 1620.

Original sin

Most people think that original sin is a biblical concept resulting from Adam first biting the apple in the Garden of Eden. However, this is not entirely true.

Original sin has been commonly ascribed to the first sin of man, Adam, in defying the command of God not to eat the forbidden fruit. The concept also involves the resulting unavoidable transmission of guilt by heredity to all of mankind. However, the Bible nowhere specifically mentions this doctrine. Original sin is a complex ideology that has developed through history in religious tradition and folklore, largely in the fifth and sixth centuries.

Also, according to Genesis 3:6, it was not even Adam, but Eve, who first ate the forbidden fruit. She then convinced Adam to do likewise, and it was his disobedience that brought into the world the evils of mortality, hedonism, and alienation from God, according to the doctrine. As a woman, and within the cultural context that prevailed as the doctrine was formed, Eve's action was not considered important.

In addition, nowhere in the Bible is the apple ever mentioned as the forbidden fruit. God's command was simply not to eat the "fruit of the forbidden tree."

Ostriches

The ostrich does not bury its head in the sand when confronted with danger, or at any other time. The animal need not rely on such an obviously useless defense when it possesses two outstanding physical attributes—speed and a powerful kick.

When on its nest and confronted with danger, an ostrich will lay its long neck and head on the ground to stay low so as not to be seen. Also, if unable to run, and if the threat is not near, an ostrich will, at times, lie on its side to escape detection. It is this behavior that has led to the popular misconception about ostriches. But even in these situations, they never bury their heads in the sand.

Instead, an ostrich depends on speed and keen eyesight to escape danger. With fifteen-foot strides, an ostrich can run at speeds of up to 40 mph. If cornered, its powerful legs can deliver vicious kicks with claws on seven-inch toes that can tear an aggressor to pieces. There is no reason for ostriches to bury their heads in the sand and not take advantage of these defenses.

Otis, Elisha

The elevator was not invented by Elisha Otis. Although the name is now nearly synonymous with the elevator, Otis's contribution was only to invent a braking system that made elevators safe.

Elevators never really had an inventor. Various types of lifts and hoists have been used by man throughout history to raise and lower things. During the 1800s, steam-powered elevators were commonly used for freight. However, the constant danger of ropes breaking made elevators extremely unsafe for people and obviously unpopular.

In 1852, Otis devised an automatic safety brake and founded his own company to manufacture elevators with the new device. To convince a still-skeptical public, he demonstrated his safety brake in an 1854 publicity stunt by placing himself in an elevator and then having the rope cut. His brake worked and, within a few years, passenger elevators and the multistory building which they made possible became common in American cities.

P

Pago Pago

Pago Pago, the capital of American Samoa in the Pacific Ocean southwest of Hawaii, is pronounced by its residents and the dictionary as "Pango Pango."

Panama Canal

The western, or Pacific, end of the Panama Canal is actually more than twenty miles farther east than is the eastern, or Atlantic, end. The canal does not run east and west as is usually thought, but runs from the northwest to southeast.

Pandas

Contrary to what they are commonly called, the panda is not a bear. Although some appear quite bearlike, pandas have been classified in the past in the raccoon family. More recently, many scientists, not really knowing how to classify them, now tend to consider these unique animals as a separate family.

In fact, there are actually two species of panda. The familiar roly-poly, black and white bearlike animal is the giant panda. The other is the red, or lesser, panda and is a much smaller,

180

catlike raccoon. Although closely related anatomically to each other, the two panda species are curiously unalike in appearance.

Quite different from a bear, the giant panda feeds exclusively on bamboo leaves and shoots. It possesses an extremely dexterous paw, including a thumb, for grasping tiny objects. Panda fur, which looks soft like a teddy bear, actually feels more like a Brillo pad. Although as large as a small bear when fully grown, the giant panda is smaller than a mouse at birth.

Panther

A panther is not a specific species of cat, nor is it a certain color of animal within a single species. The name *panther* is correctly applied to various larger cats that are distinguished by their black coloration. *Panther* usually refers to a black leopard, but is also properly used for pumas, jaguars, and cougars that are black.

Paper mache

There is no such thing as paper mache. The rigid material made of paper pulp or paper mixed with flour or glue is correctly named papier-mâché.

Parachute

Since the parachute is commonly associated with people jumping out of airplanes, it is natural to assume that the parachute was invented after the airplane. However, the history of the parachute considerably predates that of the airplane.

The first actual parachute descent took place more than one hundred years before the invention of the airplane. In 1783, a Frenchman, Louis Lenormand, created the parachute to save people who had to jump from burning buildings. By 1797, another Frenchman, Jacques Garnerin, gave the first public exhibition of parachuting by jumping from a hot air balloon from three thousand feet and safely descending to the ground.

The first regular use of parachutes was over one hundred years later in World War I observation balloons. But surprisingly, the parachute was never applied for use in airplanes during this war. The first actual bail-out from an airplane did not occur until 1922, almost twenty years after the invention of the airplane. By the next year, they were required in the U.S. Army Air Corps and considered indispensable.

Parsons table

So-called Parsons tables have nothing to do with cleric's furniture. These small, stacking tables were named for the Parsons School of Design in Manhattan, where they were first made in the early 1930s.

Pasteurization

The process of pasteurization does not involve boiling, sterilizing, or heating milk to very high temperatures. Nor does it actually kill all of the bacteria present. Pasteurization simply heats milk moderately to a temperature between 130° F and 158° F for about thirty minutes, which kills only some of the bacteria.

Pasteurization is a process that extends the storage life of certain foods, usually milk, milk products, beer, and eggs. Discovered by Louis Pasteur in 1864, its original application was for beer and wine, and not for milk as is often assumed.

By exposing the product to mild forms of heat treatment, the number of microscopic organisms are only reduced in number. In fact, after pasteurization, the bacteria count returns to levels almost as high as before the procedure was applied. However, most of the "bad" bacteria, if they were ever present, are destroyed by the warm temperatures. An advantage of this method of applying only mild heat over sterilization is that the flavor of the food is not affected by the low heat as usually takes place following the higher temperatures involved with sterilization.

Penguins

Penguins do not live at just the South Pole. In fact, of the seventeen species of penguins found in the Southern Hemisphere, only two, the emperor and Adélie, are actually confined to the Antarctic continent.

Other species of penguins range north to the shores of South Africa, South America, Australia, and New Zealand. One species, the Galapagos, even lives on the equator due to the cold water in that region from the Humboldt Current. No penguins live at the North Pole.

Pennsylvania Dutch

This ethnic group, concentrated mainly in the southeastern counties of Pennsylvania known as the Pennsylvania Dutch, is actually German. Since these settlers from the Rhineland referred to themselves in their original language as *Pennsylfawnish Deutsch*, they became inaccurately called "Dutch" in America. They did not refer to themselves as Germans for the simple reason that Germany, as we now know it, including the word, did not even exist until Bismarck formed the country nearly two centuries after these Rhinelanders arrived in the United States.

Arriving in Pennsylvania as early as 1683, these settlers retained their Old World language and customs because of their large numbers and strong ethnic and religious heritage. But not all of the Pennsylvania Dutch are the rigid traditionalists they are commonly thought to be. Some have kept their conservative ways, such as the Old Order, "plain" Amish and Mennonites, and are the ones usually sought out by tourists. However, 90 percent of the Pennsylvania Dutch are New Order, "fancy" and have blended into American society largely indistinguishable in appearance and custom.

Perry Mason surprise trial endings

Contrary to the popular image created by Hollywood, court cases seldom produce the highly dramatic, Perry Mason style surprise endings where an unknown witness suddenly appears to win the case. These finishes are very uncommon in criminal cases, and particularly rare in civil courts.

Unforeseen developments are viewed as detrimental to the concept of a fair trial and are not encouraged in the American court system. They are usually averted by pretrial procedures known as the rules of discovery, which are intended to disclose facts, documents, evidence, and witnesses that are relevant, but not privileged, to either party prior to trial. Cases can be severely damaged or dismissed if evidence is not presented during discovery.

This procedure is requisite in civil cases, and in criminal cases, informal discovery, arraignment preceedings, and pretrial hearings similarly bring forth the relevant information before the trial.

Perspiration

Although there are times when it may not seem to be true, perspiration is actually a nearly clear liquid that is completely odorless. It is the action of skin bacteria rather than the perspiration itself that produces the characteristic odor.

Human perspiration is of two types. One is water vapor given off directly through the skin as simple evaporation and is not noticeable. The other type of perspiration is the one more commonly referred to as sweat. Both kinds serve the primary purpose of body temperature regulation.

There are also two kinds of sweat. Eccrine sweat is produced over most surface areas of the body and contributes to much of the body's cooling. Apocrine sweat is produced only in areas containing hair—the scalp, armpits, and genital area.

Although sweat is 99 percent water, there is one significant difference between the two types of perspiration. Apocrine sweat contains certain fats which, after being secreted onto the skin, are broken down into unsaturated fatty acids by the ever-present bacteria on the skin, especially those flourishing under the arms and in the genital region. The creation of these acids by the bacteria are thus responsible for the familiar pungent odor usually associated with perspiration.

Antiperspirants and deodorants contain insecticides and bactericides that are similar to those used in the garden. These poisons, in diluted concentrations, kill the furry, round little bacteria that reside in the armpits, preventing the formation of the odor.

Petrified wood

Most people think that petrified wood is wood that has somehow turned into stone. Actually, it is a fossil formed by mineral replacement of the natural wood fibers.

Produced through the process of petrification, groundwater carrying dissolved mineral salts and silica invades buried wood. Over a considerable length of time, these salts react with the decomposition products of the wood. The salts and silica replace the decaying cellulose, particle by particle, forming a stonelike substitute of the original organic matter. Often, the stone replacement is so accurate that both the internal structure and the external shape are the same as the original object. In these cases, petrified wood is the result.

Petroleum production

It is a common misconception that the world's petroleum production is dominated by Middle East countries. In fact, their production is not nearly as great as most people think.

Although production levels vary slightly from year to year, according to 1985 figures, which are typical, of the top ten crude-oil-producing nations in the world, only two are from the Middle East. They are Saudi Arabia (8 percent of the world total) and Iran (4 percent).

The other producers of crude oil in the top ten of world production are the Soviet Union (22 percent), the United States (16 percent), Mexico (5 percent), the United Kingdom (5 percent), China (5 percent), Venezuela (3 percent), Canada (3 percent), and Indonesia (2 percent). Other Middle East countries not in the top ten supply less than 2 percent of the world's petroleum production.

Pigs

Although the epithet "pig" has generally been used as one of the worst insults for a dirty, greedy, and stupid person, the pig is actually a clean and very intelligent animal. Mainly because of our erroneous image of the pig has it been so maligned through the years.

Since the pig is omnivorous and will eat almost anything, the practice has always been to feed it just that—garbage. However, if given the choice, pigs will choose a less odorous and more nutritious diet. Pigs also have one other redeeming quality. Given an ample food supply, pigs will seldom overeat as do their human counterparts.

Because pigs do not perspire, they like to wallow in the mud for cooling purposes as well as to keep off pesky insects. This behavior has led to the mistaken belief that pigs are dirty, and people have then treated them as such. But given a chance, pigs will often bathe in clean water.

Studies have shown that pigs are actually more intelligent than most other animals with the exception of primates. They can easily be taught tricks and are generally recognized as the smartest farm animal.

To be technically correct, in American farm usage, a swine more than three months old is not called a pig but is correctly referred to as a hog. Pigs are actually swine that are less than three months of age. In Canada and Great Britain, swine of all ages are referred to as pigs.

Finally, pigs do not squeal with delight. Their squealing is actually a sign of distress and can reach noise levels up to one hundred fifty decibels, or about as loud as the engines on a Concorde jet.

Pilgrims and Plymouth Rock

The landing of the Pilgrims at Plymouth Rock evokes familiar images for most people. Unfortunately, many of these popular ideas are untrue.

The original destination of the *Mayflower* was not Massachusetts, where the ship actually landed. The charter of the *Mayflower* stipulated that its destination was to be Virginia. The exact reasons why the voyage terminated in New England are not known for certain. The *Mayflower*'s journal recorded only that they were running out of "victuals and beer," indicating that their provisions may have run low.

The first landing of the *Mayflower* was not at Plymouth as is usually believed, but at Cape Cod harbor on November 21, 1620. The *Mayflower* remained anchored at that location for four weeks while an exploring party set out in a small boat in search of a permanent place to settle.

Therefore, the historic landing at Plymouth was not made from the *Mayflower* as is usually depicted in paintings and sketches. When the small scouting party stepped ashore, it was done from the little open boat. They returned to the *Mayflower* and sailed into Plymouth harbor on the more well-known date of December 20, 1620.

Contrary to popular belief, all aboard the *Mayflower* were not Pilgrims. Of the 102 passengers who left England, only about forty were the religious dissidents with whom we are familiar. The rest were along simply seeking adventure or financial gain, were servants accompanying their masters, or, as with Miles Standish, were paid military leaders to protect the group.

The well-known Mayflower Compact was not written at sea, was not an attempt to create democratic rule, and was not the first establishment of democracy in America. The compact was written two days after the landing in a desperate effort to quell the turmoil and dissension that threatened the group's survival. Also, representative democracy was established first at Jamestown, Virginia, in the House of Burgesses the year before the Mayflower Compact.

The now-famous Plymouth Rock is never even mentioned in any of the Pilgrims' early chronicles. The name itself, and the entire story surrounding the rock as the place where the Pilgrims first stepped ashore, was not ever heard until one hundred twenty years after the historic landing.

In 1741, Elder John Faunce somehow identified the boulder as the original landing site. The legend started by Elder Faunce did not receive great popularity until it was revived eighty years later during the 1820 bicentennial celebration of the Pilgrims' landing when the story suddenly became widely believed.

The symbol of the first permanent English settlement in New England, Plymouth Rock was removed from its original site near the shore in 1774, at which time it accidentally split in half. The two pieces were separated for over one hundred years, while one was used as a step for a building entrance. They were re-joined in 1880 at what was believed to be the rock's original location.

The Pilgrims never did refer to themselves as Pilgrims. When leaving England, they called themselves Separatists, from the English Separatist Church to which they belonged. After landing at Plymouth, the name Old Comers was briefly used, but they later became commonly known as the Forefathers.

The term Pilgrim first appeared two centuries later in an 1820 bicentennial ceremony by Governor William Bradford, who referred to them as ''saints'' and as the ''Pilgrim Fathers.'' The name Pilgrim was used again by Daniel Webster, and its popularity was thus established.

Pineapples
The pineapple did not originate in Hawaii. The fruit was unknown there until 1790, and even then it was not seriously cultivated on the islands until a century later.

The pineapple probably first grew in South America. It found its way to the Caribbean prior to the arrival of Columbus, who was the first European to experience the fruit. From the Caribbean it eventually was brought to Hawaii by Europeans.

Columbus is also responsible for the seemingly inappropriate name for the pineapple, since it in no way resembles an apple. It reminded him of a pine cone, and since the apple was the most common fruit of the time, he called it a "pine apple."

Ping Pong

The popular table game played with paddles and a bouncy, little plastic ball is not called Ping Pong. The generic name of this game is table tennis.

Ping Pong is a registered trademark used by a particular manufacturer of table tennis games. The name Ping Pong has become one of the many trademark names, such as Kleenex, that has slipped into the common language but is actually the trademark name of a specific product.

Pink flamingos

Flamingos are not naturally pink. These long-legged and long-necked water birds are gray when young chicks, but are usually pink or red as adults because of the food they eat.

Flamingos are filter feeders. They suck in quantities of water and mud and, with sievelike filters in their bills, separate algae, diatoms, and small mollusks to eat which turn pink during digestion. The pigment is absorbed into the bird's body, and its plumage is tinged pink. Flamingos that are fed substitute foods are usually white.

Pinkie

"Pinkie" is not a childish term carried over from baby talk used to designate the little finger of the hand. The word *pinkie* is derived from the old Dutch word *pinkje*, which simply means "little finger."

Piranhas

Piranhas are believed to be such dangerous and voracious feeders that anytime part of a human body touches water inhabited by these fish, the exposed part will be instantly consumed down to the bone. However, the truth is that the danger piranhas present to humans has been greatly exaggerated. This common myth was largely encouraged and popularized after Theodore Roosevelt returned from South America with his gruesome, but inaccurate, stories of piranhas.

Piranhas are a South American freshwater fish. Despite their reputation, there is no known record of a human ever being attacked, killed, and consumed by piranhas. Although the piranha is a dangerous fish, having razor-sharp teeth and a strong jaw, most bites from piranha are actually the result of native fishermen handling caught piranhas, which will ferociously snap at anything near them.

The native people of Amazonia frequently swim and bathe in water populated with piranhas, and these fish are commonly caught for food. Attacks occasionally do occur, but their frequency and severity are much less than they are imagined to be. Amazonians actually consider the freshwater stingray and the tiny catfish called the candiru far more dangerous than piranha.

Schools of piranha will attack and consume to the bone large, particularly injured, animals, but only under highly specialized conditions. When trapped in a landlocked lagoon by receding water, a large school may become more fierce from starvation. However, this behavior is uncommon.

Finally, a noted explorer, Harold Schultz, who spent twenty-five years in the Amazon basin, has reported meeting only seven people who had been bitten by piranhas. As one ichthyologist asked, if piranhas are really as deadly as myth has it, then why aren't there any other fish left in Amazonia except piranhas?

Pirates

Contrary to popular opinion, pirates did not get rid of their unwanted captives by forcing them to walk the plank. This version of pirate cruelty was first depicted through the imagination of Howard Pyle in an 1887 engraving, and later made popular in Hollywood films. But it is completely unfounded in historic fact. Although many ways were probably used at one time or another, the classic technique for getting rid of unwanted persons on ships, as seafarers have always done, was to simply heave them overboard.

In fact, much of the popular image of pirates is incorrect.

Although piracy was an ugly business, those engaged in it were usually not lawless cutthroats. They had strict rules of order, and by the seventeenth century, there even existed a pirate government.

Pirates were actually extremely democratic, and they made efforts to prevent dictatorial control. Captains were actually elected for their leadership and naval knowledge rather than for their dueling superiority. Quartermasters provided for equal disposition of the booty, and pirate courts settled disputes.

Famous pirates such as Blackbeard and Captain Kidd were not the swashbuckling, brutish buccaneers usually depicted in movies and books. Prisoners were allowed to join the pirates or sail off on their own ships, although heavy resistance often brought harsher treatment.

Another legend popularly associated with pirates is that of buried treasure. However, the truth is, little evidence exists to support these tales, and few real finds of buried treasure have ever been reported.

The Plague

Despite the fact that hundreds of millions of people have been killed by the plague throughout history, including twenty-five million in the fourteenth century and thirteen million since 1894, the plague is not directly communicable from one person to another as one might think. The disease, characterized by an acute infection, fever and swelling of the lymph nodes, is transmitted only by the bite of infected rat fleas. As the diseased rats die, the fleas leave for other hosts, including humans.

The plague, also known as the bubonic plague and black death, is still prevalent in unsanitary tropical countries. Limited outbreaks do occasionally occur in the western United States. However, the disease can now be treated with drugs, and prevention accomplished through the control of the rodent population.

Planets and the sun

Because of the radiant properties of the sun, most people believe that it is composed of an entirely different material than are the planets, including the earth. This is incorrect. The sun burns for one simple reason— its size. It consists of the same cosmic matter from which all of the planets are made.

The sun contains 99.8 percent of the mass of the solar system and is a million times larger than the earth. The effect of its size is to produce pressure at the center so great that even atoms are crushed, exposing their nuclei, and allowing them to smash into each other. These collisions are actually nuclear reactions, and are felt and seen by us from 93 million miles away as heat and light.

The internal temperature and pressure of the earth is only high enough to liquefy rocks. Jupiter, whose diameter is eleven times that of the earth, has been calculated to possess almost enough mass for its interior to glow. The least massive star known to exist barely shines because it has just .04 percent of the sun's mass and is only forty times as large as Jupiter. Somewhere in that fortyfold difference in mass between Jupiter and this smallest known star is the borderline between a planet and a glowing star like our sun.

Plant growth

It is not true that trees and plants grow during the day in direct response to sunlight and rest at night. Just because we humans depend on this cycle of activity, plants do not sleep at night.

Although the period of maximum growth is different for all plants, it is generally true that faster growth usually occurs at night. During daylight hours, plants photosynthesize sunlight to produce food which the plant then uses at night for growth. Sunlight, in fact, actually stimulates growth inhibitors in plant cells so that the plant's energy is more effectively concentrated on food production to sustain the nighttime growth.

Plastic surgery

The surgical specialty known as plastic surgery seldom, if ever, uses any plastic. In fact, the name actually has no connection at all with synthetic polymers.

In this type of medicine, plastic derives from the Greek word *plastikos*, which means to build up or to take form. Plastic surgery deals with the appearance, form, and surgical reconstruction of body tissues.

Plastic surgery is also much older than most people think.

Ancient Egyptians, the early Greeks, Hindus, and physicians for hundreds of years have attempted to reform facial characteristics. However, great advances and modern techniques did not develop until post World War I years by surgeons attempting to repair the disfigurements of combat.

It is popularly believed that plastic surgery is a frivolous specialty concerned with cosmetic face-lifts and breast enlargements. This is incorrect. Plastic surgeons require more postgraduate medical training than do any other surgical specialists. More than 60 percent of all plastic surgery deals with reconstruction to repair serious damage from burns, injuries, or congenital abnormalities. Less than 40 percent involves cosmetic face-lifts, skin tucks, or breast implants.

Poison ivy

It is not true that everyone is sensitive to poison ivy, or to the related species poison oak and poison sumac. The sensitivity to these plants, or more specifically to the irritating oil urushiol, is not innate in humans. It is a reaction that only about half of the adult population ever acquires.

No one is sensitive to poison ivy the first time they contact it. But following the initial exposure, some people are likely to react to the irritant in some way. However, even if a reaction occurs, it varies from a very mild rash to the familiar, more severe itching and blisters. Neither the blisters nor the rash itself is contagious or infectious.

Polka

The term *polka*, which refers to both the vigorous dance and the music that accompanies it, did not originate or initially even become popular in Poland. The dance first arose among the peasants of eastern Bohemia and then spread to Prague, Czechoslovakia, in the 1830s. By 1840, the polka reached Paris, where it swept the dance floors of Europe and the United States. A regional variation later developed in Poland has continued as today's familiar Polish Polka.

Polka dots were named when the dotted fabric became popular as a dress material at the same time that the polka-dance craze was in full swing.

Pony

A pony is not a baby horse. A newborn or a very young horse, under one year of age, is called a foal. Ponies are any of several distinct breeds of small horses regardless of their age.

A pony must generally be less than fifty-eight inches tall, although their full-grown size varies from thirty-two to fifty-eight inches. The smallest pony is the Shetland, which averages about thirty-seven inches high. Ponies, despite their size, are strong, sturdy, and are well suited for riding and draft purposes, especially as children's mounts.

Foals are the young of any kind of horse. After a foal is one year old, males are called colts and females are known as fillies until they each attain sexual maturity, usually within three to five years.

Pony Express

Think of the lore and legend of the American west and a picture of the Pony Express will likely appear. The image of the brave rider galloping across the wilderness on his trusty steed with Indian arrows flying about is not at all fictitious.

However, the truth is, the Pony Express lasted only nineteen months and ended up losing over two hundred thousand dollars for the three men who founded the company. The Pony Express began its nearly two thousand-mile run on April 3, 1860, from St. Joseph, Missouri, and ended in Sacramento, California. It ceased operations on October 24, 1861.

The Pony Express mainly contracted U.S. mail and was usually made in ten days. However, the use of mounted riders and relay stations was actually similar to the one first used by Benjamin Franklin in 1775 when he established the nation's first postal service.

The transcontinental telegraph soon made the Pony Express obsolete. Its heroic and dramatic operation compressed into nineteen months the essence of the American pioneer experience. However, it was a financial disaster and, as a delivery system, wholly impractical.

Porcupines

A porcupine cannot throw its quills. The quills, which are barbed and are as sharp as needles, are only loosely attached to the skin and will come off very easily when touched. For this reason, porcupines are mistakenly thought to throw their quills.

When frightened, a porcupine can raise its quills to stick up, much as other mammals do with their hair when threatened. But they are unable to propel the quills, although porcupines do lash their quill-covered tails at an enemy.

Possession is nine-tenths of the law

The familiar saying, "Possession is nine-tenths of the law," is without legal merit. Possession does not convey any right of ownership.

Real and personal property, under the law, may be owned or possessed. But the two terms are not synonymous. Ownership is the right of title. It is evidence of the right of a person to possess, enjoy, and dispose of property to the exclusion of all others. On the other hand, possession provides only the right of custody, or use, but does not necessarily include the right of title.

Possession is a basic legal interest in property entitling the possessor to certain rights against everyone except those having the right of ownership. Consequently, you may legally possess something without owning it, as is the case when you rent an automobile.

Finding lost property does not provide the finder with absolute title. Although some rights are obtained by the temporary owner, the true owner's title is not affected simply because the property has been lost. Thus, the adage, "finders keepers," is also incorrect.

Postal Service motto

"Neither snow nor rain nor heat nor gloom of night stays these couriers from the swift completion of their appointed rounds" is not the motto of the Postal Service. In fact, the U.S. Postal Service has no official motto.

These familiar words are actually the inscription on the New York City General Post Office building. They were written by Herodotus about 500 B.C. in reference to the ancient Persian system of mounted postal couriers. The inscription was supplied only by the architect of the building. Other postal buildings display different inscriptions, none of which have any official significance as a motto.

Potatoes

It is popularly believed that potatoes were native to Ireland and introduced into the United States by Irish immigrants. Actually, the reverse of this is nearly true.

Potatoes were first cultivated by the Incas in the Peruvian Andes when the Spaniards discovered them in 1532. By 1570, the potato had been introduced into Spain and the rest of Europe, but was grown merely as a garden novelty and not as a food. Apparently, its flowers resembled those of the poisonous nightshade, and Europeans were afraid to eat the potato.

However, by the 1700s, their food value had been recognized and potatoes were popular throughout Europe, especially in Ireland. The potato was then brought to America by various European immigrants, and not just from Ireland.

Folklore also has it that Sir Walter Raleigh introduced the potato to Ireland from North Carolina. Other legends contend that Raleigh brought the potato to America from Ireland. The fact is, the potato was already firmly rooted on both sides of the Atlantic by Raleigh's lifetime.

Prepositions at the end of a sentence

Contrary to what you thought you learned in school, there is, and never has been, a rule that prohibits ending a sentence with a preposition. Although it may be better form at times to avoid the use of a preposition at the end of a sentence, it is not incorrect to do so.

This fact was best demonstrated when Winston Churchill referred to the absurdity of such a rule in his familiar remark, "This is something up with which I will not put."

Prohibition

Prohibition was a nationwide effort in the United States to stop people by law from drinking alcoholic beverages. There are several common misconceptions associated with this event.

Prohibition did not outlaw the actual possession or drinking of alcohol. The law made illegal only "The manufacture, sale, or transportation of intoxicating liquors. . . ." It also did not outlaw every alcoholic drink, but only beverages containing more than .5 percent alcohol.

Prohibition was not the short-lived experiment most people think it was. Passed as the Eighteenth Amendment to the Constitution in 1919, prohibition took effect on January 16, 1920, and ended thirteen years later in 1933.

As an attempt to legislate morality, and as an effort by rural America to stem the tide of slum conditions and disorganization in big cities, prohibition arose from the belief that drinking, especially by immigrants, was responsible for these problems. But the law actually resulted in the creation of more speakeasies than there were saloons before prohibition. It also led to the formation of bootlegging gangsters and resulted in organized crime becoming firmly established in American society. As a moral and social cure, it was an abominable failure.

Proof

The measure of the alcohol content of a distilled liquor, known as proof, does not refer to the actual percentage of alcohol in the liquid. Proof is, in fact, twice the true percentage of alcohol as measured by volume. For example, an 80-proof whiskey contains just 40 percent alcohol.

Historically, the technology to accurately measure the alcohol content of liquids appeared long after alcoholic beverages were produced and sold. However, purveyors of spirits and tax collectors, even in earlier days, needed a method to determine alcohol content.

To do so, a procedure was developed in England to test alcohol content by pouring whiskey on gunpowder and lighting the whiskey. If the gunpowder ignited after the alcohol burned away, it was "proof" that the whiskey had not been diluted. Whiskey that just passed the test was called 100-proof.

After the discovery of the hydrometer, a 100-proof mixture was found to contain slightly less than 50 percent alcohol. In the United States, this was simplified into a system that defined the proof of distilled liquor to be double the actual alcohol content. However, measures of proof vary markedly from country to country and refer to entirely different measures of alcohol content.

Pyramids

The largest pyramids in the world are not in Egypt. Although the Egyptian pyramids are tall, the pre-Columbian pyramids in Mexico rival and, in some cases, exceed in size and splendor those found in Egypt.

The pyramids of Mexico are of unknown antiquity, but were probably constructed for the Aztec and Toltec gods between the sixth and second centuries B.C.

The largest is Quetzalcoatl at Cholula de Rivadabia in Mexico. Although not as tall as the Great Pyramid of Cheops in Egypt, its base occupies 45 acres, and the pyramid contains 4.3 million cubic yards of material. Egypt's Great Pyramid sits on 13 acres and contains 3.4 million cubic yards of stone.

Another Mexican pyramid, Teotihuacan, or the Pyramid of the Sun, has a circumference at its base of 2,800 feet compared to the Great Pyramid's 755-foot circumference. Teotihuacan is 210 feet tall, while Cheops is 480 feet in height.

Although actually larger in total size than those in Egypt, the pyramids of Mexico have generally not received the same attention as the ones in Egypt for several reasons. The pyramids in Mexico are not true geometric pyramids, but are usually stepped, or layered in shape. The Mexican pyramids were constructed with slightly less precision than those in Egypt, since they were built mainly from adobe, earth, and rubble.

In contrast, with accurately and laboriously cut stone blocks, the pyramids of Egypt are just as famous as engineering and construction marvels as for their size.

Finally, the Mexican pyramids did not contain tombs as did the ones in Egypt. Because they were built simply as a base for temples and worship, they lacked the mystery, treasures, and popular appeal of the Egyptian pyramids.

Q

"If ignorance is bliss,
there should be more happy people."

Victor Cousins

Quarterhorse

The quarterhorse was not originally named for its size, nor did the name initially refer to a specific breed or species. In colonial America, any horse that was suited to running a quarter-mile race, the standard length horse race of the time, became known as a quarterhorse. The lineage or breed did not matter; only the agility and ability to run fast over short, rough paths gave these horses their name.

A modern quarterhorse has developed into a distinct breed. Although weighing about the same as a thoroughbred, a quarterhorse is shorter and stockier. It is ideal for ranch work and in rodeo contests that require short, sudden bursts of speed and maneuvering. Because horse races are now generally much longer than a quarter mile, the quarterhorse is no longer considered a suitable race horse.

Quicksand

It is a popular misconception that quicksand possesses some sort of strange power enabling it to suck in anyone who falls into it. However, this is an image largely created by Hollywood which is unsupported by reality.

Quicksand is a condition in which loose, fine sand becomes so saturated with water that it behaves like a liquid. It usually occurs near the mouth of a large river, near a shoreline underlaid by stiff clay, or above an underground spring where a steady subterranean water supply exists.

However, the specific gravity of quicksand is so high that the substance is actually more buoyant than water. A human body will not sink more than three-quarters below the surface in quicksand and will then float. Sudden, jerking movements will only hasten the descent to that level.

It is even possible to swim in quicksand, although it is not recommended. The best method to extricate oneself is to lie on your back and then slowly float or roll out. In any event, the quicksand will not suck a person under as Hollywood has led us to believe.

R

"Get your facts first,
and then you can distort them as much as you like."

Mark Twain

Rabbits and hares

The furry, hopping animals popularly called rabbits and hares are often incorrectly named. Rabbits and hares are entirely different animals, and their names cannot be used interchangeably. In fact, this confusion extends to even some proper names for these animals. For example, jackrabbits are actually hares, while the Belgian hare is really a rabbit.

Although distinctions between the two are basically anatomical and outwardly slight, rabbits are somewhat smaller than hares and are usually burrowing animals. They are born helpless, furless, and become highly gregarious.

In contrast, hares are somewhat larger, can hop around just minutes after birth, and have black-tipped ears. Hares are generally solitary animals.

Incidentally, Welsh rabbit is neither rabbit nor a hare. It is actually melted cheese on toast. A similar term also popularly used is Welsh rarebit, and is an incorrect derivative of Welsh rabbit. When only Welsh noblemen were allowed to hunt rabbits, the peasants concocted their own poor man's version of Welsh "rabbit."

200

Raindrops

Raindrops do not really resemble teardrops as they are usually pictured nor do they fall as fast as most people think they do. A raindrop is a balance between the aerodynamic forces it experiences while falling and its own weight. The result is actually a shape more like the typical hamburger bun.

Water vapor condenses in the atmosphere as small, spherical droplets. However, these droplets form only clouds, fog, or mist since their weight is insufficient to cause them to fall to the ground.

If the droplets accrete sufficiently in size, raindrops are produced. Smaller drops lightly fall as drizzle and retain a basically round shape. As the size of a raindrop increases, aerodynamic forces, mainly in the form of air resistance, flatten them out on the bottom and create a rounded, mushroom cap-shaped top. Faster-falling, heavier raindrops even acquire a concave undersurface which forms into an exploding bubble if its speed becomes too great.

Raindrops usually fall at a much more gentle rate than they appear. Mist barely falls at all, while drizzle descends at about 1 to 2 mph. The largest raindrops in the heaviest storms fall at about 20 mph, which is about as fast as a drop can fall and still be held together by its surface tension before breaking up. Raindrops in typical rain showers fall at an average speed of about 7 mph.

Raleigh, Sir Walter

As the English colonizer, courtier, and writer who sponsored and encouraged the first English settlements in North America, Sir Walter Raleigh is well known for many things. But he never laid down his cloak for the queen, went to America, or brought tobacco to England as are usually attributed to him.

The story that Raleigh placed his cloak across the mud for Queen Elizabeth is a quaint anecdote originated by Thomas Fuller in the late 1600s. As an author, Fuller was a more-than-imaginative historian who often elaborated on historical fact. Fuller fabricated the story about the cloak, years after Raleigh's death, for its romantic appeal.

Largely responsible for the early English colonies in what is now Virginia and North Carolina, Raleigh himself never journeyed to America as is often assumed. As the queen's favorite, Raleigh was forbidden by her to leave England. Although the capital of North Carolina is named in his honor, his adventures in the New World took him only to South America and Newfoundland.

Raleigh also did not introduce tobacco to England. Tobacco from America was taken to Spain, then to France, and later introduced into England by Sir Francis Drake in 1586. With a vested financial interest in the product, Raleigh did encourage its use in England and contributed to the popularity of smoking. It is for this reason that he is often associated with the introduction of tobacco into England.

Reading left to right

There is nothing inherent in the human brain or our visual system that requires that we read from left to right or top to bottom. Many languages have been written in different directions, and the brain is perfectly capable of adapting to symbols arranged in any order.

The early Greeks tried writing from right to left and left to right several times before settling into a system going from left to right. Several current languages are written from bottom to top or from right to left such as Chinese, Hebrew, and Arabic. With training and a little practice, anyone can learn to read and write in any direction.

.niaga kniht retteb dah uoy neht ,ti od tonnac uoy kniht uoy fI

Red Square

Red Square in Moscow was not named by the current socialists in power after the Communist party. It was known as the Red Square long before the Russian Revolution took place that ultimately led to the present Soviet government.

In fact, this historic hub of Moscow was once a thriving sixteenth century market comprising the commercial center of the city. The name Red Square derives from the market's seventeenth century Old Russian name of *krasnaya* simply meaning "beautiful."

Reindeer

Reindeer may look like deer and even have a deerlike name, but they are not true deer. Instead, they are actually caribou. Referred to as reindeer in Northern Europe and Asia, they are the same species as the caribou found throughout the Western Hemisphere.

Revere, Paul

Nearly every schoolchild has heard of the midnight ride of Paul Revere. Yet, the familiar story usually told represents one of the more interesting examples of misinformation in American history. The truth is, Paul Revere's famous ride was not made alone, and he never even made it to his intended destination because he was arrested along the way.

Revere's involvement in events defiant to England did not begin that spring night of April 18, 1775. As a skilled and well-known artisan, Revere also became a leader in colonial opposition to the king. For many years, he had been a paid messenger rider for the patriots, was involved in the Stamp Act riots, and was an "Indian" at the Boston Tea Party. Revere also did not volunteer his services for the famous ride. He rode that night as a paid messenger.

Revere became immortalized in American folklore mainly through the popular poem of William Wadsworth Longfellow. The poem, correctly titled "Paul Revere's Ride," and not, as is commonly believed, "The Midnight Ride of Paul Revere," was actually written ninety years after the ride took place. Fortunately, Longfellow was a better poet than historian.

A significant omission made by Longfellow was the fact that Revere did not ride by himself. Knowing that British regulars were about ready to move to arrest John Hancock and Samuel Adams in Lexington, and also to confiscate supplies and weapons at Concord, Revere set out for the two towns on a borrowed horse with William Dawes.

The two men were successful in warning Hancock and Adams in Lexington, and were then joined by Dr. Samuel Prescott as all three were to ride to Concord. However, Revere and Dawes were stopped by a British patrol, detained for the night, and sent back to Lexington in the morning. It was Prescott who actually completed the journey to Concord to alert the residents there of the British advance so that the important supply of weapons and ammunition could be protected. The "shots heard round the world" fired the next day at Concord, beginning the Revolution, came from the supplies saved by Prescott.

Revere is also credited with signaling with lanterns from the church "one if by land and two if by sea" to warn of the British movement. However, it was really the church sexton, Robert Newman, who received the information from Revere and signaled from the steeple. Also, as Revere rode along, he did not shout, "The British are coming." Instead, the warning actually was, "The regulars are out."

In his later years, Revere regarded his ride as merely an exciting, isolated incident from a time when many heroic events took place. He was most proud of his skill and versatility in his work as an artist and silversmith. If not for Longfellow singling him out for recognition in his poem, this is how he likely would now be remembered.

Rhinoceros horn

The horn of the rhinoceros, the only animal with such a growth on its nose, is not a horn at all. The rhino's horn is simply matted hair hardened by secretions of keratin.

Myths concerning the rhinoceros's horn are largely responsible for the rhino now being an endangered species. It has been a persistent belief that these horns possess medicinal and magical powers, and that they even contain an aphrodisiac. These ideas have resulted in extensive killings of the rhinoceros, and poachers now present a serious threat to the survival of the species. However, there is absolutely no evidence to support any of these myths concerning the powers of their horns.

Rickshaw

The rickshaw is not a traditional method of transportation in the orient, nor was it invented by an Asian. It was first built by an American Baptist minister, Jonathan Scobie, in 1869.

While living in Yokohama, Japan, Scobie needed a means of transport for his invalid wife, so he invented a hand-drawn passenger cart. The rickshaw became an immediate success, and many more were soon built by Scobie to provide employment for his Christian converts.

Right to bear arms

It is usually assumed that the United States Constitution allows every American the unlimited right to possess firearms for individual use and protection. But it would be difficult to find those actual words or that specific meaning in the Constitution.

The right to bear arms is a controversial subject whose current legal status has been strictly a matter of interpretation by the courts. The only reference for these definitions for a right to bear arms is contained in the second article of the Bill of Rights of the Constitution. It states, in its entirety,

> "A well regulated militia, being necessary to the security of a free state, the right of the people to keep and bear arms, shall not be infringed."

The unlimited right to bear arms has not been recognized in common law. Courts have interpreted the second article of the Bill of Rights to apply to the constitutional guarantee of the people to bear arms in order to maintain a militia, or national guard.

This right cannot be infringed by gun-control laws as long as there is a reasonable relationship between the use and possession of a firearm and the preservation of a well-regulated militia. However, certain prohibitions involving the ownership, possession, use, and transport of firearms are permissible. These restrictions are regulated by state and federal laws to protect the safety of the public insofar as the maintenance of a state militia is not impaired.

Ring around a rosie

Every child has happily joined hands with friends and recited the familiar nursery rhyme, "Ring around a rosie, a pocket full of posies. Ashes, ashes, we all fall down." Few people realize to what this seemingly happy little rhyme actually refers.

This nursery rhyme began about 1347 and derives from the not-so-delightful Black Plague, which killed over twenty-five million people in the fourteenth century. The "ring around a rosie" refers to the round, red rash that is the first symptom of the disease. The practice of carrying flowers and placing them around an infected person for protection is described in the phrase, "a pocket full of posies." "Ashes" is a corruption or imitation of the sneezing sounds made by the infected person. Finally, "we all fall down" describes the many dead resulting from the disease.

Ringworm
The infections of the skin, hair, and nails commonly known as ringworm are not caused by worms at all. Ringworm is the result of a group of fungi that feed on people as they penetrate into the skin. The fungi spread outward in a circle, while those in the center gradually die, producing the familiar rings on the skin.

Technically referred to as tinea, but commonly called ringworm of the scalp, jock itch, and athlete's foot, these fungi are spread only by direct contact. Before it was known that the disease was the result of a fungus, it was thought that the infection was caused by small worms. In fact, *tinea* is Latin for "gnawing worms."

Robin
The American robin is actually a thrush. Its name was erroneously chosen by early European settlers because of its similarity to the European species of the same name. However, the resemblance between the American and European robin is slight, although they both have reddish breasts. To add to the confusion, the European robin redbreast is really a warbler.

The original failure to correctly identify the bird as a thrush partly stems from the fact that a thrush usually has a spotted breast. Since the breast of the American robin is clear, it was not recognized as a thrush. However, young robins do have the characteristic speckled breast of a thrush.

Roosevelt, Franklin D.
In his March 4, 1933 inaugural address, President Franklin Roosevelt said, "The only thing we have to fear is fear itself." Because these words were made famous by him, Roosevelt is usually given credit for originating the expression. However, the phrase had been in existence long before it was used by the President.

In 1580, Michel Montaigne wrote, "The thing of which I

have most fear is fear." Francis Bacon said, "Nothing is terrible except fear itself." Similar remarks were later made by the Duke of Wellington and Henry Thoreau. It is likely that Roosevelt's speech writers were familiar with the previous uses of this expression.

Ross, Betsy

Although folklore has elevated Betsy Ross to the level of a national legend, there is absolutely no evidence connecting her with making the first American flag. The tale originated under dubious circumstances, yet it quickly became accepted as fact by many Americans.

The story did not first appear until nearly one hundred years after the event allegedly took place. William Canby, the grandson of Elizabeth (Betsy) Griscom Ross, related the story at a meeting of the Historical Society of Pennsylvania in 1870.

Canby claimed that his grandmother, Betsy Ross, was visited by George Washington and two members of the Continental Congress in June 1776, and was asked to sew a flag. According to Canby, Betsy complied and produced the first U.S. flag. The story was later published during the U.S. centennial celebration of 1876, and the public sentiment was delighted with the tale.

However, there has never been a stitch of evidence to substantiate the story. Canby's account was based solely on his aunt's memories of what an elderly Betsy had supposedly told her. There is no record of any Continental Congress committee headed by Washington that planned a flag, and no record exists of any payment for one. Although Betsy Ross was a seamstress, the only proof of her flag-making consists of one voucher for flags made for the Pennsylvania militia.

The true history of the United States flag has become so cluttered by myth and folklore that the actual facts are difficult, and in some cases impossible, to establish. It is known, however, that the official U.S. flag was adopted years after the Betsy Ross event supposedly occurred. Her legend must be regarded as an example of exaggerated family sentiment which, although in consistent with the facts, nevertheless grew into popular folklore and has even found its way into history books.

Rough Riders

The famous charge up San Juan Hill by Theodore Roosevelt's Rough Riders was, indeed, a rough ride. Instead of horses, the cavalry unit was on foot in their famous assault up the hill while their trusty steeds were still in Florida.

Actually, the Rough Riders were officially named the First U.S. Volunteer Cavalry. The nickname was taken by Roosevelt from a term that Buffalo Bill Cody had used to describe himself and his horse-riding pals.

Roosevelt's Rough Riders were sent to Cuba in 1898 in connection with the Spanish-American War. However, their horses had to be left behind in Florida. During their charge, not a single horse was actually used.

The role of Theodore Roosevelt with the Rough Riders has also been exaggerated and romanticized through the years. Roosevelt was not actually in command of the Rough Riders for most of their existence. That position was held by Colonel Leonard C. Wood. Although Roosevelt participated in the earlier assault of Kettle Hill, he only supported the charge up San Juan Hill from his position on Kettle.

Russia

The name Russia is often incorrectly used to refer to the country named the Soviet Union. More accurately, the term Russia indicates either prerevolution Russia or the single Soviet republic, the Russian Soviet Federated Socialist Republic. The name of the country is the Union of Soviet Socialist Republics, or the Soviet Union.

Russia, the Russian Soviet Federated Socialist Republic, is one of fifteen unions, or national republics, within the Soviet Union. It is somewhat similar to a United States state or Canadian province, and Russia is the largest, most populous, and well-known of the Soviet republics.

S

"To treat your facts with imagination is one thing,
but to imagine your facts is another."

John Burroughs

Sailing

Despite what common sense would seem to dictate, some sailing craft can, in fact, travel at speeds greater than the actual wind speed that propels them. This improbable event occurs commonly with ice racing boats and, in some cases, with sailboats on water.

When going downwind, a sailing craft of any kind can reach a speed no greater than the natural wind speed. But across the wind, the flow of air over an airfoil-shaped sail, and the lateral resistance of the boat going sideways, produces a strong force to drive the boat ahead. This creates a wind flow that is a combination of the natural wind and the sideways pull from the boat's sails. It is similar to the lift provided by an airplane wing, except it is a lateral pull rather than a vertical one.

This effect is most apparent with ice racing boats, which experience little resistance from the ice surface. An ice boat can actually sail on a wind of its own making to obtain speeds four or five times greater than the true wind speed. It is not uncommon for twelve-foot ice yachts to attain speeds of sixty to ninety mph in much slower winds, while smaller "skeeters" are capable of being propelled at 125 mph in winds of only fifteen to thirty mph.

This phenomenon does not usually occur with sailboats, primarily due to the enormous drag from water resistance over the hull. However, some smaller, specialized sailing craft, such as catamarans, can utilize these principles and, despite friction, can sail at or slightly greater than the speed of the wind.

Saint Patrick

The popular belief that Saint Patrick was Irish is pure blarney. Patrick, his real name is not even known for certain, was born in 390 in England, where he spent much of his early years.

While a youth in England, Patrick was captured by Irish marauders and taken to Ireland, where he spent nearly six years as a slave. He used his time in captivity to pray, and it was during these years that Patrick decided to become a priest. After either escaping or being freed, he returned to his family in England.

Patrick spent twelve years at a monastery in England training for the priesthood, and returned to Ireland in 435 to organize a church. By the time of his death in 460, he had established the Christian Church in Ireland, although it took many other evangelists and several generations to accomplish the conversion of the entire country.

However, Patrick was made the patron saint of Ireland for his early and crucial role in converting the country to the faith. As was then the custom, his death day of March 17, and not his birthday, is now commemorated as Saint Patrick's Day.

The legend that Saint Patrick drove the snakes from Ireland is untrue. There is no evidence to support this folk tale, and the story did not even appear until hundreds of years after his death.

Salmonella

The infectious disorder known as salmonella has nothing to do with salmon, or any other kind of fish. The name derives from its discoverer in 1885, Dr. Daniel Salmon, an American microbiologist.

Salmonella is actually not a specific bacteria, but a general term applied to over three hundred types of related bacteria found in food. Most cases occur in the home, and not in restaurants as most people think. The effects of salmonella can vary, depending on the bacteria involved, from mild symptoms of infection to death.

Samson and Delilah

It is not true that Samson lost his strength because Delilah cut off his hair. In the first place, Samson's hair was never cut off. It was shaved, and it was not even shaved by Delilah, but by another man. According to the Bible (Judges 16:19), Delilah made Samson "sleep upon her knees; and she called for a man, and she caused him to shave off the seven locks of his head."

The popular misconception of this biblical story was encouraged by Cecil B. DeMille's 1949 film *Samson and Delilah*. The story involves the Israelite Samson and his love for the Philistine woman Delilah, and her betrayal of him.

Samson's fate was more serious than simply losing his hair. He was also imprisoned, had his eyes gouged out, and ended his own life in an attempt to destroy the temples in one of the Bible's rare suicides.

San Diego Chargers

The San Diego Chargers of the National Football League did not acquire the name "Chargers" from any athletic skills involved with running the football down the field. The name derives from the fact that the team's original owner, Baron Hilton, also owned the Carte Blanche credit card company. Hence, the name San Diego Chargers.

San Francisco earthquake

The earthquake that struck San Francisco on April 18, 1906, resulted in the loss of about five hundred lives and caused the destruction of twenty-five thousand buildings. Yet, it was not the earthquake that produced most of the damage as most people believe. The resulting fire that swept the city caused twenty times more casualties and property loss than did the earthquake itself.

In addition to demolished buildings, the damage from the earthquake included hundreds of fallen electrical wires, broken gas lines, and toppled fireplaces which set off the inferno. Three days of fire burned a path over three miles wide through the city.

Fire fighting was rendered hopeless since most of the water

mains had also broken during the earthquake. Dynamite was used to create firebreaks, but to no avail. As a last resort, artillery guns were brought in and were fired on the city in order to carve out a five hundred-foot wide clearing that was generally successful in stopping the fire.

Sanctuary

The idea persists that certain consecrated places, such as a church, serve as a refuge where offenders against the law cannot be seized or arrested. Despite these beliefs, there is no such thing or place that provides sanctuary for those persecuted for political, moral, or criminal reasons.

The principle of sanctuary derives from Old English law and generally remained in effect in many countries until the eighteenth century. This idea has been perpetuated in the popular mind by many Hollywood movies, including *The Hunchback of Notre Dame*. However, the privilege of sanctuary has been abolished, and even a church now provides no such legal protection.

Sardines

There is actually no living fish called a sardine. A sardine is not a sardine until it is packed into a sardine can.

International standards exist that allow each country to establish its own definition of what constitutes a sardine. There are currently twenty-one different fish species that are recognized as acceptable for sale as sardines. The most common fish used world-wide are young herring or pilchard. The Maine sardine industry, now the only American production center, uses juvenile Atlantic herring.

It is the oils and seasonings that are added to the fish that give sardines their distinctive taste. The little fish are still cut and packed head-to-tail into the can by hand. Sardines are packed together like sardines into their cans because, depending on the type of oil used, the oil is often more costly than the fish itself.

Scalping

It is generally assumed that scalping was unique to the American Indian, was practiced only on white victims, and involved slicing off all the hair and skin from the head. None of these ideas accurately represents the custom of scalping.

The practice of scalping has been found in numerous societies throughout history, including parts of Europe. North American Indians, prior to the arrival of Europeans, infrequently scalped. The early practice of scalping was actually more related to the Indian custom of cutting off various body parts as trophies following warfare.

Indian scalping commonly appeared only after the French and English settlers arrived in America. Two factors contributed to this change. First, the introduction to the Indians of the steel knife made scalping physically possible. Second, high bounties were offered by the white colonists to the Indians for the scalps of other Indians. As early as 1703, Massachusetts paid bounties for scalps, as did New Hampshire in 1725. During the French and Indian War, the French also paid for Indian scalps. It was also during the inter-European wars in North America that the practice of scalping was extended to whites for the first time.

Scalping usually consisted of merely slicing off a small patch of skin only an inch or two in size, often behind one ear, on either an alive or dead person. Although the entire skin of the head was at times removed, the practice was generally more limited in completeness to just the removal of a small slice. On live victims, this usual form of scalping was not fatal.

Scan

To scan something means to look at or examine all parts of a thing intently, completely, and point by point. It also means the opposite—to glance at casually and quickly, but not thoroughly. Skim means to read quickly, noting only the main points.

Sea level

Except for tides, most people believe that the term *sea level* refers to some constant, uniform height of the ocean surface that is the same everywhere on all seas of the world. It is not. There is no such thing as an absolute, specific sea level that is the same at every locality at any time.

Sea level is defined as the position of the air-sea interface. Although it is the reference datum to which all terrestrial elevations and submarine depths are made, ocean surfaces are not uniform as one might expect.

In reality, sea level is in a constant state of change and is most influenced locally by tides, which vary from one to two feet to as much as fifty feet. But it is also affected by less regular and predictable factors such as atmospheric pressure, wind and waves, long-term climatic changes, coastline configurations, gravitational pull of mountains, and currents.

In addition to these fluctuations, there are variations in the apparent uniform level of the sea that are not so well understood. The surface of each ocean usually contains irregularities of as much as several feet at different locations. It is believed that the sea level of the Pacific is about two feet higher than at the same latitude in the Atlantic. It is known that the level of the oceans in the Northern Hemisphere drops about eight inches in the spring without rising anywhere else. No one knows why this occurs. Sea level, which has risen and fallen several hundred feet through geological history, is currently rising this century at the rate of .05 inches per year, probably due to the melting of polar ice.

Since sea level is not a precise term, the concept of mean sea level is used instead. The U.S. Geodetic Survey makes regular measurements at numerous locations over the complete nineteen-year cycle of tides and determines the average sea level for a location. It is this theoretical figure that is actually used when referring to sea level at a specific location.

Sea life

It is a popular misconception that life in the ocean is more abundant in warm water than in cold water. In fact, the opposite is true. Marine life of all kinds—animal and vegetative—is more abundant in the colder waters of the earth.

The reason for this is that cold water is able to hold more dissolved gases, particularly oxygen and carbon dioxide, than warm water. This, in turn, provides the essentials for plants to photosynthesize.

Antarctic waters are teeming with life of all kinds, especially plankton and krill, producing the "soup" that supports whales, seals, and many kinds of fish. A similar abundance exists in the cold waters around the Arctic. Many of the world's most productive fishing grounds are found in cold-water locations. Warm, tropical waters are often clear and, although more beautiful and containing some exotic species of fish, are generally lacking the quantity of life found in colder water.

Seashell roar

The sound produced when a seashell is placed over the ear is not the sound of the ocean roaring. It is actually the sound of blood rushing through the veins in the ear and a composite of echoes of ordinary nearby sounds. This effect can also be produced simply by putting any cup-shaped object over the ear.

Seasons

In the Northern Hemisphere, the sun is not closer to the earth in the summer than it is in winter. Although this may seem logical, seasons are not really determined by the distance between the earth and the sun. In fact, the earth is actually about three million miles closer to the sun around January 3 and farthest in July.

Seasons are caused by the tilting of the earth's axis of rotation of about 23° from the plane of its orbit. As a result of this tilting of the earth, there are more hours of sunshine and more direct rays of sunlight on various parts of the earth at certain times of the year. These times are called summers. The more nearly perpendicular rays provide more energy in given areas with less solar energy reflected back into space by atmospheric gases and particles, and generally produce warmer weather.

At 45° north latitude on June 22, these effects produce about four times (300 percent) as much solar energy in the form of heat as is received at the same location on December 22. Although about 7 percent more heat is received when the earth is closer to the sun in late December than early January, the effects of tilting are so much greater than the variation in distance factor that the latter is almost negligible in affecting the season.

Shark attacks

Most people believe that staying near the shore in shallow water while swimming in the ocean will reduce the likelihood of a shark attack. This can be a dangerous misconception.

The fact is, the great majority of shark attacks take place in ordinary wading depths of fewer than five feet of water and within ten feet from shore. This does not mean that sharks regularly swim in shallow water, only that most swimmers are within this area. However, it also means that shallow water is not necessarily a haven from shark attack.

Sharks actually prefer deeper water, since their usual method of attack is to approach the victim from the rear and below. After the initial assault, a shark will usually swim away and circle the victim until it bleeds to death. Sharks do not relentlessly tear apart their victims as is commonly imagined. It is during this reprieve when most rescues of attack victims are made.

A shark will be more likely to attack anything in the water that resembles its primary food—the sea lion. A splashing swimmer near the surface, even in shallow water, will elicit an attack from a hungry shark, while a submerged diver will often be ignored.

Contrary to our fears acquired from the movie *Jaws*, the typical attack involves a shark about seven feet long and weighing two hundred pounds. The shark is only seen before the attack by about one-third of the victims, and less than one in five people attacked are actually killed. Less than 10 percent of the three hundred known species of sharks are dangerous to man. Also, in the United States, bees kill about one hundred times as many people each year as do sharks.

Ship locks

It is commonly, but erroneously, believed that ship locks, which raise and lower ships in order to navigate around waterfalls and other obstructions, operate by mechanically pumping water into and out of the locks. However, no pumps of any kind are used in this type of lock.

Water is moved, and the ships raised and lowered, entirely by the action of gravity. A lock is filled simply by closing the gate at the lower end and allowing water to flow in from the upper end. It is emptied by opening the gate at the lower end and letting the water drain out.

Ship's tonnage

When referring to the tonnage of large ships, the term *ton* does not mean the actual weight of the ship. Nor does it have anything to do with the standard two thousand-pound ton normally used to weigh heavy objects. In fact, there are actually three kinds of tonnage used, based on different measuring criteria, often making it impossible to compare one ship's tonnage with that of another.

Originally, tonnage was a measure of the carrying capacity of a ship. The word derives from the *tun*, a large cask or barrel in which wine, ale, or other liquids were transported. One *tun* was roughly equal to one large barrel, and *tunnage* was the number of barrels a ship could carry.

This method proved inadequate, and led to the development of a more precise, if less uniform, system that retained the original terms. As applied to American merchant ships, tonnage is classified under both space and weight tons. The terms are intended for different kinds of vessels and are not interchangeable.

Gross tonnage is a measure of space and applies to passenger ships. It is the total measure of the enclosed capacity within a ship, with one hundred cubic feet considered one ton. Net tonnage is also sometimes used, and is the gross tonnage minus those areas required for propulsion machinery, fuel, and crew quarters.

Deadweight tonnage is a measure of weight of a ship's carrying capacity and is used for freighters and tankers. It is the weight, in avoirdupois tons of 2,240 pounds, of everything a ship can carry fully loaded, except the weight of the ship itself, and remain at its navigable waterline.

Displacement tonnage refers to warships and is the weight of the ship and its full load given in tons of seawater displaced when loaded to its loadline. In displacement tonnage, thirty-five cubic feet of seawater is considered to be one ton.

Shooting stars

A shooting star is not, of course, really a shooting or falling star. It is actually a small piece of cosmic matter that has become visible as it burns up in the earth's atmosphere.

These pieces of cosmic debris are called meteoroids while

drifting through space. They are rock or dust particles, usually iron, stone, or an intermediate mixture.

The streaking light popularly called a shooting star is produced as the meteoroid heats up from friction with air as it enters and passes through the earth's atmosphere. This begins to occur at about sixty miles above the earth's surface. At this point, the burning particle is referred to as a meteor. If the meteor reaches the ground, it becomes a meteorite.

Meteors and meteorites are much smaller than most people think, especially when one considers the sometimes spectacular displays of light they produce. The average weight of a faint shooting star is actually just a fraction of an ounce. Bright fireballs usually weigh just two or three pounds. Although they have caused some minor damage, no human has ever been reported killed by a meteor anywhere in the world at any time through history.

Shriveled skin

Skin that has been submerged under water, such as in the bathtub, does not appear shriveled up because it is shrinking, as is usually believed. The skin is actually expanding from the absorption of water.

Human skin is quite different in structure and function over different areas of the body. One of these differences is that skin on the palms, fingers, soles, and toes is somewhat thicker than in other places.

Because the internal body fluids of humans are more concentrated than fresh water, water is absorbed by skin immersed in water through the process of osmosis. These areas of thicker skin become saturated, expand, and, because of the skin's relative denseness, wrinkles appear. Skin color becomes white from the opaqueness produced by the increased water content of the skin.

Skin elsewhere on the body soaks up water after prolonged immersion, but because it is thinner, there is more room for moisture so that wrinkles do not appear so quickly. Wrinkling does not occur from ocean salt water since seawater is more like the fluids in our body and osmosis does not take place.

Silkworm

The silkworm is not a worm. It is a caterpillar, the larva of a moth, that spins a silken cocoon, especially one that is suitable for commercial silk production. The commonest is the Chinese silkworm.

Sitting Bull

The famous Sioux leader, Sitting Bull, did not participate in the battle of the Little Big Horn, was not a war chief, and Sitting Bull was not even his real name.

Like most well-known Indians in American history, the name Sitting Bull was applied by the white man. His real name was Tatanka Yotanka, and although a chief of the Hunkpapa Sioux, he was not a war chief. Sitting Bull was a medicine man whose reputation, both as a warrior in battle and for being able to invoke the spirits, had earned him the position of a great leader among the Sioux.

Under Sitting Bull, the Sioux were abiding by the permanent terms of a treaty that placed them on a reservation in the Black Hills of South Dakota. After the discovery of gold in the region, the U.S. government rescinded the treaty and attempted to relocate the Sioux to another reservation.

When Sitting Bull refused to move, the U.S. Army sent a force against his camp to remove the Indians. Thousands of Sioux warriors then joined Sitting Bull at the Little Big Horn. However, on June 25, 1876, it was Crazy Horse who actually led the warriors against Custer, while Sitting Bull remained in the Sioux village and made medicine, apparently with great success.

Skull

The human skull is not one solid bone as is usually imagined, nor does it consist of just the top of the head as most people think. The skull, technically referred to as the cranium, is actually composed of twenty-two separate bones. There are eight cranial bones and fourteen facial and jaw bones in the human skull. Only one of them, the mandible, or jaw, is movable.

In infants and very small children, the cranial bones are disconnected segments but are held together by connective tissue stripes called sutures. At certain sites, these sutures are especially weak, creating the familiar soft spots, or fontanels, in an infant's head.

When growing is complete, the bones of the skull fuse together along the suture lines. These unions contain small amounts of fibrous connective tissue which are examples of immovable joints.

Although the skull may structurally be one piece when fully developed, it is still composed of separate bones. Many old skeletal remains that appear to have cracked or broken skulls are actually just missing some of these pieces. The softer connective tissue has decomposed, leaving little support between the individual pieces of bone in the skull, causing them to fall out.

Skyscrapers swaying

Skyscrapers do not sway nearly as much as most people believe, and if they do, the sway is not actually a back-and-forth swing.

In the first place, what is often referred to as sway is not really a motion like that of a pendulum, but is more like a bend or lean in the structure. In either case, tall buildings are designed to operate like an elastic cantilever, so that any motion is not likely to result in the collapse of the building.

This sway, or bend, is usually a matter of only a few inches off the vertical. Buildings such as the Empire State Building and the Sears Tower in Chicago bend only several inches in moderate winds. In contrast, they are designed to bend up to three feet in 100 mph storms.

Affecting sway as much as wind are the design criteria and the external-surface construction materials. Each structure has its own personality for swaying, and height alone is not the most relevant factor.

If support steel is on the exterior, sunlight will bend the structure so that the top of the building will lean away from the sun. Differences in temperature on the sides of the building generated by the sun's heat produces this effect. This bend is not on a straight axis, but the building actually forms a curve. If support steel is in the interior of the structure, the bend from the sun's heat will be negligible.

To the occupants of a tall building, internal vibrations are more perceptible than is the movement of the whole structure. In skyscrapers, the objects inside the building may vibrate more than does the building itself, and these vibrations are often mistaken for building sway.

Snake charmers

Snake charmers do not hypnotize and render harmless snakes by the sounds of their flutelike instrument. Instead, it is actually the swaying of the charmer and his instrument that makes the snake appear passive.

The flute is used simply to create the impression that the music is attracting the snake's attention. However, like all snakes, the cobra is deaf to normal sounds, including those produced by a flute. The snake actually responds to the visual stimuli of the swaying charmer.

It also boosts the confidence of the snake charmer to know that the snake's mouth has often been sewn shut or that the fangs may have been removed. In addition, cobras are night hunters and cannot see well enough in daylight to accurately strike anyway. Also, snake charmers, who are experts at handling snakes, know enough to remain outside the striking distance of the snake as it is coiled up in the basket.

Snake in the Garden of Eden

The Bible makes no mention of a snake in the Garden of Eden. According to Genesis (3:2–14), it was a "serpent" that tempted Eve and convinced her to eat the "fruit of the tree of knowledge of good and evil."

A serpent in antiquity did not usually refer to a snake, but to any creeping thing that was especially noxious or venomous. The term also extended to imaginary creatures. But in any case, the word *snake* is not used to refer to the creature which tempted Eve.

Snakes

Most people seem to have an aversion to snakes and regard them as totally repulsive. Yet the snake's image as one of the most hated creatures is largely based on several common misconceptions.

Contrary to a very popular belief, snakes are not wet and

slimy. The skin is actually quite dry, and feels somewhat like leather. The outer surface is covered with a layer of scales which produce a slightly rough texture. There is also an inner layer of pigmented skin, responsible for coloration and markings, which is covered by the thicker outer skin. As light reflects off the two layers of skin, an appearance of wetness is created.

A snake does not move along the ground as fast as most people think they can travel. This mistaken notion probably stems from the illusion that such a repulsive, legless creature can slither along the ground so smoothly.

Actually, snakes are much slower than they appear. Most travel at speeds of 2 to 4 mph, while the fastest known snake can attain a speed of just 7 mph. These speeds are only about half the average running speed of an adult or normal child.

However, snakes do not normally chase people anyway, since very few are aggressive and most usually flee from humans unless cornered or startled. In fact, snakes actually move very little. Only when hungry, during mating, or to adjust their body temperature will one usually be seen slithering around.

Snakes do not bite or chew their food. They bite only to inject venom into their victim in order to kill it for a meal. Once incapacitated, a snake's victim will only be eaten by being swallowed whole—never by being bitten or chewed. Snakes are also very irregular feeders eating on the average of once every seven to ten days. Larger pythons may eat only seven or eight meals a year.

Most people believe that nearly all snakes are poisonous. The fact is, poisonous snakes account for only about three hundred of the three thousand snake species. It is also true that even when a poisonous snake bites, 25 to 50 percent of the time no venom is even injected.

Deaths from snakebites are far more common worldwide and much less frequent in the United States than most people realize. Although most are accidental bites, surprisingly, thirty-five thousand to forty thousand people die annually from snakebites, mostly in India and Southeast Asia, where an abundance of poisonous snakes exist and much of the population goes barefooted.

In the United States, three thousand to four thousand snakebites occur annually, but deaths vary only from two to fifteen a year because of prompt medical attention. By comparison, more than one thousand people in the U.S. die every year from bee and wasp stings.

Snow

If a survey were conducted, it would likely reveal that most people believe that snow is simply frozen rain. However, in this case, most people would be wrong.

Snow forms in below-freezing temperatures in the atmosphere directly from water vapor by condensing into a very small crystal of ice. It develops into ice crystals from a vapor without ever passing through the liquid state. On the other hand, rain that freezes as it falls is called sleet and not snow. In fact, it is estimated that half of the rain that falls initially forms as snow crystals that melt when falling.

As used in everyday conversation, it is technically incorrect to refer to falling snow or snow on the ground as snow. Snow is actually a tiny, six-sided crystalline ice particle. As they begin falling these crystals usually combine with other crystals to produce the more familiar snowflake.

However, snowflakes are not snow in the true sense, but are large aggregates of ice crystals, often as many as several thousand in a single flake, forming beautiful symmetrical shapes with an infinite variety of patterns. Once on the ground, snow quickly loses its crystalline shape because of heat and pressure, and soon becomes an assemblage of granular ice forms that cannot be considered as true snow either.

Snow is not white, but is transparent and colorless, much like glass or ice. Its characteristic white appearance is caused by the many surfaces in the ice crystals reflecting light which is then seen as white.

Sonic boom

A sonic boom is usually thought to be a sudden event that occurs only at the moment and place where the sound barrier is broken by a supersonic aircraft. This is not true. The boom is actually a continuous wave of compressed air that moves with the aircraft and is heard continuously along its path as long as it maintains speeds in excess of the speed of sound.

At subsonic speeds, the pressure waves created by an aircraft as it flies through the air are able to move ahead of the plane. However, at supersonic speeds they cannot escape in a forward direction since the source is moving faster than the waves themselves. When the speed of an aircraft is greater than the speed of sound, these shock waves produce a sonic boom that continuously travels along behind the aircraft in a cone-shaped path with the nose of the plane at its vertex. The intersection of this cone with the ground is the moving line along which at all points the sonic boom is heard.

The intensity of a sonic boom is relatively unaffected by the speed of the aircraft. Instead, it varies more according to its size, weight, shape, and weather conditions.

SOS

The international distress signal known as SOS does not stand for Save Our Ship, Save Our Soul, or anything else for that matter. The three dots, three dashes, and three dots were chosen simply because they were an easy-to-remember, -transmit, and -understand Morse code signal. It was only a coincidence that it formed the acronym "SOS" in Morse code and triggered the popular imagination to account for its meaning.

SOS, as the radiotelegraph international distress call, is now nearly obsolete due to modern communications technology. The verbal distress signal, Mayday, is today the more common call, since radio and satellite communications are now in such widespread general use. Mayday, incidentally, has nothing to do with "May Day," but is from the French *m'aidez*, meaning "help me."

Sounds at night

The sounds at night of barking dogs, noisy trucks, or a loud party do not seem louder simply because it is otherwise more quiet at night than during the day. Sounds do actually carry better at night, and are more noticeable, due to the elastic properties of air and differences in the refraction of sound at night.

The velocity of sound, which is not a constant, travels through warm air faster than through cold air. During the day, when the upper levels of air are cooler than ground levels, the upper part of a sound wave moves slower than the lower parts. The entire sound beam is consequently refracted upward and slightly away from a ground listener.

At night, the upper levels of air are warmer than ground levels. The sound wave is refracted downward toward a ground listener. It is for this reason that sounds can usually be heard more clearly and over much greater distance at night than during the day.

Spanish Armada

It is fairly well known that the Spanish Armada represented one of the most powerful and invincible naval forces in history. Although it may have been just that, what is not so well known is that the Armada was defeated and nearly destroyed without sinking even a single enemy ship.

The Spanish Armada was an assemblage of one hundred twenty-four ships, eleven hundred guns, and twenty-seven thousand men. In anticipation of an impending invasion by the Armada during the summer of 1588, England amassed one hundred ninety-seven ships with two thousand guns. Under Sir Francis Drake, the English force led the Armada north into the North Sea in a ten-day running battle with their faster, more maneuverable ships and longer range guns.

A fierce storm appeared that battered and sunk many of the larger and heavier Spanish ships, and, combined with over one hundred thousand rounds fired by British guns, the Armada was virtually destroyed without any British ships sunk. Less than half of the ships in the Armada were able to return to Spain, many of them damaged.

The defeat of the Armada is regarded as the most significant naval battle in history. It prevented an invasion of England, was a turning point in naval tactics, and paved the way for colonial expansion throughout the world by England and France, including the colonization of North America.

Spanish fly

Nearly everyone has been intrigued with the idea of Spanish fly. But the alleged aphrodisiac has always been more talked about than available—and for a good reason. Spanish fly is really a dangerous chemical that can cause severe blistering and internal discomfort.

Spanish fly does not really come from flies. Nor is it uniquely

Spanish. The substance, cantharidin, is derived from the golden-green European blister beetle. The chemical is extracted from the dried body, especially the wing sheaths, of the beetle.

Externally, Spanish fly is a powerful blistering agent. Taken internally, it produces diarrhea, vomiting, depression, internal bleeding, and genitourinary pain. This is hardly an amorous response. However, in very small doses, it has been used in medicine as a diuretic.

The nearly legendary properties of Spanish fly have never been adequately explained. In medicine and scientific tests, it has not been shown to demonstrate any qualities whatsoever to deserve its reputation as an aphrodisiac, and its indiscriminate use can result in serious medical problems.

Spareribs

The term *spare* in spareribs does not refer to the sparsity of meat on the bones of this popular food. Instead, it derives from the early Germans who roasted pig ribs on a spit, which was then called a *sper*.

In English, this became *spar*, and by the sixteenth century, the meat was referred to as *sparrib*. In later years, it was simply assumed that *sparrib* came from the separate words *spare* and *rib*, so that the popular version of the meat's name became sparerib.

Speed of sound

It is a misconception that the speed of sound is an absolute constant velocity as is the speed of light. The speed of sound depends on the medium through which it travels and, as a result, has widely varying speeds.

The natural speed with which the molecules making up a substance move determines the speed of sound through that substance. The closer together the molecules, the faster the sound wave passes through it. Thus, sound travels through solids faster than through liquids and through liquids faster than through gases.

In air at sea level and at 0° Centigrade, the speed of sound is 743 mph, but 3,300 mph in water, 11,000 mph in steel, and 13,000 mph in glass. Particularly in air, but also in any substance, temperature also affects the elasticity of the molecules and thereby the speed of sound.

Spiders

A spider is not an insect as most people think. An insect is characterized as having six legs, three body parts, antennae, and wings. But spiders are eight-legged, have just two body segments, and do not possess antennae or wings.

Spiders do not eat their prey as most people believe, either. They drink them. Insects have biting jaws and mouth parts used for tearing and chewing their victims. However, spiders inject an enzyme into their prey that digests and dissolves the tissues. The spider then sucks these juices from their victims for nourishment.

Spruce Goose

The world's largest airplane, the "Spruce Goose," is not made of spruce, nor is "Spruce Goose" the real name of the aircraft. Although constructed entirely of wood, the famous plane built by Howard Hughes is actually made of birch.

As a nickname for the H.2 *Hercules*, Spruce Goose was a name also commonly given to several early all-wooden airplanes. The press picked up this nickname used by airplane enthusiasts, and soon everyone was calling it the "Spruce Goose," although Howard Hughes greatly disliked the name.

Built at a reported cost of forty million dollars, and designed to carry seven hundred troops, it has the largest wingspan of any plane ever built. However, it flew only one time in November 2, 1947, for about one thousand yards at a height of seventy feet. The "Spruce Goose" is now on permanent display in Long Beach, California.

Squash

When used to refer to the popular vegetable, the word *squash* has nothing to do with smashing or squashing the cooked food as the name implies. Squash derives from the early Indian word for the plant, *askutasquash*. It meant simply "something eaten raw." The Pilgrims shortened it to squash, but, unlike the Indians, cooked it before serving.

Squirrels

Contrary to popular belief, squirrels do not really know where they bury and hide their nuts. Although a typical squirrel may hide thousands of nuts a year, it can only remember for about twenty minutes where they are hidden. A squirrel may dig up less than a tenth of the nuts it has actually buried.

To compensate for its bad memory, squirrels have an excellent sense of smell and can find buried nuts for a prime source of food. However, the nuts that the squirrel digs up are seldom the ones it buried. Most squirrels eat any food they can find, regardless of who buried it.

Star of David

The six-pointed star formed by imposing two triangles, one inverted, over each other and now used as the Jewish religious symbol was not originally Jewish. The Star of David is an ancient symbol and has been used for centuries as a secular and magical representation.

The earliest recorded appearance of the design can be traced to its secular use in the thirteenth century. The first formal Jewish use of the Star of David occurred in the seventeenth century when a prayer group adopted the design as its official symbol. Zionists began using it late in the nineteenth century, and it officially became part of the flag of Israel in 1949.

Statue of Liberty

The correct name for the Statue of Liberty is "Liberty Enlightening the World." It was thus originally named by its designer and builder, Frederic Bartholdi, in 1886, and remains today its proper title.

The statue was originally not in New York as most people think. Bedloe Island, now Liberty Island and the site of the Statue, was in New Jersey until the island was ceded to the state of New York. New Jersey later appealed New York's claim to the island, but after it came under the jurisdiction of the United States as a national monument in 1924, the dispute ended.

Although it is believed that the Statue of Liberty was a gift from the French people, only the statue itself was built and paid for by France. The 150-foot pedestal was an American contribution. Lack of funds for the base nearly doomed the entire project until a nationwide campaign among schoolchildren raised the money necessary to finish the base.

The statue is also a miniature Eiffel tower. Its inner supporting structure was designed by Gustave Eiffel and is very similar in construction to the famous Paris tower which he later built.

Statutes of limitations

There is no such thing in capital cases as a statute of limitation. Although most states have statutes of limitations for all other crimes, murder cases are exempt. A suspect may be brought to trial at any time after a murder has been committed.

It is also incorrectly assumed that the statute of limitations is an automatic protection or right. This is not so. In a defense, the right to impose the protection of the statute must be pleaded, or asserted, before the court by a suspect. Failure to do so amounts to a waiver of the privilege, and the statute of limitations will not be applied.

Steam

The cloud of moisture that comes out of a boiling teapot is not steam. Steam is invisible. It is the vapor state of water, and subsequently, pure, dry steam cannot be seen and is completely odorless. Only when it is cooled or mixed with cooler water particles can minute droplets be seen as a condensed, visible cloud or mist.

What is seen coming out the spout of a boiling teapot is merely condensed water droplets attached to the vapor molecules of steam, or the cooled, condensed steam. The little space of "air" usually seen between the spout opening and the mist above it is actually steam.

Stomach digesting food

Contrary to popular belief, food is not digested in the stomach. The stomach plays only a very small role in the process of digestion. Its primary purpose is simply to store ingested food and prepare it for the digestive process.

After food is chewed and mixed with saliva, it is known as bolus. The bolus enters the stomach where hydrochloric acid, pepsin, and other enzymes are mixed with it for three to four hours in preparation for digestion. This mixture is known as chyme, and is occasionally evident as the delightful substance that we vomit. It is the storing and mixing of the chyme that is the primary purpose of the stomach.

Digestion actually takes place in the small intestines. When the chyme is properly prepared, a valve at the bottom of the stomach opens, allowing the contents to enter into the intestines. Bile from the liver combines with pancreatic and intestinal juices which permits the absorption of the mishmash into the intestinal wall. The process of digestion is completed when the large intestine removes water from the undigested residue about twelve hours later and eliminates it from the body about a day later.

Stomach growling

Those rumbling, gurgling, and splashing sounds usually referred to as the stomach growling actually have very little to do with the stomach. Technically called borborygmus, the sounds are also not caused by hunger pains as is usually believed.

Borborygmus is produced in the small and large intestines by the passage of air and liquefied food moving through the intestines during digestion. The mushed-up food and gases, mostly methane, are pushed and squeezed through the convoluted openings, up and down hills, and back and forth about twenty feet through the intestinal tract, creating the familiar and normal sounds of growling. Actually, then, they should be called growling intestines instead of a growling stomach.

As a part of digestion, these sounds are not directly related to the sensation of hunger, although the psychological anticipation of eating can generate increased muscular contractions in the intestines setting off even more rumbling. To distinguish various tones, higher pitched sounds are produced in narrow intestinal passages, while lower rumblings result from lower pressure in large passages.

Strawberries

The "straw" in strawberries has nothing to do with the straw often used in their cultivation. The name comes from an old English description of the runners that the plant throws, or strews, over the ground. They were once referred to as "strayberries," and the name simply changed to strawberries over time.

Strawberries are not even berries. The part we eat is actually a fleshy fruit receptacle, housing on its surface numerous single-seeded fruits. It is an aggregate fruit and is not considered a true berry by botanists.

Suicide rates

Despite the popular belief that suicide rates are highest among the young, especially teenagers, figures indicate that the age group with the highest rate of suicide is above seventy years of age. Suicide rates for those over seventy are about three times the rate for those ten to nineteen years old.

Although the media tend to devote considerable attention to suicide among the young, their rates are, in fact, rather low, particularly for those under fifteen. Suicide rates tend to increase with age and reach a peak for persons seventy to eighty-five years of age. White males over sixty-five have a suicide rate at least fifty times greater than do teenagers under fifteen.

The high rates among the elderly are reflected in suicide rates for major U.S. cities. Tampa–St. Petersburg, Florida, a popular retirement area, has the highest suicide rate of any large American city. Of the six major U.S. cities having the highest suicide rates, four are retirement centers, such as Tampa, Ft. Lauderdale, Miami and Phoenix.

Another common myth associated with suicide is that rates tend to fluctuate based on time of the year. Most people believe that suicides increase in winter months, especially at Christmas, and decline in the summer.

However, statistics show that the opposite is true. Suicide rates are not generally related to bad weather, winter, or holiday depression. Incidence of suicide declines in autumn, reaches its lowest level in midwinter, slowly rises in early spring, and peaks in the summer months of May and June. Suicides at Christmas and Thanksgiving actually show a slight decline before and on the holiday itself, then a gradual climb back to normal rates afterward.

Finally, despite considerable attention to homicide in this country, the fact remains that Americans kill themselves at a higher rate than they do each other. Statistics show that suicides now outnumber murders in the United States each year.

Sun

Most people believe that the sun is simply a big ball of fire. It is not. The sun consists of superheated gases, mostly hydrogen and helium, fueled by atomic reactions at the core, and is quite different from fire.

The sun is, in effect, a giant thermonuclear furnace generated by a continuous sequence of nuclear fusion reactions at its interior. The immense quantities of heat and light produced by this process create the impression from ninety-three million miles away that it is just a fiery mass. But mere fire alone could never create even a billionth of the energy output of the sun.

It also appears from earth that the sun has a definite size and surface. However, this is only an illusion caused by the great distance from which it is viewed and the nature of its composition. Although there does exist a visible edge, or photosphere, to the sun, in reality the sun consists of layers of mixing solar gases with varying temperatures, directions, and visual characteristics.

The apparent surface of the sun is just that—only a visual one. The "surface" is actually a transition region of brighter and darker gases of different densities which create a surface of light rather than one with any definite physical properties. The so-called surface is actually the boundary between the opaque convective zone of the interior and the transparent atmosphere of the sun.

In fact, the "surface" of the sun is known to oscillate back and forth about two miles every two or three hours. The layers immediately above this visual surface, the chromosphere and corona, actually shine by themselves with about the intensity of a full moon since these layers also consist of very hot gases. However, radiance from this area is not usually visible because of the brilliance of the sun's central region. The corona, the outermost layer of solar gases and still part of the sun, extends out into space for millions of miles.

Sunday and the Sabbath

Sunday and the Sabbath are not the same day. The Sabbath was set aside in the fourth of the Ten Commandments as the seventh day of the week, Saturday, and ordained by God as the day of rest for the benefit of his people. Hebrews recognized the Sabbath on Saturday, lasting from sunset on Friday to sunset on Saturday. For Muslims, the Sabbath is Friday.

The early Christian Church soon substituted Sunday as the Sabbath for the Christian day of rest and worship. Its significance came from the resurrection of Christ, which took place on Sunday, the first day of the Jewish week.

Sunrise and sunset

When the sun appears just above the horizon during a sunrise or sunset, it is really not even there at all. Because of refraction of the sun's rays in the atmosphere, the true position of the sun during a sunrise is still three to four minutes away from its apparent location. In a sunset, the sun has already sunk below the line of sight even though it still appears on the horizon.

All sunrises and sunsets, then, are an illusion created by the bending, or refraction, of the light from the sun as it enters the thicker atmosphere of the earth. Consequently, in a sunrise, the rays of light from the sun are bent allowing us to see it before the sun is really there. The opposite occurs in a sunset.

The effect of this refraction, at the equator, is that the sun appears to rise about two minutes earlier than it otherwise would if its rays were not bent, and it delays the image of the sunset also about two minutes. This extension of apparent daylight increases to about four minutes each for sunrise and sunset at higher latitudes. The combined time of the illusion adds about eight minutes of daylight to the day in some locations in the United States.

Sutter's Mill

John Sutter did not discover the gold on his property in 1848 that led to the greatest gold rush and westward migration in U.S. history, nor did he become rich from the discovery.

Gold was actually discovered by Sutter's carpenter, John Marshall, while building a sawmill on the American River. Within a few years, Sutter's workers had all quit to look for gold and squatters had moved in and taken over his land.

Sutter, a Mexican citizen, had established a huge personal empire in California. But the combination of squatters and the unfortunate coincidence of the Mexican government ceding California to the United States, unaware of the discovery of gold, nine days after the discovery meant that Sutter had only questionable title to his fifty thousand acres under U.S. law. He went bankrupt in 1852 and lived off a small California pension the rest of his life.

Swallowing

Food doesn't just fall down the esophagus when we swallow as most people think. Instead, it is gradually pulled down the ten-inch passage to the stomach in five to ten seconds. As a result of this pulling action, it is possible to swallow food while standing on your head.

Swallowing is a complex act for moving food from the mouth to the stomach. A series of closures to temporarily inhibit respiration occur while constrictive and peristaltic waves move the food in rhythmic muscular contractions down the esophagus.

Liquids make the trip in about one second, mostly due to gravity. Semifluids are pulled down in about five seconds, while solids take about ten seconds to be drawn into the stomach.

Swastika

The swastika was not invented by Hitler or Nazi Germany. As a symbol of prosperity and good fortune, the swastika has been widely distributed throughout the ancient and modern world.

The word itself is Sanskrit in origin and has been known to exist in Asia since the third millennium B.C. The pattern has been found on ancient coins, in early Christian art, and was used by Polynesians and North, South, and Central American Indians before Europeans discovered the New World.

The belief by some Germans that the swastika was an Aryan symbol led to its rise in the early 1900s by Austria and Germany as a sign of anti-Semitism. As a result of this association, Hitler placed a black swastika in a white circle on a red cloth when he created a banner for the National Socialist party in 1919. This banner became the official flag of the Third Reich, and was also displayed in all official emblems of both the Nazi state and party.

Sweetbread

Sweetbread is not a bread. It is the thymus or pancreas of a young animal, usually a calf, but sometimes a lamb or pig.

Sweetbread is considered a delicacy, but is low in nutritional value. It is prepared by blanching and cutting the organ into pieces to be fried, served in a sauce, or at times combined into a pie or rice dish.

Swimming after eating

It is not true that swimming immediately after eating causes cramps and that the activity should be avoided for at least one hour following a meal. This is an old wives' tale that is not supported by the evidence.

The American Red Cross does not set a time limit for swimming after eating. They also indicate that there is no scientific evidence proving that cramps are related to swimming and eating. In fact, the Red Cross recommends that people engaged in any physical activity, including swimming, receive proper nourishment before the exercise.

The popular misconception that swimming after eating causes cramps stems from the erroneous belief that digestion draws blood away from the body's muscles. However, even if this were true, some glucose from food becomes available almost immediately after eating to fuel the muscles, regardless of the distribution of the blood supply. It is also true that muscle cramps are, in fact, actually caused by fatigue and chilling rather than by digestion. Swimming after eating is not a real concern, and is demonstrated in the fact that long-distance swimmers actually eat while in the water to avoid fatigue and muscle cramps.

Switzerland

It is popularly believed that Switzerland is a non-military country lacking any significant armed forces. This is not true. Switzerland does not have an army, it *is* an army.

Constitutionally neutral since 1815, it is unlawful for Switzerland to make war, except in self-defense, or to enter into any political alliance with another nation. Switzerland does not belong to the United Nations and has only limited political and economic ties with Europe.

But Switzerland's neutrality must not be confused with its lack of military preparedness. It is one of the few countries that has a program of universal military conscription for all men between the ages of twenty and fifty. Conscientious objectors and the physically unqualified are liable for alternate service or subject to a special tax. Participation requires active duty, frequent inactive training, and reserve duty for twelve years. There is also a large, well-trained women's auxiliary force.

Switzerland has developed extensive mobilization plans and defensive strategies to destroy every tunnel, bridge, and pass leading into the country. Its national militia is supported with highly mobile, modern, well-equipped armored units. Switzerland is the only country in the world where military personnel can take their equipment and ammunition home when not on duty.

The per-capita military spending of Switzerland is higher than many other European countries. According to 1980 figures, Switzerland has a standing army of five hundred eighty thousand men on forty-eight-hour mobilization. This compares to France's three hundred twenty thousand and Britain's one hundred sixty-seven thousand. Switzerland's air force consists of three hundred seventy-seven combat aircraft, while France has four hundred sixty and Canada two hundred forty-seven.

T

"It is impossible to defeat
an ignorant man in an argument."

William McAdoo

Tapeworms

Contrary to popular belief, tapeworms produce surprisingly few physical disturbances in infected individuals. Although often very large in size, tapeworms do not usually cause increased appetites or weight loss as is commonly believed. In fact, tapeworms in the human intestine ordinarily cause no symptoms at all. Mild weight loss or vague abdominal complaints may appear only in severe, multiple infestations. They are usually detected only after segments are found in an infected person's bedding or clothing.

Tapeworms are normally acquired from eating uncooked, infected beef, fish or pork. They are parasitic flatworms that attach themselves to the intestinal wall, range in length from less than an inch to thirty or forty feet, and can live up to thirty years.

Beef tapeworms produce only minor, often unnoticeable symptoms, while tapeworms from fish can cause anemia, since the worm competes for vitamin B12 in the host's body. The most dangerous aspect of tapeworm is from the eggs of infected pork. After ingestion, these eggs develop in the stomach and then pass into the bloodstream to form cysts in muscles and the brain.

However, as with most tapeworms, weight loss and appetite change are not apparent.

Teeth

Although teeth grow in the jaw and contain tissue that resembles bone, they are not actually bone, and are not considered a part of the skeletal system. In terms of histological development, teeth form as an outgrowth or projection of the skin and represent, in vertebrates, the modified descendants of skin plates similar to the scales on a fish. In fact, human teeth and the scales of a shark are much the same in basic structure.

A tooth is composed mostly of a bonelike, but not bony, yellowish substance called dentin, which is much softer than bone. To protect the dentin, a layer of white and very hard enamel, much harder than bone and the hardest substance in the body, surrounds the tooth. It is the appearance and strength of the enamel that has led to the erroneous impression that teeth are bones.

Also, teeth are not really connected to the jaw in any direct way. Instead, they are semipermanently fixed in separate sockets which originate in epidermal layers. Unlike the bones in our bodies, the position of a tooth can be changed, as any teenager with braces demonstrates.

Ten-gallon hat

A ten-gallon hat does not really hold ten gallons. Its true volume is about three-quarters of a gallon, or three quarts.

The descriptive, yet inaccurate, name for these hats is believed to have come from the Spanish term *sombrero galon*, which referred to a fancy, braided hat worn by Mexican vaqueros. In Mexico during the 1800s, it was popular to adorn hats with ribbons and other ornamentation. The bigger the hat, the more embellishments that could be added. These large hats were then jokingly called ten-*galana* hats for the number of decorations on them, and Americanized as "ten-gallon" hats.

Tennis seed

The term *seed*, when used to rank players in tennis tournaments, has nothing to do with plant seeds or anything that grows. The term derives from the word *conceded*, meaning which players are conceded, or assumed, to be the best in ranking for a tournament. Casual usage altered it to *ceded*, and tennis, being the game of propriety that it is, adopted the real word *seed* to replace the improper *ceded*.

Tetanus from rusty nails

The notion that tetanus can be acquired by stepping on a rusty nail is a dangerous misconception. It erroneously associates tetanus with rusty metal, while it obscures the real sources of contact of the disease.

Tetanus, also known as lockjaw, is an acute infectious disease of the nervous system characterized by spasms and painful convulsions. It has nothing to do with the rust or dirt on a nail. Tetanus is acquired from bacteria that originate in the feces of infected animals, especially domestic and farm animals.

The disease can enter the body through any open wound, not just a puncture wound caused by a nail. Any cut or animal bite can infect a person if the tetanus bacteria is present. Of course, a cut from a rusty nail can cause the disease, but not because of the rust.

The tetanus bacteria can be anywhere in the soil or on objects around infected material, particularly near farm manure, and can survive in the ground for many years. The toxin secreted by the tetanus bacteria is extremely potent—one milligram can kill about twenty million people. There is no known treatment for the disease, which is usually fatal. However, tetanus immunizations are safe and effective in preventing the disease.

Thanksgiving

The first Thanksgiving celebrated by the Pilgrims in 1621 consisted of venison, geese, lobster, clams, bass, corn, vegetables, and dried fruits, but turkey and pumpkin pie were probably not served.

The "fowls" and "wild Turkies" described in accounts of the three-day feast enjoyed by the Pilgrims and Indians referred to a variety of ducks, geese, and guinea fowls of the pheasant family, not generally to the wild North American turkey, a bird considerably different than today's common turkey. Also, since the Pilgrims' supply of flour brought on the *Mayflower* had been used up, it was impossible to make a pumpkin pie. Boiled pumpkin was the vegetable of the day.

A day of Thanksgiving was not an idea unique to the early settlers in America. The Pilgrims were well acquainted while in England with annual Thanksgiving celebrations, which had been known throughout history as an ancient and universal custom. In fact, the first Thanksgiving was more like a harvest festival, with none of the accounts mentioning any giving of thanks in solemn, religious piety as it is usually imagined. In keeping with long-standing English custom, Thanksgiving was filled with "revelry, sports, and feasts." However, because of a poor harvest the next year and the arrival of new settlers to feed, the Pilgrims never again celebrated a Thanksgiving.

The custom of a Thanksgiving did not actually catch on quickly in the United States. Although each colony occasionally had Thanksgiving observances at various times and for different reasons, it was not until 1777 that all thirteen colonies practiced such a celebration. Since this observance was connected with the Revolutionary War, it too was a one time event. To unify a hodgepodge of different observances in separate states, Thanksgiving finally became an official national holiday in 1863.

Thoreau, Henry David

The popular perception of Henry David Thoreau is that of a writer who returned to nature by becoming a recluse at Walden Pond. The truth is, Thoreau was never the literary hermit as legend portrays him.

Thoreau's "Walden experiment" lasted just over two years between 1845 and 1847. On land owned by his friend, Ralph Waldo Emerson, and just two miles from the town of Concord, Massachusetts, Thoreau and a small group of friends constructed a cabin. His sole purpose was to achieve a simple life, to be one's own master, and, less philosophically, to have more time to write.

But in day-to-day matters, Thoreau was seldom alone and secluded from the world. He was also generally bored with the whole episode. Thoreau regularly walked to Concord, often to dine with friends and family, and frequently entertained visitors at Walden. In fact, his famous book on the experience, *Walden*, contains a chapter titled "Visitors."

Thoreau's well-known commitment to civil disobedience, leading him to jail rather than paying his taxes to support the

Mexican War and slavery, is also exaggerated. Thoreau spent just one night in jail. He reluctantly returned to Walden when an unidentified lady paid his taxes the next morning.

Thoroughbreds

A Thoroughbred is not just any horse with a pure line of breeding, and it is not similar to the term *pedigree* as used with dogs and other animals. Thoroughbreds are actually a distinct breed of horse, just as are Appaloosa, Arabian, and the quarterhorse.

All modern Thoroughbreds descend from the male line of just three Arabian sires bred with Royal mares in England between 1748 and 1758. Thoroughbreds have sensitive temperaments, are taller, sleeker, and, with their longer strides and stamina, are ideal for racing.

Three wise men

Typical manger scenes displayed at Christmas depict three wise men appearing on camels when Jesus was born. However, these ideas, and many other notions about the wise men, are not supported by the information contained in the Bible.

The Bible (Matthew 2:1–12) never mentions the number of wise men. It only refers to the "wise men from the east." Western religions have placed the number at three, probably since three gifts were given to Jesus by the wise men—gold, frankincense, and myrrh. Eastern religions have claimed that there were twelve wise men. However, the Bible provides no support for any of these assumptions. Even the names now attributed to them, Gaspar, Melchior, and Balthasar, did not appear until the sixth century and have no biblical authority.

The wise men, or magi as they are also called, were not kings as most people believe. They were probably learned men, especially in astrology, who were themselves sent by a king—King Herod.

Contrary to popular belief, there is nothing in the Bible indicating that the wise men rode on camels, or any other animal for that matter. Although they may have ridden, theologians now consider it more likely that they walked.

It is not true, as most people believe, that the wise men appeared at the manger the night Jesus was born. According to the Bible, it was only the shepherds who came to the manger that night. The wise men visited the "house of the child," not the manger. The time of their visit is not agreed upon by biblical authorities, and varies from twelve days to more than a year after the birth of Jesus.

Thumbs-down signal

The thumbs-down sign generally thought to be the signal for death given by ancient Romans in the Coliseum is nearly the opposite of what was actually used. It is now agreed by Latin scholars that a motion with the hand extended and the thumb turned inward and moving slightly upward, somewhat like a dagger being thrust into oneself, was the signal for death. The sign for life was an outward motion of the hand with the thumb extended away from the body.

This misconception arose from a popular 1873 painting by the French artist Jean Gérôme, who made history by showing the thumbs-down sign for the death of the gladiator. The error arose from a mistranslation for the Latin word for "turned in." Gérôme interpreted the Latin to be "turned down." Other artists followed Gérôme's original depiction, and largely from this rendering in Hollywood films, the misconception became perpetuated and popularized.

Tidal wave

A tidal wave has nothing to do with tides, tidal action, or large storms. These unusually large, and often enormously destructive, sea waves are produced by earthquakes, landslides, or volcanic activity on the bottom of the ocean floor.

To avoid this confusion, the Japanese word *tsunami* has now been adopted to replace the term *tidal wave*. Tsunamis are not nearly as dangerous to ships on the open water as they are to shoreline areas, where tremendous damage and loss of life can occur from these fast-moving walls of water.

Tides

Tides do not occur only as the result of the moon's gravitational effect on the earth. Nor do they involve just the oceans. The sun creates its own tidal movements, and the combined forces of the moon and sun affect the water, land, atmosphere, and even the human body.

Because the moon's gravitational pull is more than twice that of the sun, solar tides are considerably smaller and occur less frequently than tides produced by the moon. The sun's effect on tides is primarily in combination with that of the moon as variations in their relative positions produce variations in tidal range. Exceptionally high "spring tides" and low "neap tides" occur twice monthly when the sun and moon are in aligned or opposite positions.

The combined gravitational forces of the sun and moon also produce "tides" on the surface of the land and on the atmosphere. The North American continent may rise at times as much as six inches due to these effects. Even lakes are affected, with measurable changes in larger lakes amounting to several inches. The earth's atmosphere is known to bulge several miles due to tidal forces. Also, the human body will gain and lose weight, although slight, in tune to the cycles of the tides. Even the female menstrual cycle, although not in synchronization, is nevertheless identical to the twenty-eight-day lunar cycle.

Titanic

The sinking of the *Titanic* was not the worst disaster in maritime history as is commonly believed. The sinking of the German vessel *Wilhelm Gustloff* by a Russian submarine in the Baltic Sea in 1945 resulted in the death and drowning of over seventy-seven hundred people, mostly women and children. This toll was nearly five times the 1,513 lives lost in the *Titanic* sinking.

It is also popularly believed that the hymn "Nearer, my God, to Thee" was played by the *Titanic's* band as the ship sank. This, too, it not true. As the ship took on water and it steadily became apparent that the *Titanic* would sink, the band played ragtime. Once the bridge entered the water, the hymn "Autumn" was played. However, the song ended abruptly as the huge ship turned and slipped beneath the surface, taking the bandsmen who had played until the very end.

Toadstools

The often inedible or even poisonous mushroomlike fungi are not called toadstools because toads actually use them as stools. The word derives from the German *tod* and *stuhl*, meaning "death stool," in reference to the poisonous nature of many of these fungi.

Tongue-tie

Tongue-tie is not just a popular expression used to describe the psychological experience of being speechless. Tongue-tie, or ankyloglissia, is a specific physical malady in which the muscle tissue under the tongue is attached to the gums behind the lower front teeth instead of to the floor of the mouth. Tongue-tie restricts the mobility of the tongue, interferes with swallowing, and makes speech very difficult.

Tower of London

The Tower of London is not just a single tower as its name suggests. It is a large, ancient, royal fortress in London occupying nearly thirteen acres.

Dating from the year 1078, the original structure was called the White Tower, although it was then only five stories tall. It became known as simply the Tower, and when a whole fortress grew up around it, the name Tower of London was applied to the entire walled-in complex.

The Tower of London was a royal palace until the seventeenth century. It is now a barracks, armory, and a museum containing the famed British crown jewels.

Tree growth

It would seem logical to most people to think that the trunk, branches, leaves, and any other material comprising a tree come out from the ground as the tree grows. However, this impression is not entirely correct. A far greater portion of a tree, or any other plant for that matter, actually comes from the air and not the ground.

Between 90 and 95 percent of a tree's nutrition is taken from the atmosphere. Plant fiber and tissue are formed when chlorophyll, aided by sunlight, combines with carbon dioxide from the air to produce starches, sugars, and other materials necessary for growth. However, only water and a small but essential amount of minerals in the water come from the soil. In simple terms, a plant breathes and eats through its leaves from the air and drinks from the ground with its roots.

Contrary to popular opinion, when a tree grows, it does not rise up from the ground with all parts continuously moving higher. Growth only occurs upward from existing material at the ends of branches or at the top of the tree. An existing branch or romantically carved heart in a trunk will never be any higher above the ground even as the tree grows taller.

Tree sap

The little spots that appear on car windows when parked under most deciduous trees are not tree sap. This actually is the excretory material from little insects in the tree called aphids. This excretory product is referred to as honeydew. It is a sweet, sticky digestive leftover from aphids, and is a prime source of food for ants.

Truck farming

Truck farming has nothing to do with the truck as a form of motor transportation used to deliver crops to market. Truck farm refers to garden produce and commodities grown for sale in the market. The word *truck* used in this manner is a derivative of an old French word *troque*, meaning "for barter." The large, motorized transport vehicle known as a truck comes from the Greek word *trochos*, meaning "wheel."

Truck farms have also been around considerably longer than the motor truck. The truck farm, and referred to as such, appeared in 1785 in the United States. Most fresh vegetables grown in the country are now produced on farms of this type.

Truman, Harry

Harry S Truman did have a middle name. It was just the letter S with no period. Although it is often written as Harry S. Truman, it is not correct to do so.

After his birth, Truman's parents could not agree on which of Harry's grandfathers to honor, Anderson Shippe Truman or Solomon Young. They decided to give him the letter S without a period after it as his official middle name to recognize both men.

Truth is stranger than fiction

Lord Byron did not write, "Truth is stranger than fiction." His actual words were, " 'Tis strange—but true; for truth is always strange—stranger than fiction."

Tuberculosis

Contrary to popular belief, tuberculosis is not a disease that only affects the lungs. Although tuberculosis of the lungs is the most common type in the United States, comprising 90 percent of the active human cases, the infectious bacteria can establish themselves in every human tissue or organ.

Because the disease is usually acquired by the inhalation or ingestion of infected material, the lungs and intestines are the most likely locations of the illness. However, tuberculosis is a group of infectious diseases, and only because of modern drugs are the other types so uncommon in developed countries.

Tulips

Tulips did not originate in Holland. Instead, they are native to Central Asia, particularly Turkey, where they were introduced into Europe and Holland during the middle of the sixteenth century. In fact, the word *tulip* is not even Dutch, but comes from the Turkish word *tuliband*.

After arriving in Europe, the tulip's popularity increased rapidly, and a tulip mania swept Holland in 1634. As a result of this tulip craze, Holland became established as the center for tulips throughout the world. Wild speculation in tulip-bulb prices led to enormous amounts of money often paid for individual bulbs. The highest recorded price then paid for a single bulb was fifty-two hundred dollars.

Nowadays, the Netherlands, Belgium, and England are the tulip-growing centers of the world. Most of the four thousand kinds of garden tulips now grown have been the product of years of breeding and selection. In fact, it is known that today's tulips are completely horticultural in origin and that no existing wild species is a source of any current garden tulip.

Turkeys

The familiar bird referred to as a turkey has little connection with the country of the same name. The term is derived from the bird's circuitous route around the world lasting a hundred years and ending up transplanted nearly where it began.

There are now two kinds of birds in the United States called a turkey. One is the North American wild turkey, which is now nearly extinct in much of the country, and the other is the domestic, or common, turkey.

In the sixteenth century, Spanish conquistadores brought back to Spain some North American wild birds that they had seen the Aztecs hunt and, to a limited extent, domesticate. In Europe, these birds were confused with another bird originally called the Guinea fowl, which originated in Guinea, West Africa.

This African fowl had been brought to Europe by Portuguese travelers through Turkey and, for reasons not completely understood, the Guinea fowl acquired the name *turkey*. As the wild bird from America spread throughout Europe and to England, it also acquired this name.

However, it was in England where the North American bird was bred into several new and different domesticated varieties, while still retaining the name *turkey-cock*. Nearly a century later, English colonists in America encountered the wild North American bird and misnamed it the turkey because of its similar appearance to their domestic varieties.

The North American wild turkey became extinct in New England by the mid 1800s, and is now gone from the entire eastern United States. Many so-called wild turkeys are, in reality, actually varieties of escaped domestic birds.

Twain, Mark

The familiar saying, "Everybody talks about the weather, but nobody does anything about it," is usually attributed to Mark Twain. But the phrase was actually first written in an editorial in the *Hartford Courant* by his friend and cowriter Charles Warner. Despite repeated attempts to give proper credit to Warner, Twain is incorrectly recognized for originating the remark.

Twelve-meter yachts

America's Cup sailboats, referred to as twelve-meter yachts, have no one feature that is twelve meters in length. A twelve-meter boat is not twelve meters long, and any part of the boat this size is twelve meters only by coincidence.

The designation as a twelve-meter yacht is actually the result of a complicated formula which is as follows: length plus twice the girth difference plus the square root of the sail area minus freeboard plus 2.37 equals twelve meters. The winner of the 1987 America's Cup, the *Stars and Stripes*, has an overall length of about eighteen meters, but is classified by this formula as a twelve-meter boat.

Twelve-meter boats are not the fastest sailing boats either. Although the America's Cup has come to represent yacht-racing superiority, many other classes of sailing yachts and boats are actually faster than twelve-meter sailboats.

Twenty-four dollars for Manhattan

Nearly everyone has heard the story that Manhattan Island was purchased from the Indians for twenty-four dollars. Although Peter Minuit did execute a deed of purchase for the land in 1626 with the local Indians, no money of any kind was ever involved. Only an unknown quantity of trinkets and goods valued by the Dutch at sixty guilders was exchanged in the transaction. For this reason, no one really knows what the real purchase price was in dollars. In fact, there was no such thing as a dollar for another one hundred fifty years.

It was not until the 1840s that a New York newspaper writer speculated on the value of the deal in American dollars. He somehow arrived at the amount of twenty-four dollars for the value of the goods traded two hundred years earlier, despite fact that no record was ever made by the Dutch listing the specific items traded. The twenty-four dollars estimate became established in popular literature and has persisted to this day with little question.

Twilight

The term *twilight* is commonly thought to mean the period of incomplete darkness in the evening after the sun is below the horizon. However, twilight also correctly refers to the period between full night and sunrise in the morning. Both morning and evening twilight are caused by the reflection of sunlight from the upper levels of the atmosphere that are illuminated before or after the sun is visible.

Two-by-fours

The familiar piece of lumber known as a two-by-four is not, and never has been, two inches by four inches. The size of a standard two-by-four is one-and-one-half inches by three-and-one-half inches. Similarly, all other board sizes are actually smaller than their apparent dimensions.

But contrary to popular belief, this situation is not the result of the lumber industry having gradually reduced the size of boards through the years in order to increase profits. As a long-standing and accepted practice in the industry, logs are first roughly cut to ''nominal'' sizes which indicate their retail measurements, such as a two-by-four. These rough surfaces are then planed and smoothed, which reduces their dimensions considerably. However, the traditional use of nominal dimensions for lumber is a widely accepted convention in the industry and poses no problems to the knowledgeable user of lumber, either the craftsman or carpenter.

Typhoid Mary

The infamous disease carrier known as Typhoid Mary was not the cause of a major outbreak of typhoid fever as most people think. Mary Mallon, better known as Typhoid Mary, was the direct cause of just fifty-one original cases of typhoid fever and only three deaths during the early 1900s.

As a carrier, Typhoid Mary was immune to the typhus bacteria, but could pass on the disease to other people. Following an outbreak of the disease in New York City, Mary Mallon was identified by health authorities as the carrier.

However, she managed to elude authorities for eight years while working as a cook and a domestic. Finally taken into custody, she was committed by the New York City Health Department, despite an appeal to the U.S. Supreme Court, to an isolation center on New York's North Island where she died thirty years later of a stroke.

U–V

Unleaded gasoline

Most people think that unleaded gasoline should cost less and not more than regular gasoline, since refiners do not have to add lead in the first place, making it cheaper to produce. However, this assumption is not necessarily correct.

Tetraethyl lead is added to regular gasoline to improve its octane rating in order to reduce engine knocking. Because the use of lead in motor fuels is now restricted due to environmental hazards, gasoline without lead results in excessive engine knocking in today's high compression engines.

Since there are no economical alternatives to lead as an anti-knock compound in gasoline to solve this problem, refiners are forced to either produce a purer and more expensive product, or add more costly chemicals to increase the quality and octane rating of gasoline. In either case, the savings made by not adding lead are more than offset by the costs involved with these other methods.

Van Gogh, Vincent

Vincent van Gogh did not cut off his ear. The famous expressionist artist only sliced off a portion of his left ear lobe which erroneously has led to stories of a more serious injury.

The event followed two months of hard work, immoderate drinking, and an argument the day before with his friend and fellow painter Paul Gauguin. Van Gogh's deteriorating mental condition precipitated the self-mutilation on December 23, 1888. Although just a small part of the lobe was cut off, it is true that he wrapped it in paper and presented it to a local prostitute.

Van Gogh spent most of his life, not as a painter, but as an art dealer, schoolteacher, and preacher. He painted for only ten years, during which he completed hundreds of works and revolutionized art. Even though many are now worth millions of dollars, he sold just one painting during his lifetime.

Verbal

The word *verbal* does not refer to just spoken words. *Verbal* is defined as "of, in, or having to do with words of any kind." It includes spoken words as well as those that are written. Thus, the words on this page are defined as verbal.

Verbal and oral are often thought of as meaning the same thing, while verbal is usually contrasted in meaning to written words. These ideas are incorrect. Oral and written words are simply specific kinds of words that are both verbal. In its correct meaning, verbal is actually distinguished from abstract thoughts, ideas, or actions.

Vespucci, Amerigo

It is not true that America was named after an Italian mapmaker simply because he placed his own name on maps of the New World. Although Amerigo Vespucci, like Columbus, had never even seen the North American continent, the newly discovered land was named in his honor largely because of popular ignorance of his actual accomplishments.

Unlike Columbus, Vespucci was at least the first to realize that a new continent had been discovered. A merchant and explorer, Vespucci made several journeys along the eastern coast of South America between 1497 and 1504. Few reliable documents exist of his explorations, which have caused some historians to speculate that Vespucci was an opportunist, if not a liar. However, enough is known of his journeys to credit him with first establishing proof of the existence of a new continent.

Following his voyages, a geographer and mapmaker named Martin Woldseemuller issued maps in 1507 showing the new continent of South America, and proposed naming it after its discoverer, Amerigo. The name "America" became popular with the public, and it was later commonly extended to North America as people became aware of its existence, even though Vespucci never even saw the North American continent.

Vietnam causalities

Despite the fact that the Vietnam War produced large numbers of battle deaths, the extraordinary truth is that while the war was in progress, almost twice as many Americans were killed in the United States by firearms as were killed in Southeast Asia. During the war years of 1963 to 1973, there were 46,752 battle deaths reported in the Vietnam War. This compares to 84,633 Americans killed by firearms on the "homefront" during the same period. In addition, since 1900, there have been more Americans murdered with handguns in the United States than the number of American servicemen killed in all foreign wars combined.

Volcanoes

The lava that erupts from volcanoes does not come from the center of the earth as is commonly believed. Because the earth's mantle is about eighteen hundred miles thick, it would not be possible for any type of molten material to travel that distance through the solid rock of the earth's interior and remain a liquid.

The lava actually originates as magma in pockets of molten rock at depths no greater than twenty miles below the surface of the earth. These reservoirs are relatively small in size, and are probably due to the liquefying of local basalt rock formations. The heat and pressure, even at these depths, would be sufficient to melt these rocks, especially in areas where mountains are forming as continental plates are crushing into each other.

Vomiting

Despite the wretched sensation produced in the stomach when vomiting, the stomach actually plays virtually no role in the physical act of ejecting undigested matter through the mouth. In addition, it is not just the contents of the stomach that are forced out during vomiting, but also much of the material from the upper small intestine as well.

Vomiting is a very complex act controlled by a vomiting center at the base of the brain. The first stage is strong, reverse contractions of the upper small intestine followed by contractions of the lower portion of the stomach. These successive contractions force the partially digested material from the small intestine and lower stomach into the main body of the stomach.

The stomach remains completely relaxed while abdominal muscles around it and the diaphragm push in unison to compress the stomach and squeeze out the contents. Respiration is, in this rare instance, involuntarily stopped to prevent aspiration of the vomit into the lungs. The digestive tract, from almost the beginning of the large intestine, up ten feet of small intestine and into the stomach, is emptied in this way.

W–X–Y–Z

"An idea or belief is not necessarily true or false
because your parents, your friends,
or you or your children have believed it."

Abel J. Jones

Wagon trains

Although wagon trains in westward expeditions did pull into
a large circle at night, it was not for the purpose of creating a
protective wall against possible Indian attack. Rather, the circular formation familiar to viewers of old western movies was
actually to form a corral to keep in the horses, mules, and oxen.
Of course, it also provided excellent protection from attack.

Wagon trains first began in the 1820s and were used extensively, not to move settlers, but to transport freight. The movement of people did not begin until after 1841. Also, horses
were seldom used to pull the wagons. Instead, oxen and mules
were the usual draft animal.

Although death on the westward trail was a way of life, the
danger from Indians has been much exaggerated in folk history.
Of about three hundred thousand deaths believed to have taken
place on wagon trains heading west, only three hundred sixty-
two deaths have ever been confirmed as resulting from Indian
attack. By far, the greatest killer on the trail was disease.

War is hell

William Tecumseh Sherman did not say, ''War is hell.'' This popular version of his speech was created through the process of folk editing from his actual words. In speaking before a group of war veterans Sherman said, ''There is many a boy here today who looks on war as all glory, but, boys, it is all hell.'' The remark was met with an outburst of applause.

Warranties

Although most consumers look upon the written warranty that comes with a purchased product as a benefit, the fact is these expressed product warranties actually are intended to protect the manufacturer and to limit the duration of the protection for the consumer. Without an expressed, limited warranty, there usually exists an implied warranty that generally is broader in coverage.

Under the Uniform Commercial Code, the basic law of sales in every state except Louisiana, consumer purchases are protected by implied warranties of merchantability and fitness. The law implies that a product is fit to be sold and used for its ordinary, intended purpose in terms of design, quality, and safety.

However, these implied warranties can be limited for duration and, to some extent, coverage by reasonable, expressed warranties, such as a ''limited one-year warranty.'' These expressed warranties are intended to protect the manufacturer by limiting the coverage of the implied warranty.

Washington and the cherry tree

The popular story of George Washington chopping down the cherry tree and, in the process, displaying his honesty is simply a delightful example of American folklore. There is no basis in fact for the tale.

The account derives from the first published biography of George Washington. However, not written as a serious essay, this biography was actually the cheerful prose, largely fictitious, of Mason Locke Weems, better known as Parson Weems. Weems idolized Washington in life and, with his biography, intended to glorify his reputation in death.

Weems was known to resort to historical reconstruction, and his first volume was little more than a complimentary sketch of

Washington written two months after his death. The tree-chopping story did not even appear until eight years later in the sixth edition of the book.

There is no other historical evidence to support Weems's legend. Since Washington's father died when George was just eleven years old and because Weems did not even begin his profile until after Washington had died, there seem to have been few reliable sources for the information.

Although it is popularly believed that Washington chopped down the cherry tree, the story by Weems did not even mention cutting down a tree. Instead, the account only says that young George "hacked and barked it so the tree probably never got the better of it."

Washington's Birthday

George Washington was not born on Washington's Birthday. This oddity was not the fault of Washington's mother, but resulted from the conversion to the Gregorian calendar during the middle of Washington's life.

By the sixteenth century, astronomers had observed a significant discrepancy between the existing Julian calendar, which was instituted in 46 B.C., and the true solar year. Consequently, in 1582, Pope Gregory XIII implemented a revised calendar, which came to be known as the Gregorian, or New Style, calendar. It required the elimination of ten days to rectify the accumulated celestial error, and included the present system of leap years to maintain its accuracy.

In addition, the day usually celebrated as the first day of the new year varied from one country to another. In colonial America, as elsewhere, New Year's Day had been observed on March 25. The Gregorian calendar also restored January 1 as the first day of the year.

However, not all, in fact not many, countries immediately adopted the new system. Britain and her colonies did not switch until 1752, at which time it had become necessary to eliminate eleven days due to an even greater error in the Julian calendar.

This conversion in 1752 was made during the twentieth year of Washington's life. As a result, although he had been born on February 11, 1731 Old Style, the date became February 22, 1732 New Style, when colonial Virginia adopted the new calendar.

Washington officially celebrated his birthday on February 11 until 1796, the year he left the presidency, when he began to use the February 22 New Style date for some reason. However, dates for events that occurred prior to the conversion of the Gregorian calendar were generally not converted. Most events in Washington's life, as well as other historical incidents, are unconverted Old Style dates, except for his birth date, which is usually given in New Style but not so specified.

Washington's Farewell Address

George Washington's Farewell Address is generally believed to have been delivered as an oral valediction. It was not. His famous address given upon leaving public life was presented to the people only through the press on September 17, 1796. The address, which became a major influence on American politics, was largely written by Alexander Hamilton as an attempt to counter the presidential candidacy of Thomas Jefferson.

Watch jewels

The jewels in a so-called jeweled watch are really synthetic materials that are worth only a small mount of money. Although diamonds and sapphires were originally used in the early 1700s, by the late 1800s they had commonly been replaced by synthetic "jewels." Today, nearly all jeweled watches use synthetic materials.

In the modern stem-wind watch, there are between seven and twenty-three jewels used as bearings at key friction points. They affect quality and durability by reducing wear on the various levers, balance wheels, and rollers.

Synthetic jewels are usually produced from fused powdered alumina. They are highly polished, precisely sized, and held in place only by friction. But the intrinsic value of these "jewels" is negligible.

Watt, James

The steam engine was not invented by James Watt. His contribution was to improve existing engines, and in so doing, became one of the most important figures in the Industrial Revolution.

Early steam engines had been devised by at least 1698, and

possibly as early as 1639. In 1711, Newcomen had improved these somewhat-primitive machines into a fairly practical source of steam power.

While repairing a Newcomen steam engine in 1764, Watt realized that a more efficient engine could be made if the steam were condensed in a separate chamber. By 1769, Watt had completed his steam engine, which greatly improved the power and efficiency of older models. In so doing, he created the source of power that powered the Industrial Revolution.

Waves

Despite the illusion that waves seem to move along the surface of water, they are actually not horizontally moving lines of water at all. In a wave, there is virtually no transport of the water itself. The wave's action is essentially a circular pushing motion through and under the water.

An object floating on the surface in open water does not get pushed along by a wave. It will move forward with the wave crest, but reverse its motion in the trough. Actually, a floating object in open water will follow a circular vertical orbit. One circle is completed with the passage of each wave, but no horizontal motion occurs except that produced by the wind or near the shore where the circular flow is interrupted as the wave breaks.

Contributing to the impression that waves move water horizontally along the surface is the apparent movement of a surfboard rider. However, as waves approach the land, friction from the seafloor with the wave's motion beneath the surface disrupts the normal motion of the wave, causing the top to pitch forward as a breaker. This combines with gravity, pulling the surfboard down while the wave crest is pushing it upward. These forces produce the familiar horizontal motion of the surfer.

Webster's Dictionary

Any dictionary having the name Webster in the title has nothing to do with the first American dictionary created by Noah Webster. None of these books are put out by the same company that published Webster's original dictionary, nor are they current authorized editions of the original publisher.

Like the title of any other book, the name Webster cannot be copyrighted in a title. Anyone can, and some do, publish a dictionary and call it *Webster's Dictionary*, just as anyone could write a book about tornadoes and title it *Gone With the Wind*.

Actually, Webster's first dictionary did not even use his own name. He titled it, *The American Dictionary of the English Language*.

Weeks in a year

Everyone thinks that there are 52 weeks in a year. This is not entirely true. 52 weeks multiplied by seven days in a week equals only 364 days. Yet there are, of course, 365 days in a year. So the year actually contains 52 weeks and one day, and 52 weeks and two days in a leap year.

Weight of feathers and gold

A pound of feathers does weigh more than a pound of gold. This is because there are two systems for measuring weight. One is the avoirdupois pound, which contains sixteen ounces. The other is the troy-weight pound, containing only twelve ounces.

Feathers, and most other large and course commodities, are measured by avoirdupois weight. Gold, and other precious metals and stones, are measured by troy weight. Thus, a pound of feathers actually weighs four ounces more than a pound of gold.

Weissmuller, Johnny

Johnny Weissmuller's famous and incredible Tarzan of the Apes call in his Tarzan films was not entirely his own. It was a combination of several different sounds, including his own scream, a high C hit by a soprano, and a hyena's howl recorded on tape and played backward.

Wells Fargo

Although the name *Wells Fargo* is associated with the history and folklore of the American west, both Henry Wells and William Fargo were Easterners who lived in New York. Formed in 1852 after the gold rush, Wells Fargo became the largest stagecoach network in the United States. But Wells went west just one time, and Fargo never ventured from his New York home.

Whistler's Mother

James Whistler's famous painting, now hanging in the Louvre in Paris, is not, and never has been, titled *Whistler's Mother*. It was, indeed, a portrait of his mother, Anna McNeill Whistler, but it was originally titled *An Arrangement in Gray and Black*. Following its popularity, Whistler retitled it *Portrait of My Mother*.

Witch burning at Salem

It is commonly believed that many witches were burned to death at the stake during the Salem, Massachusetts witch hunts, and that witch burning was carried on for a considerable length of time. The fact is, neither of these beliefs are true.

No witches were ever burned to death at Salem. During the infamous witch hunts of 1692, one hundred fifty accused people were arrested and nineteen were executed as "witches and wizards." Of those executed, eighteen were hanged and one was crushed to death by stones. Ten others were convicted but not executed. Two accused dogs were also put to death.

The witch-hunting hysteria lasted for only a few months during the year 1692. It began when several young girls accused a West Indian slave, known for his tales of voodoo, of bewitching them. Since many English and Americans at the time believed in witches, their story attracted considerable attention. A special court was convened to try the suspected witches, but it ignored both existing English judiciary rules and the wise clerical advice presented to convict some of the accused as witches.

The madness ended a few months later when the governor dissolved the court. Twenty years later, the Massachusetts legislature made reparations to the heirs of the executed victims.

Wolves

Wolves are not the hostile, vicious, or dangerous animals that most people think they are. Their behavior is much like the domestic dog, and aggressive only in connection with procuring food or protecting their young, as is the case with many animals. The wolf can be tamed and domesticated to live as a house pet as easily as any dog. In fact, all dogs are descended from wolves within the last twelve thousand years and are not significantly different from wolves in behavioral characteristics.

Wolves are highly gregarious animals with well-developed family systems and possessing a complex social organization. Despite occasional pack hunting, the wolves' diet generally consists of field mice, fish, and carrion. Whatever deer or caribou the wolf eats are usually the sick, old or injured culled from the herd. There has never been a single verified case of a healthy wolf attacking a human in North America.

Nor is the term *wolf*, when applied to a human male and used symbolically to refer to an aggressive womanizer, accurate. The male wolf mates for life, is completely monogamous, and, unlike most males in the animal world, helps in the rearing of the pups.

World War I deaths

In spite of the popular image of combat in World War I involving trench warfare, poison gases, and legions of infantry engaged in pitched battles, more U.S. Army soldiers were killed as the direct result of disease, primarily influenza, than died in action. Of the nearly one hundred thirteen thousand Americans who lost their lives in World War I, more than half, or almost sixty-three thousand, died from disease. In fact, until the end of World War I, disease-related deaths outnumbered battle deaths in every war throughout history.

World's highest mountain

Depending on how you look at it, Mount Everest is not the highest mountain in the world. Measured from the center of the earth, Chimborazo, in the Ecuadorian Andes of South America, is the point on the earth's surface that sticks out farthest into the atmosphere.

As measured from sea level, Everest is higher compared to Chimborazo—29,028 feet to 20,561 feet. However, because the earth is not a perfect sphere, but bulges at the equator by several miles, sea level at the equator is actually about fourteen miles farther away from the center of the earth than at the north or south poles.

Because Chimborazo is located less than 2°, or ninety-eight miles, from the equator, compared to about 28° degrees, or more than fifteen hundred miles, from the equator for Everest,

Chimborazo is actually 7,057 feet farther from the center of the earth than is the summit of Mount Everest.

Actually, the world's tallest mountain is usually not even considered a mountain at all. From base to peak, Mauna Kea, a peak in the Hawaiian Trough of the Pacific Ocean and part of the Hawaiian Islands, has a height of 33,476 feet, of which 13,796 feet are above water. For this reason, Mauna Kea is generally regarded as an island instead of a mountain.

Wright, Orville and Wilbur

The first airplane flight made by Orville and Wilbur Wright is considered a momentous and historic event, and the two fliers are now regarded as legendary heroes. However, the belief that the Wright brothers were immediately accorded recognition and fame for their flight is not exactly the way things turned out for the two men.

Following their first flight in 1903, the Wright brothers experienced an exasperating and fruitless attempt to have their accomplishment recognized and accepted by a skeptical world. In part, this was due to the continuing debate as to who, in fact, actually made the first airplane flight. Several other claims, some legitimate, confused the public. However, historians now agree that for a manned, self-powered takeoff with sustained, controlled flight in a heavier-than-air craft, the Wright brothers were the first.

In addition, in 1903, the prevailing attitude toward men flying was simply one of indifference and skepticism that flight was anything more than a stunt. There seemed to be no practical value to the airplane, especially the hazardous contraptions first flown. Even the army refused to believe or attach any significance to the Wright brothers' first flights.

After considerably improving their airplane between 1903 and 1905, the Wrights still received little attention, acclaim, or profit from their invention. Because of this indifference, they completely gave up flying for three years until 1908.

Still convinced that Americans had no interest in their flying machine, the Wrights went to Europe, where they performed dozens of exhibition flights in France. The French became enthusiastic about flying, and the interest soon spread to the United States. By 1909, six years after the first flight, the army signed a contract with the Wrights, finally enabling them to form their own airplane company.

However, complete recognition for their historic flight was still nearly forty years away. Even the Smithsonian museum erroneously had failed to credit the Wrights with the first manned airplane flight. Their original flying machine was not even accepted by the Smithsonian until 1948, when it was returned from a London museum, which had previously been the only one interested in displaying it.

Writer's cramp

Writer's cramp is usually thought to be a nonexistent medical term used jokingly by students to refer to a tired, sore hand caused by too much writing. However, writer's cramp is, in fact, a real condition characterized by the spastic inability to voluntarily control the hand as a result of excessive writing. It is a paralysis of the muscles of the thumb and the two adjoining fingers with no specific organic disease, which prevents a person from holding a pen to write. But strangely, all other uses of the hand remain unaffected.

Identified as early as 1830, writer's cramp is also known as scrivener's palsy and graphospasm. Rest of up to six months can be needed to return normal use of the hand for writing. However, the condition is now less common as an occupational neurosis due to the typewriter and other printing devices.

Yankee Doodle

"Yankee Doodle," the famous colonial Revolutionary marching song, and one of America's traditional patriotic tunes, was originally a British war ballad intended to make fun of, slander, and chide the colonists for their hapless disarray. Now regarded mostly as a children's song, "Yankee Doodle" was once considered almost as a national anthem that embodied the spirit of American patriotism.

The song originated as a British tune from the French and Indian War. Although its authorship is clouded in folklore, its words were believed to have been written by a British surgeon, Dr. Richard Shackbury. However, many other versions of the song were commonly sung, and new lyrics were regularly improvised.

The British sang "Yankee Doodle" derisively at the colonists, but following several early military successes by the Americans during the Revolutionary War, the colonists took the song and defiantly and proudly played it back to the British. The upstart Americans enjoyed this irony so much that "Yankee Doodle" instantly became the unofficial colonial national anthem. In fact, it was played by Washington's troops during the ceremonies at the British surrender to end the war.

The familiar verse from "Yankee Doodle," "Stuck a feather in his cap, And called it macaroni," usually confuses most people. It does not refer to pasta. Macaroni refers to the Macaroni Club in London, which was an organization of effete young men who wished to bring European elegance to England. The British were poking fun at the American bumpkins for trying to be elegant Macaroni dandies by sticking feathers in their caps.

Zip codes

The lowest Postal Service zip code, which is an acronym for Zone Improvement Plan, is not 00001 as one might expect. The Readers Digest Association in Pleasantville, New York, has the lowest zip code in the U.S. Postal Service—00401. The highest zip code, although close to 99999, is Ketchikan, Alaska—99950.

Bibliography

A complete bibliography for a book intended for the general reading public is not usually necessary. In this case, it is also not practical. Because more than 590 different topics were researched, literally hundreds of reference sources were used. Although the majority of fallacies presented in this book are disproved with information that is found in readily available encyclopedias and books, many other questions were not so easily answered. Everything from complex medical texts to Chinese cookbooks was used. Also, information received from nearly fifty professional associations and societies proved invaluable when other sources were incomplete.

However, since much of the information contained in this book contradicts what many people believe, a partial bibliography will be presented. The following represents the primary, but certainly not complete, list of reference sources.

Encyclopedia Britannica
Encyclopedia Americana

Both of these excellent sources can, and did, answer almost any question, disproved most popular misconceptions, and provided a wealth of factual information.

Fabulous Fallacies, Tad Tuleja, 1982
The Dictionary of Misinformation, Tom Burnam, 1975

These are the only recent books dealing with popular fallacies. Thanks especially to Mr. Burnam for resurrecting the popular approach to misinformation.

266

A Dictionary of Common Fallacies, Philip Ward, 1978
Common Fallacies Regarding United States History, Orville
  Lindquist, 1948
Popular Fallacies, A. S. Ackerman, 1950
The Prevalence of Nonsense, Ashley Montagu and Edward Dar-
  ling, 1967

These thorough but outdated books demonstrate the fact that
one generation's fallacy is another's nonsense. Nevertheless,
without the efforts of the authors, maybe these notions would
still be our misconceptions.

Bartlett's Familiar Quotations
I Hear America Talking, Stuart Flexner, 1976
Information Please Almanac, 1988
Morris Dictionary of Word and Phrase Origin, William and
  Mary Morris, 1977

Some dependable and useful information was provided in these
books.

American Trivia, Jay Hyams and Kathy Smith, 1983
Book of Facts, Isaac Asimov, 1981
Browsers Book of Beginnings, Charles Panati, 1984
Can Elephants Swim?, Robert M. Jones, 1967
Imponderables, David Feldman, 1986
Information Roundup, George Stimpson, 1948
Polar Bears Like It Hot, Joseph Rosenbloom, 1980
2201 Fascinating Facts, David Louis, 1983
The Book of Strange Facts and Useless Information, Scott Mor-
  ris, 1979
The Ignorance Book, Webb Garrison, 1971
The Straight Dope, Cecil Adams, 1984

Although these books do not deal with fallacies per se, they
contain an assortment of remarkably interesting information,
including numerous misbeliefs. And a special thanks to George
Stimpson for being one of the first to take a serious approach to
intellectual oddities.

About the Author

Born and raised in Michigan, J. ALLEN VARASDI obtained a bachelor's degree in psychology and sociology from Wayne State University, Detroit. Following service in Vietnam, he received a master's degree in sociology from Wayne State. *Myth Information* is his first book, the result of years of fascination with the incongruity between belief and fact.